Public Speaking

Public Speaking

Presley Haywood

Public Speaking
Presley Haywood
ISBN: 978-1-64172-107-3 (Hardback)

Published by Larsen and Keller Education,
5 Penn Plaza,
19th Floor,
New York, NY 10001, USA

Cataloging-in-Publication Data

Public speaking / Presley Haywood.
p. cm.
Includes bibliographical references and index.
ISBN 978-1-64172-107-3
1. Public speaking. 2. Business presentations. 3. Communication in management.
4. Oral communication. I. Haywood, Presley.
PN4193.B8 P83 2019
808.51--dc23

For more information regarding Larsen and Keller Education and its products, please visit the publisher's website www.larsen-keller.com

Table of Contents

Preface

Public speaking is the act of delivering a speech to a live audience. It is done to inform, persuade or entertain. Traditionally, public speaking involved simple oratory structure. The modern approach to public speaking, however integrates modern technologies for sophisticated communication. Some of these include address systems or microphone and audience response systems. Any individual desirous of success in the spheres of politics, law, or any public platform has to acquire the art of fine public speaking. The use of wit and humor, use of digressions and an appeal to the listener's emotions often characterize good public speaking. Modern public speaking involves telecommunication and videoconferencing. This book is compiled in such a manner, that it will provide in-depth knowledge about the theory and practice of public speaking. The topics included herein are of the utmost significance and bound to provide incredible insights to readers. In this book, constant effort has been made to make the understanding of the difficult concepts of public speaking as easy and informative as possible, for the readers.

To facilitate a deeper understanding of the contents of this book a short introduction of every chapter is written below:

Chapter 1, Public speaking is the act of delivering a speech in front of an audience. It can be for the purpose of persuasion, entertainment or for imparting information. This chapter will introduce briefly all the important aspects of public speaking such as debate, eloquence, keynote, homiletics, etc. **Chapter 2**, The most important requirements in public speaking are the message to be conveyed, the medium of communications and the audience for whom the message is intended. Lasswell's model of communication describes the five elements of public speaking. The aim of this chapter is to give an overview of the basic elements of public speaking and includes vital topics related to medium of public speaking, the targeted audience, effect of the speech delivery, etc. **Chapter 3**, Public speaking can serve the purpose of motivating people, telling a story or transmitting information. Some of the public speaking skills required to be an expert orator are self-confidence, strategic planning, good body language and ability to engage an audience, which have been discussed in great detail in this chapter. **Chapter 4**, Some of the tools of communication used in public speaking are public address system, microphone and loudspeaker, while in the modern age, video conferencing is a common and important tool of public communication. This chapter closely examines these tools to provide an insight into public speaking. **Chapter 5**, Effective communication involves a number of skills related to listening, observing, questioning, interpersonal processing, gestures, evaluating and speaking. The diverse communications skills, communication types, theories of communication, etc. have been elucidated in this chapter.

I would like to share the credit of this book with my editorial team who worked tirelessly on this book. I owe the completion of this book to the never-ending support of my family, who supported me throughout the project.

Presley Haywood

1

Introduction to Public Speaking

Public speaking is the act of delivering a speech in front of an audience. It can be for the purpose of persuasion, entertainment or for imparting information. This chapter will introduce briefly all the important aspects of public speaking such as debate, eloquence, keynote, homiletics, etc.

Public speaking skills refer to the talent of effectively addressing an audience. Whether it is in front of a group of people you already know or a crowd of complete strangers, your ability to communicate to them with clarity and confidence is known as your public speaking skills.

There may or may not be an opportunity for interaction between the speaker and audience. The basic difference, however, between a casual talk and public speaking is that the latter is more purposeful and meant for celebratory, entertainment, influencing, or informative purposes.

Although there is evidence of public speech training in ancient Egypt, the first known piece on oratory, written over 2,000 years ago, came from ancient Greece. This work elaborated on principles drawn from the practices and experiences of ancient Greek orators. Aristotle was one of the first recorded teachers of oratory to use definitive rules and models. His emphasis on oratory led to oration becoming an essential part of a liberal arts education during the Middle Ages and the Renaissance. The classical antiquity works written by the ancient Greeks capture the ways they taught and developed the art of public speaking thousands of years ago.

In classical Greece and Rome, rhetoric was the main component of composition and speech delivery, both of which were critical skills for citizens to use in public and private life. In ancient Greece, citizens spoke on their own behalf rather than having professionals, like modern lawyers, speak for them. Any citizen who wished to succeed in court, in politics or in social life had to learn techniques of public speaking. Rhetorical tools were first taught by a group of rhetoric teachers called Sophists who are notable for teaching paying students how to speak effectively using the methods they developed.

Separately from the Sophists, Socrates, Plato and Aristotle all developed their own theories of public speaking and taught these principles to students who wanted to learn skills in rhetoric. Plato and Aristotle taught these principles in schools that they founded, The Academy and The Lyceum, respectively. Although Greece eventually lost political sovereignty, the Greek culture of training in public speaking was adopted almost identically by the Romans.

In the political rise of the Roman Republic, Roman orators copied and modified the ancient Greek techniques of public speaking. Instruction in rhetoric developed into a full curriculum, including instruction in grammar (study of the poets), preliminary exercises (progymnasmata), and preparation of public speeches (declamation) in both forensic and deliberative genres.

The Latin style of rhetoric was heavily influenced by Cicero and involved a strong emphasis on a broad education in all areas of humanistic study in the liberal arts, including philosophy. Other areas of study included the use of wit and humor, the appeal to the listener's emotions, and the use of digressions. Oratory in the Roman empire, though less central to political life than in the days of the Republic, remained significant in law and became a big form of entertainment. Famous orators became like celebrities in ancient Rome—very wealthy and prominent members of society.

The Latin style was the primary form of oration until the beginning of the 20th century. After World War II, however, the Latin style of oration began to gradually grow out of style as the trend of ornate speaking became seen as impractical. This cultural change likely had to do with the rise of the scientific method and the emphasis on a "plain" style of speaking and writing. Even formal oratory is much less ornate today than it was in the Classical Era.

Despite the shift in style, the best-known examples of strong public speaking are still studied *years* after their delivery. Among these examples are Pericles' Funeral Oration in 427 BCE addressing those that died during the Peloponnesian War; Abraham Lincoln's Gettysburg Address in 1863; Sojourner Truth's identification of racial issues in "Ain't I a Woman?"; and Mahatma Gandhi's message of nonviolent resistance in India.

Impact of Public Speaking on your Career

- Demonstrates knowledge: If you can clearly articulate your thoughts, it's a good way to show your knowledge. It can be said that knowledge is of limited value if it isn't applied, and if key people with you work don't know that you have it. By being good at public speaking, you can show that you're knowledgeable on the job.
- Increases knowledge: This one may be a bit counter-intuitive, but by preparing for a presentation, you actually have a chance to become more in tune with the subject matter itself. The key to making a good presentation is knowing your stuff. Very simple to the point of sounding nearly ridiculous, but it makes sense when you think about it. Along those lines, not only does knowing the subject matter inside and out help lead to a winning presentation, you make yourself understand it better.
- Develops and shows confidence: If you can effectively speak to a large group, it can only help develop your confidence in some way, right? It did for me in the workplace. Also, a good presentation that is effectively delivered with confidence can help your standing in the workplace. People often gravitate toward confidence, as long as it isn't excessive of course.
- Differentiates you in the workplace: Not everyone is good at public speaking, depending on what job you have or where you work. If you can stand out, you can only help your career.
- Helps you avoid career risks: If nothing else, being at least competent versus being terrible at it doesn't put you at a disadvantage. I remember seeing a joint presentation by two colleagues some years ago, both speaking for about an hour. The subject matter they each spoke about was related. The first guy was a good presenter, engaging and able to keep the attention of the room. The second guy seemed to be much less dynamic, had way more

"uh" and "um" filler, and was quite simply much less polished as a presenter. I walked away thinking more highly of the first guy than the second guy. It may not have been fair, and frankly my opinion at the time didn't matter much anyway. But a few other people in the room were more senior-level people, and I have a hard time believing that they didn't see the difference too.

- May make you more promotable: At senior levels of leadership, people will need to be comfortable making presentations to the point of being polished and persuasive. Having good public speaking ability can be a good attribute to help you position yourself for a move up.

Tips to Improve Public Speaking

- Nervousness is Normal, Practice and Prepare.

  All people feel some physiological reactions like pounding hearts and trembling hands. Do not associate these feelings with the sense that you will perform poorly or make a fool of yourself. Some nerves are good. The adrenaline rush that makes you sweat also makes you more alert and ready to give your best performance.

  The best way to overcome anxiety is to prepare, prepare, and prepare some more. Take the time to go over your notes several times. Once you have become comfortable with the material, practice—a lot. Videotape yourself, or get a friend to critique your performance.

- Know Your Audience and Your Speech is about them, not You.

  Before you begin to craft your message, consider who the message is intended for. Learn as much about your listeners as you can. This will help you determine your choice of words, level of information, organization pattern, and motivational statement.

- Organize Your Material in the Most Effective Manner to Attain Your Purpose.

  Create the framework for your speech. Write down the topic, general purpose, specific purpose, central idea, and main points. Make sure to grab the audience's attention in the first 30 seconds.

- Watch for Feedback and Adapt to It.

  Keep the focus on the audience. Gauge their reactions, adjust your message, and stay flexible. Delivering a canned speech will guarantee that you lose the attention of or confuse even the most devoted listeners.

- Let Your Personality Come Through.

  Be yourself, don't become a talking head—in any type of communication. You will establish better credibility if your personality shines through, and your audience will trust what you have to say if they can see you as a real person.

- Use Humor tell Stories and Use Effective Language.

  Inject a funny anecdote in your presentation, and you will certainly grab your audience's attention. Audiences generally like a personal touch in a speech. A story can provide that.

- Don't Read Unless You have to Work from an Outline.

  Reading from a script or slide fractures the interpersonal connection. By maintaining eye contact with the audience, you keep the focus on yourself and your message. A brief outline can serve to jog your memory and keep you on task.

- Use Your Voice and Hands Effectively and Omit Nervous Gestures

  Nonverbal communication carries most of the message. Good delivery does not call attention to itself, but instead conveys the speaker's ideas clearly and without distraction.

- Grab Attention at the Beginning and Close with a Dynamic end

  Do you enjoy hearing a speech start with "Today I'm going to talk to you about X"? Most people don't. Instead, use a startling statistic, an interesting anecdote, or concise quotation. Conclude your speech with a summary and a strong statement that your audience is sure to remember.

- Use Audiovisual Aids Wisely

  Too many can break the direct connection to the audience, so use them sparingly. They should enhance or clarify your content, or capture and maintain your audience's attention.

Necessity of Practice

Good communication is never perfect, and nobody expects you to be perfect. However, putting in the requisite time to prepare will help you deliver a better speech. You may not be able to shake your nerves entirely, but you can learn to minimize them.

Speech

Speech means what the speaker says in front of the audience. It is fully audience-oriented system. Generally the political leaders, the managers, the business man or the workers' leaders use this system sometimes. It can build tension or it can relax tension. This system is practiced in public gathering, at company meetings, inauguration and seminars etc. It needs to considerable skills otherwise it is not effective.

So, speech is the formal talk that the speaker addresses through spoken language words in front the audience gathered in a place to hear massage.

The important characteristics of a good speech are as follows:

- Clear: Clarify is the first major characteristic of a good speech. Successful of speeches are fully dependent on the clarity of the idea. Otherwise it will bring a bad result.
- Informal talk: A good speech is closer to a personal and informal chat between two intimate friends. When somebody speaks, there should be a perfect report between the speaker and the audience.

- Concreteness: Abstractions kill a speech. The successes of the speeches are depended on its concreteness.
- Concise: The concentration of an average audience does not last more than fifteen to twenty minutes. So the speeches should be concise.
- Interesting: Quotations anecdotes and humorous touches often make a speech interesting quotations should be only form accepted authorities. They should be familiar but not worn-out. Anecdotes should be new, brief and in good taste. Humor should be topical, spontaneous and gentle.
- Audience-oriented: A good speech is always tuned to the wavelength of the audience. Before giving the speeches the speaker consider some the points carefully that means is the audience general or specialized one or how large the audience or what is the age group of the listener and what are the social, religious, political and economic views of the listeners.

Most of the people do not feel comfortable speaking before others. With effort, everybody can improve their speaking quality. Preparation should always start well in advance. In presenting a *good speech* the following steps should be followed:

- Selection of the topic: The first step in the formal speech morning is to determine the topic of the presentation. Before selection of the topic at first the speaker should consider his knowledge about the topic than they will consider the interest of the audience. Where the topic will be presented and lastly he should consider the occasion. The selection should be justified by all above factors.
- Preparation of the presentation: After selection of the topic the speaker should gather the information that the he needs for this speech. After collection of the information the speaker should organize the information. In presentation stage the greeting usually comes first and gain attention in the opening. In the second stage the speaker prepared the main body of the speeches and lastly conclusion. In the introductory stage the speaker can use the gossip, humor, quotations, questions etc. The middle should be devoted to the discussion and in conclusion it should summarize the main points.
- Determination of the presentation method: With the speech organized, the speaker is ready to prepare its presentation. At this time, the speaker needs to decide on the method of presentation that is, whether to present the speech extemporaneously, to memorize it or to read it.
- Audience analysis: One requirement of good speech making is to know the audience. The speaker should study his audience both before and during the presentation.
- Appearance and physical actions: When the listeners hear the speech, they are looking for the speaker. What they see is a part of the message and can affect the success of the speech. The speaker should understand the communication effects of the listeners see. The speaker must be careful about the communication environment, personal appearance, posture, walking, facial expression, get gestures etc.
- Use of voice: Good voice is an obvious requirement of good speaking. Like physical

movements, the voice should not hinder the listener's concentration on the message. More specifically, it should not detract attention from the message. The speaker should be careful about lack of pitch variation, lack of variation in speed, lack of vocal emphasis and unpleasant voice quality etc.

Production

Speech production is a multi-step process by which thoughts are generated into spoken utterances. Production involves the selection of appropriate words and the appropriate form of those words from the lexicon and morphology, and the organization of those words through the syntax. Then, the phonetic properties of the words are retrieved and the sentence is uttered through the articulations associated with those phonetic properties.

In linguistics (articulatory phonetics), articulation refers to how the tongue, lips, jaw, vocal cords, and other speech organs used to produce sounds are used to make sounds. Speech sounds are categorized by manner of articulation and place of articulation. Place of articulation refers to where the airstream in the mouth is constricted. Manner of articulation refers to the manner in which the speech organs interact, such as how closely the air is restricted, what form of airstream is used (e.g. pulmonic, implosive, ejectives, and clicks), whether or not the vocal cords are vibrating, and whether the nasal cavity is opened to the airstream. The concept is primarily used for the production of consonants, but can be used for vowels in qualities such as voicing and nasalization. For any place of articulation, there may be several manners of articulation, and therefore several homorganic consonants.

Normal human speech is pulmonic, produced with pressure from the lungs, which creates phonation in the glottis in the larynx, which is then modified by the vocal tract and mouth into different vowels and consonants. However humans can pronounce words without the use of the lungs and glottis in alaryngeal speech, of which there are three types: esophageal speech, pharyngeal speech and buccal speech.

Speech Errors

Speech production is a complex activity, and as a consequence errors are common, especially in children. Speech errors come in many forms and are often used to provide evidence to support hypotheses about the nature of speech. As a result, speech errors are often used in the construction of models for language production and child language acquisition. For example, the fact that children often make the error of over-regularizing the -ed past tense suffix in English (e.g. saying 'singed' instead of 'sang') shows that the regular forms are acquired earlier.Speech errors associated with certain kinds of aphasia have been used to map certain components of speech onto the brain and see the relation between different aspects of production: for example, the difficulty of expressive aphasia patients in producing regular past-tense verbs, but not irregulars like ‹sing-sang' has been used to demonstrate that regular inflected forms of a word are not individually stored in the lexicon, but produced from affixation of the base form.

Perception

Speech perception refers to the processes by which humans can interpret and understand the sounds used in language. The study of speech perception is closely linked to the fields of phonetics and phonology in linguistics and cognitive psychology and perception in psychology. Research in speech perception seeks to understand how listeners recognize speech sounds and use this information to understand spoken language. Research into speech perception also has applications in building computer systems that can recognize speech, as well as improving speech recognition for hearing- and language-impaired listeners.

Speech perception is categorical, in that people put the sounds they hear into categories rather than perceiving them as a spectrum. People are more likely to be able to hear differences in sounds across categorical boundaries than within them. A good example of this is voice onset time (VOT). For example, Hebrew speakers, who distinguish voiced /b/ from voiceless /p/, will more easily detect a change in VOT from -10 (perceived as /b/) to 0 (perceived as /p/) than a change in VOT from +10 to +20, or -10 to -20, despite this being an equally large change on the VOT spectrum.

Repetition

In speech repetition, speech being heard is quickly turned from sensory input into motor instructions needed for its immediate or delayed vocal imitation (in phonological memory). This type of mapping plays a key role in enabling children to expand their spoken vocabulary. Masur (1995) found that how often children repeat novel words versus those they already have in their lexicon is related to the size of their lexicon later on, with young children who repeat more novel words having a larger lexicon later in development. Speech repetition could help facilitate the acquisition of this larger lexicon.

Problems Involving Speech

There are several organic and psychological factors that can affect speech. Among these are:

1. Diseases and disorders of the lungs or the vocal cords, including paralysis, respiratory infections (bronchitis), vocal fold nodules and cancers of the lungs and throat.

2. Diseases and disorders of the brain, including alogia, aphasias, dysarthria, dystonia and speech processing disorders, where impaired motor planning, nerve transmission, phonological processing or perception of the message (as opposed to the actual sound) leads to poor speech production.

3. Hearing problems, such as otitis media with effusion, and listening problems, auditory processing disorders, can lead to phonological problems.

4. Articulatory problems, such as slurred speech, stuttering, lisping, cleft palate, ataxia, or nerve damage leading to problems in articulation. Tourette syndrome and tics can also affect speech. Various congenital and acquired tongue diseases can affect speech as can motor neuron disease.

5. In addition to dysphasia, anomia and auditory processing disorder can impede the quality of auditory perception, and therefore, expression. Those who are Hard of Hearing or deaf may be considered to fall into this category.

Brain Physiology

Classical Model

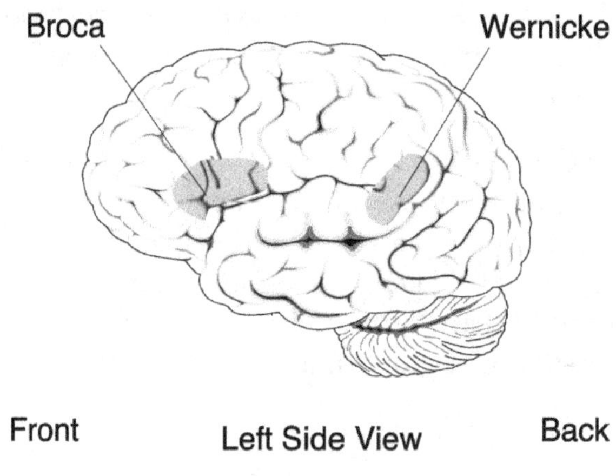

Broca's and Wernicke's areas.

The classical or Wernicke-Geschwind model of the language system in the brain focuses on Broca's area in the inferior prefrontal cortex, and Wernicke's area in the posterior superior temporal gyrus on the dominant hemisphere of the brain (typically the left hemisphere for language). In this model, a linguistic auditory signal is first sent from the auditory cortex to Wernicke's area. The lexicon is accessed in Wernicke's area, and these words are sent via the arcuate fasciculus to Broca's area, where morphology, syntax, and instructions for articulation are generated. This is then sent from Broca's area to the motor cortex for articulation.

Paul Broca identified an approximate region of the brain in 1861 which, when damaged in two of his patients, caused severe deficits in speech production, where his patients were unable to speak beyond a few monosyllabic words. This deficit, known as Broca's or expressive aphasia, is characterized by difficulty in speech production where speech is slow and labored, function words are absent, and syntax is severely impaired, as in telegraphic speech. In expressive aphasia, speech comprehension is generally less affected except in the comprehension of grammatically complex sentences. Wernicke's area is named after Carl Wernicke, who in 1874 proposed a connection between damage to the posterior area of the left superior temporal gyrus and aphasia, as he noted that not all aphasic patients had suffered damage to the prefrontal cortex. Damage to Wernicke's area produces Wernicke's or receptive aphasia, which is characterized by relatively normal syntax and prosody but severe impairment in lexical access, resulting in poor comprehension and nonsensical or jargon speech.

Modern Research

Modern models of the neurological systems behind linguistic comprehension and production recognize the importance of Broca's and Wernicke's areas, but are not limited to them nor solely to the left hemisphere. Instead, multiple streams are involved in speech production and comprehension. Damage to the left lateral sulcus has been connected with difficulty in processing and producing morphology and syntax, while lexical access and comprehension of irregular forms (e.g. eat-ate) remain unaffected.

There are some advantages of good speech, they are given below:

1. Easy to understand: If the speaker delivers his or her speech on the basis of the audience level, it becomes easy understanding. So, the main advantages of speech are understandable.
2. Time saving: Direct speech between the speaker and the listener saves time to communicate information.
3. Good relation: Speech can help to develop the relation between the speaker and the audiences. It is possible to establish friendly relation among the parties concern through direct speech.
4. Cost saving: Direct speech saves money, because it does not require any device or writing instruments like pen, paper, computer, telephone etc.
5. Suitability: It is very suitable to communicate with both illiterate and literate people. But written communication is suitable only for literate people.
6. Quick means: Speech is a quick mean of communication. Many formalities are to be needed for written or other communications. But it does not take any formality.
7. Direct feedback: There is a quick and direct feedback of oral communication, because the audience can interact directly to the speaker.
8. Mass communication: Direct speech is suitable for mass communication. The speaker can communicate with many people at a time through speech.

There are some limitations and disadvantages of speech. These limitations are stated below:

1. Inaccuracy: The main disadvantages of speech or inaccuracy. If the speaker fails to understand the need of the audiences, speech becomes worthless.
2. Complexity: This form of communication increases the complexity in the communication channel. If the number of audience is large, it is difficult to understand the meaning of the speech.
3. Delay: It is a lengthy process to take decision making because it takes more times for personal discussions to each other. If the audiences do not understand the meaning of the speech it takes more time to take a final decision.
4. Irrelevancy: Sometimes the speaker delivers an irrelevant speech which makes the audience displeasure or disgust.
5. No record: Usually no records are kept in this form of communication. So speech cannot be sued as legal document unless it is taped.
6. Lack of secrecy: In this form of communication, the important and secret information may be disclosed.
7. Conflict: Speech cannot be kept in mind for long. So it can create many conflicts among the parties concerned.

8. Expensive: Sometimes the organization pays the T.A. And D. A. To the audiences. So it is also expensive.

Keynote

A keynote speech is a kind of speech that has a main underlying theme. The keynote speech is generally used in gathering such as a political and industrial convention. On the other hand, the keynote speech also has a purpose to motivate and inspire the audience just like a persuasive speech.

Anatomy of a Keynote Speech

- Prepare your keynote speech ahead of time.
- Deliver it to a small audience, get feedback and use it to a larger audience.
- Learn from the keynote speech of other great speakers.
- Select your topic carefully.
- Convince, engage, and make the audience aware of what you are saying.
- Ask for feedback from your audience.

Keynote Speech Outline

- The introduction: The first part of your keynote introduction speech. Introduce yourself and acknowledge the audience. Tell the audience what you are going to talk about and what benefits they can get.
- The body: Also called the main point. This is the heart of your keynote speech and this is the part where you deliver your entire speech and explain your main topics and ideas.
- Summarize what you have just said and give something that the audience will be left thinking after your keynote conclude speech. Also, use this part to thank the organization for inviting you.

Tips for Writing a Good Keynote

1. Be in Tune With Your Purpose: If you're going to hold an audience's attention for more than 5 minutes, you've got to begin by holding firm to your purpose your calling what gets you out of bed in the morning. If it's missing, all you can ever hope to deliver is a speech — which is NOT what people want to hear. If your purpose is clear, you're home free and won't need a single note card.

Mark Twain said it best: "If you speak the truth, you don't need to remember a thing."

2. Be Passionate: Realize that you are on the stage to let it rip. Completely. People are sitting in the audience because they want an experience, not just information. They want to *feel* something, not just hear something. So play full-out. Pull the rip cord.

3. Connect With Your Audience: You may know a lot of stuff. You may have a double Ph.D, but unless you know how to connect with your audience, your knowledge ain't worth squat.

If you were a tree falling in a conference room, no one would hear it.

So tune in. Establish rapport. Connect. And that begins by respecting your audience and realizing you are there to serve.

4. Tell Stories: That's how great teachers have communicated since the beginning of time. Storytelling is the most effective way to disarm the skeptic and deliver meaning in a memorable way.

"The world is not made of atoms," said poet, Muriel Rukyser. "It's made of stories."

5. Have a Sense of Humor: There's a reason why HAHA and AHA are almost spelled the same. Both are about the experience of breakthrough. And both are sparked when the known is replaced by the unknown, when continuity is replaced by discontinuity.

Hey, admit it. At the end of the day, if you can't find the humor in business, you're screwed. So, why wait for the end of the day. Find the humor now.

6. Get Visual: It's become a corporate sport to make fun of power point, but power point can be a thrill if it's done right. A picture really is worth a thousand words.

If you want to spark people's imagination, use images more than words. The root of the word imagination is *image.*

7. Have Confidence: Do you know what the root of the word "confidence" is? It comes from the Latin "con-fide" — meaning "to have faith." Have faith in what?

That's not ego. It's the natural expression of a human being coming from the place of being called.

So, if you're about to walk out on stage and are feeling the impostor syndrome coming on, stop and get in touch with what is calling you. Let *that* person speak.

8. Trim the Fat: When Michelangelo was asked how he made the David, he said it was simple that he merely took away "everything that wasn't."

The same holds true for you, oh aspiring-kick ass-presenter-at-some-future high-profile-conference (or, at the very least, pep-talk-giver to your kid's Junior High School soccer team). Keep it simple. Or, as one wise pundit put it, "Minimize your jargon footprint."

9. Celebrate What Works: If you want to raise healthy kids, reinforce their positive behaviors — don't obsess on the negative.

If you want to raise a healthy audience, give them examples of *what's working* out there in the marketplace. Feature the "bright spots," as Chip Heath likes to say. Share victories, best practices, and lessons learned.

10. Walk the Talk: Good presenters are genuinely moved. Being genuinely moved, it's natural for them come out from behind the podium and actually move around the stage — as in, walking the talk.

Don't hide behind the podium. Forget your notes. If you have to depend on notes to give your presentation, guess what? You're not being present.

People aren't sitting in the audience to watch you read from your notes. They're sitting there to watch you blast off and inspire them to get out from behind *their* podium and accomplish the extraordinary.

Eloquence

Eloquence is the art or practice of using fluent, forceful, and persuasive discourse.

Over the ages, authors have variously described eloquence as "words sweetly placed and modestly directed" (William Shakespeare), "a painting of thought" (Blaise Pascal), "the poetry of prose" (William Cullen Bryant), "the appropriate organ of the highest personal energy" (Ralph Waldo Emerson), and "the art of clothing the thought in apt, significant and sounding words" (John Dryden).

There are four kinds of speakers in the business world:

1. The *incoherent*, who meander, use tons of jargon, and talk of things interesting mostly to themselves.
2. The *coherent*, who can verbally communicate facts and opinions but seldom say anything memorable.
3. The *articulate*, who speak succinctly and clearly but whose words are seldom persuasive.
4. The *eloquent*, who use language and body language to win the hearts and minds of their listeners.

Eloquent people sound smart, regardless of how intelligent they are. The opposite is true as well. Smart people who are incoherent often come off as if they're of limited intelligence.

Fortunately, eloquence is a skill that can be taught, practiced, and mastered. Here are nine easily mastered techniques to quickly make yourself more eloquent and smarter sounding.

Stand or Sit with Spine Straight but Relaxed

Eloquence is more than just how you use language. It's also how you use your body language. The position of your back is the foundation of your body language and therefore the root of your eloquence.

Slumping communicates a lack of confidence in yourself and your words. The other extreme, a ramrod straight back, says "fight or flight." A straight but relaxed spine puts you in a mental and physical state from which words flow smoothly and easily.

Keep your Chin up

The position of your head is just as important as the position of your spine, a fact reflected in many common expressions. To "hold your head high," for example, is to show pride and determination. To be "downcast" means you're already beaten down.

An upright head is essential for eloquence for physiological reasons as well. A tense neck tends to strangle your words, preventing you from speaking clearly.

Focus on your Listeners

Eloquence is meaningful only if people are listening to you, and they won't listen if you're thinking about something else or if your eyes are wandering all over the room. Eloquence without attention is mere speechifying.

Two special cases: Avoid glancing sideways; it makes you seem dishonest. If you must check your notes, use your eyes to look downward without nodding your head.

Speak Loudly Enough to be Heard

For maximum eloquence, speak loudly enough so people farthest from you can hear but not so loudly that it's uncomfortable for those in front.

If you're unsure of your volume, ask somebody in the back if they can hear you clearly. If they answer yes, say "How about this?" in a voice slightly less loud. If they answer no, crank your voice up a notch.

However, never raise your voice to a yell. Yelling makes you sound insane rather than eloquent. If you find yourself in that position, either ask for a microphone or request that people move closer.

Buttress Words with Appropriate Gestures

Use your hands to emphasize key points. The easy way to learn this skill is to watch how celebrities and popular public speakers use gestures as they speak. Note how their hand movements seem to "emerge" from their words.

If you're not actively using a gesture, keep your hands still. Fiddling with your glasses, rattling your papers, scratching yourself, and so forth will distract the audience from your message and "cancel out" your eloquence.

Strategically Position your Body

Add power to your words by moving your body appropriately. For example, if you're speaking to a group from a stage, you might move from one spot to another to signal that you're introducing a new idea.

Similarly, when sitting at the conference table, incline forward slightly when you want to emphasize a point. Reorient your sitting position when you move from one subject or concept to another.

Use Vivid Words that everyone Understands

Cliches are the opposite of eloquence. Use unexpected but common words or phrases that illustrate points in a memorable manner. Example: "common as houseflies" rather than "dime a dozen."

Also avoid words that your audience might not understand. Using fancy words makes you sound snobby, not smart. If you absolutely must introduce a term unfamiliar to the audience, define it in plain language.

Speak at different Speeds

Speaking at a single speed quickly turns whatever you're saying into a monotonous drone. Instead, slow down and speed up depending upon the importance of what you're communicating at the time.

If you're summarizing or going over background, speak more quickly than when you're providing new information. When you're describing introducing an important concept, slow down to give listeners time to absorb it.

Use Pauses to Create Emphasis

Silence isn't just golden; it's also the crowning glory of eloquence. For example, a slight pause before you're about to say something important create suspense. It leads your audience to "hang on your every word."

Similarly, a pause after you've said something important emphasizes its importance and gives listeners a moment to reflect on its importance. A perfect example of the eloquence that comes with pausing is Martin Luther King's "I Have a Dream" speech.

Debate

A debate is an organized argument or contest of ideas in which the participants discuss a topic from two opposing sides. Those who agree with this statement or idea are the "Pro" side. Those who will not agree with this statement or idea are the "Con" side. Each side will show in an organized and clever way why they believe to have the right answers. They will use examples and evidence to support their ideas while working towards a conclusion.

Debate

Many different types of debates are used at the high school and collegiate level, as well as in the political arena. Every kind of debate has two sides, but there are two general types of debates: problem debates, which are centered on philosophical questions, such as whether something is right or wrong, and mechanism debates, which deal with practical problems, such as how something should be done.

Team Policy Debate/National Debate Tournament

Team policy debates feature two teams of two debaters each. The format consists of eight speeches, four constructive speeches and four rebuttals, and four periods of cross-examination. Emphasis is put on presenting large amounts of evidence as quickly and as coherently as possible.

The National Debate Tournament (NDT) also features two teams of two debaters each with the same format of eight speeches as team policy debates. The primary difference between team policy debates and the National Debate Tournament is that the team policy debates are for younger debaters in the upper middle and high school grades, whereas NDT is used at the collegiate level.

Cross-Examination Debate Association

Cross-Examination Debate Association, or CEDA, debates are a newer type of two-on-two collegiate debate. Unlike NDT debates, CEDA debates have resolutions that are not related to policy. CEDA debates are intended to be based on values, but, like NDT, a lot of evidence can be presented.

Lincoln-Douglas Debate

Lincoln-Douglas debates were inspired by the debates between Abraham Lincoln and Stephen A. Douglas during a senatorial race in the 1850s. They are one-on-one debates that focus on arguing for or against competing moral and ethical values. There traditionally has been a strong emphasis on speaking persuasively, logically and clearly in Lincoln-Douglas debates.

Spontaneous Argumentation

Spontaneous argumentation, or SPAR, debates feature two debaters who draw a topic at random (traditionally out of a hat). The debaters then spend a few minutes preparing what they will say before engaging in a brief debate on the topic. It is often used in college and university classrooms and helps decrease speaker anxiety and build confidence. Because the debates do not require serious research, they focus more on presentation and style than on content.

Parliamentary Debate

Similar to SPAR debates, parliamentary debates require no prior research. Resolutions are established only 10 minutes or so before a round of debate begins, so wit, logic and persuasiveness are strongly emphasized. These debates are referred to as "parliamentary" because of their resemblance to the debates that occur in British Parliament. There are two teams of two debaters in parliamentary debates, and a round consists of six speeches: four constructive speeches and two rebuttal speeches.

Benefits of a Debate

Debate teaches how to dress respectably.

- Debate provides preparation for effective participation in a society with representative government: Our form of civil governance has relied upon debate to empower citizens with greater knowledge and to help spread that knowledge. This allows fellow citizens to more effectively participate in the democratic process.
- Debate offers preparation for leadership: The fundamental requirement of all leaders in any position is to provide direction and be able to explain why that direction is needed.
- Debate offers training in argumentation: From its earliest beginnings to today, debate has been the best practice for argumentation. As an educational method, it offers short-term and long-term motivations and rewards.
- Debate provides for investigation and intensive analysis of significant contemporary problems: While education in general might only touch upon various recent issues, debate topics cover ground students may never discuss and in much greater depth than most curriculums will allow. Some debaters comment that after researching and debating a public policy topic for a year they are now more interested in that topic in general. Consider the seven-year history of the homeschool league and the seven topics debated by homeschoolers:
    - 2002-2003 - Resolved: That the United States should significantly change its trade policy within one or both of the following areas: the Middle East and Africa.
    - 2001-2002 - Resolved: That the United States should substantially change its federal agricultural policy.
    - 2000-2001 - Resolved: That the United States should significantly change its immigration policy.
    - 1999-2000 - Resolved: That the 16th amendment to the United States Constitution and all federal, personal, and corporate income taxes should be repealed and replaced with an alternate plan.

    - 1998-1999 - Resolved: That the United States should substantially change the rules governing federal campaign finances.
    - 1997-1998 - Resolved: That Congress should enact laws which discourage the relocation of U.S. businesses to foreign countries.
    - 1996-1997 - Resolved: That the United States should adopt a more narrow policy for foreign military intervention.
- Debate helps integrate knowledge: Debate topics are multi-faceted and cut across several disciplines. This allows debaters to gain knowledge from unique disciplines outside the student's normal academic subjects.
- Debate develops proficiency in purposeful inquiry: Often debate topics are on the cutting edge, dealing with new technology and different ideas from the norm of the day. By learning to research and inquire into new sources, debaters find ways of collecting data new to them.
- Debate emphasizes quality instruction: Since classical rhetoric was taught in ancient times, argumentation and debate instruction has relied more upon interactive coaching and a closer relationship between coach and student than most other educational settings.

A two-brother team getting ready for a round

- Debate encourages student scholarship: While some parents and students worry that debate might interfere with other education, most report that it enhances their work in general education with better note taking skills, research skills, organization, and presentations. The competition encourages students to pursue their regular course work with vigor and use their full capabilities. David Zarefesky, former associate dean of the School of Speech at Northwestern University, remarked that "debaters gain research skills at a pretty sophisticated level, certainly compared to undergraduates in general in intensity it is equivalent to working on a master thesis".
- Debate develops the ability to make prompt, analytical responses: Cross-examination demands quick and decisive responses to questions about argumentation made before.

- Debate develops critical listening skills: Debaters develop excellent listening skills from their first debate when they learn that they must know their opponent's arguments as well as their own. Through making accurate and practiced note taking of the "flow" of a debate round, debaters learn to glean and analyze information as they hear it.
- Debate develops proficiency in writing: While the greater part of debate is perceived to be speaking in front of people, a good portion is research and preparation of argumentation before ever standing in front of another team or judge. This researching, writing, and arguing ability will carry over to many other fields such as preparing research and background papers and answering essay questions on exams.
- Debate encourages mature judgment: Debaters learn the value of suspending judgment until both sides are scrutinized. After debating both sides of an issue for an entire year, debaters know that the complex issues of today have many sides that need to be examined.
- Debate develops courage: Most people would rather be in the casket at a funeral than giving the eulogy. It takes discipline, preparation, and a bit of bravery to stand up and defend a position in front of a judge and another team arguing the exact opposite.
- Debate encourages effective speech composition and delivery: Debate not only requires work in knowing speech material, but in the presentation of the material. Debaters will present before hostile teams and in front of class.
- Debate helps develops social maturity: The business-like atmosphere of a debate tournament coupled with the diversity within the debate community forces debaters to react to various situations. Along with the competitive prospect of losing or winning, debaters learn appropriate manners and proper behavior.
- Debate develops computer competencies: Most research by debaters is now done on various types of computer systems. Whether Internet, college library catalogs, or databases, debaters learn how to find, organize, and use the information they collect.
- Debate uses students' skills to their utmost: To argue requires students to: research issues, organize and analyze data, synthesize different kinds of data, evaluate the conclusion drawn from the data, understand how to reason the conclusions, recognize and critique different methods of reason, and comprehend the logic of decision making.

Homiletics

Homiletics is from the Old English word "homily" that refers to a sermon. Homiletics refers to the practice of preparing and preaching messages. In academic studies, homiletics fits within the area of practical theology or pastoral studies. As such, homiletics has historically been closely connected with church pastors and trainers of pastors.

Homiletics consists of three main areas. The first area consists of biblical interpretation. Study of a particular passage or theme is required to develop the material necessary to effectively preach to an audience.

The second area consists of the structure of a sermon. Books on homiletics usually focus primarily on this aspect. The structure includes developing a main theme for a sermon, an outline, supporting material, illustrations, introduction, conclusion, applications, and any visual aids or props involved in preparing for a message.

The third area focuses on presentation or communication of the sermon. Once a biblical message has been studied and developed, it must also be effectively communicated to a particular audience. Communication can include a study of the particular audience, non-verbal communication such as clothing or gestures, and actual methods of verbal communication, even including one's accent, rate of speech, or enunciation.

A fourth important and often-neglected area should also be included in homiletics. This is the area of spiritual preparation. Unlike other speeches, a sermon's goal is to impact the spiritual life of its hearers. Good homiletics should also include much prayer for the sermon, the preacher, and its audience. In addition, the preacher must be spiritually prepared through how he lives his own life. The spiritual maturity of the audience must also be considered. Preaching to an audience of new believers, for example, is a much different dynamic than preaching to an audience of seminary students.

Christian Tradition: The Preaching of Jesus

The Sermon on the Mount

Jesus preached and commissioned his apostles to do so. His preaching included two forms of sermon, the missionary and the ministerial (to which correspond the *magisterium* and the *ministerium* of the Church), the former to outsiders, the latter to those already part of his movement. Of the latter we have a striking example in the discourse after the Last Supper.

It cannot be said that his preaching took any definite, rounded form, in the sense of a modern sermon; his aim was to sow the seed of the word, which he scattered abroad, like the sower in the parable. His commission to His Apostles included both kinds. For the former or missionary preaching, Paul the Apostle's sermon referred to in Acts 20:7-11 exemplifies the second kind of preaching. In this the apostles were supported by assistants who were elected and consecrated for a purpose, for example, Timothy and Titus; as also by those who had been favoured with charismata. The homily referred to in Justin Martyr's *Apology* gives an example of ministerial, as distinct from missionary, preaching.

Missionary Preaching

St Paul preaching the *Areopagus sermon* in Athens

In missionary preaching the apostles were also assisted, but in an informal way, by the laity, who explained the Christian doctrine to their acquaintances amongst unbelievers who, in their visits to the Christian assemblies, must have heard something of it. This is particularly true of Justin Martyr, who, wearing his philosopher's cloak, went about for that purpose. The sermons to the faithful in the early ages were of the simplest kind, being merely expositions or paraphrases of the passage of scripture that was read, coupled with *extempore* effusions of the heart. This explains why there is little or nothing in the way of sermons or homilies surviving from that period. It also explains the strange statement made by Sozomen (Hist. Eccl., VII, xix), and by Cassiodorus in his "Tripartite History", which Duchesne apparently accepts, that no one preached at Rome. (Sozomen wrote about the time of Pope Xystus III, in office 432-440) Thomassin's explanation of Sozomen's statement is that there was no preaching in the sense of an elaborate or finished discourse before the time of Pope Leo, with the exception, perhaps, of the address on virginity by Pope Liberius (in office 352-366) to Marcellina, sister of St. Ambrose, on the occasion of her taking the veil, which is regarded as a private discourse.

And the reason for this he attributes to the stress of persecution. Neander says of Sozomen's statement: "The remark could not extend to the early times; but suppose it did, it meant that the sermon was only secondary. Or the fact may have been that this Eastern writer was deceived by false accounts from the West; or it may have been that the sermon in the Western Church did not occupy so important a place as it did in the Greek Church."

Early Church

According to middle second-century writer Justin Martyr, the practice of the early church was for someone to read from the "Memoirs of the Apostles or the Writings of the Prophets," meaning readings from what was to become the Christian Bible. A discourse on the text followed the reading. This was the same practice as that of the synagogues, but now with the New Testament writings added, except that in Christian churches the same person who read the scripture also explained it and there was no set lectionary of readings. Origen, a third-century theologian, preached through most books of the Old Testament and many of the New, which we have today. Origen's sermons on the scripture are expository and evangelistic. By the fourth century, a system had developed where a readings from the Law, Prophets, Epistles, and Gospels were read in that order, followed by a sermon. John Chrysostom is recognized as one of the greatest preachers of this age. His sermons begin with exegesis, followed by application to practical problems.

The office of preaching belonged to bishops, and priests preached only with their permission. Even two such distinguished men as Augustine of Hippo and John Chrysostom preached, as priests, only when commissioned by their respective bishops. Origen as a layman expounded the scriptures, but it was by special permission. Felix, a priest and martyr, preached in the third century, under two bishops, Maximus and Quintus. Priests were forbidden to preach in Alexandria; but that was on account of the Arian controversy. A custom springing from this had spread to the north of Africa; but Valerius, Bishop of Hippo, broke through it, and had St. Augustine, as yet a priest, to preach before him, because he himself was unable to do so with facility in the Latin language -- "cum non satis expedite Latino sermone concionari posset". This was against the custom of the place, as Possidius relates; but Valerius justified his action by an appeal to the East -- "in orientalibus ecclesiis id ex more fieri sciens". Even during the time of the prohibition in Alexandria, priests, as we know from Socrates and Sozomen, interpreted the Scriptures publicly in Cæsarea, in Cappadocia, and in Cyprus, candles being lighted the while -- *accensis lucernis*. As soon as the Church received freedom under Constantine, preaching developed very much, at least in external form. Then for the first time, if, perhaps, we except St. Cyprian, the art of oratory was applied to preaching, especially by St. Gregory of Nazianzus, the most florid of Cappadocia's triumvirate of genius. He was already a trained orator, as were many of his hearers, and it is no wonder, as Otto Bardenhewer expresses it, "he had to pay tribute to the taste of his own time which demanded a florid and grandiloquent style". But, at the same time, he condemned those preachers who used the eloquence and pronunciation of the theatre. The most notable preachers of the century, St. Basil and the two Gregories, Ambrose, Augustine and Hilary, were all noted orators. Of the number the greatest was St. Chrysostom, the greatest since St. Paul, nor has he been since equalled. Even Gibbon, while not doing him justice, had to praise him; and his teacher of rhetoric, Libanius, is said to have intended John as his successor, "if the Christians had not taken him". It is a mistake, however, to imagine that they preached only oratorical sermons. Quite the contrary; St. Chrysostom's homilies were models of simplicity, and he frequently interrupted his discourse to put questions in order to make sure that he was understood; while St. Augustine's motto was that he humbled himself that Christ might be exalted. In passing we might refer to a strange feature of the time, the applause with which a preacher was greeted. St. Chrysostom especially had to make frequent appeals to his hearers to keep quiet. Bishops commonly preached outside their own dioceses, especially in the great cities; polished sermons were evidently in demand, and a stipend was given, for we read that two Asiatic bishops, Antiochus and Severianus, went to Constantinople to preach, being more desirous of money than of the spiritual welfare of their hearers.

Decline in The West

After the age here described preaching was on the decline in the West, partly because of the decay of the Latin language, and in the East, owing to the controversies on Arianism, Nestorianism, Eutychianism, Macedonianism, and other heresies. But still preaching was regarded as the chief duty of bishops; for instance, Cæsarius, Bishop of Arles, gave charge of all the temporal affairs of his diocese to deacons, that he might devote all his time to the reading of the Scriptures, to prayer, and to preaching. The next great name in preaching is that of St. Gregory the Great, particularly as a homilist. He preached twenty homilies, and dictated twenty more, because, through illness and loss of voice, he was unable to preach them personally. He urged bishops very strongly to preach; and, after holding up to them the example of the Apostles, he threatened the bishops of Sardinia in the following words: "Si cujus libet Episcopi Paganum rusticum invenire potuero, in Episcopum fortiter vindicabo". An edict was issued by King Guntram stating that the assistance of the public judges was to be used to bring to the hearing of the word of God, through fear of punishment, those who were not disposed to come through piety. The Synod of Trullo laid down that bishops should preach on all days, especially on Sundays; and, by the same synod, bishops who preached outside their own diocese were reduced to the status of priests, because being desirous of another's harvest they were indifferent to their own "ut qui alienæ messis appetentes essent, suæ incuriosi". At the, bishops were strongly exhorted to preach; and the Council of Mainz, in the same year, laid down that bishops should preach on Sundays and feast days either themselves or though their vicars. In the Second Council of Reims, can. xiv, xv, it was enjoined that bishops should preach the homilies and sermons of the Fathers, so that all could understand. And in the Third Council of Tours, in the same year, bishops were ordered to make a translation of the homilies of the Fathers into the rustic Roman tongue, or theodesque—the rustic Roman tongue being a species of corrupt Latin, or patois, understood by the uneducated. Charlemagne and Louis the Pious were equally insistent on the necessity of preaching. The former went so far as to appoint a special day, and any bishop who failed to preach in his cathedral before that day was to be deposed. Pastors, too, were ordered to preach to their people as best they could; if they knew the Scriptures, they were to preach them; if not, they were at least to exhort their hearers to avoid evil and do good.

Middle Ages

Preaching from a mediaeval pulpit

It has been commonly said by non-Catholic writers that there was little or no preaching during that time. So popular was preaching, and so deep the interest taken in it, that preachers commonly found it necessary to travel by night, lest their departure should be prevented. It is only in a treatise on the history of preaching that justice could be done this period. As to style, it was simple and majestic, possessing little, perhaps, of so-called eloquence as at present understood, but much religious power, with an artless simplicity, a sweetness and persuasiveness all its own, and such as would compare favourably with the hollow declamation of a much-lauded later period. Some sermons were wholly in verse, and, in their intense inclusiveness of thought, remind one of the Sermon on the Mount:

- Magna promisimus; majora promissa sunt nobis.
- Servemus hæc; adspiremus ad illa.
- Voluptas brevis; pœna perpetua.
- Modica passio; gloria infinita.
- Multorum vocatio; paucorum election.
- Omnium retribution.

Preaching of The Time

Francis of Assisi Preaching before Honorius III

The characteristics of the preaching of the time were an extraordinary use of Scripture, not a mere introducing of the Sacred Text as an accretion, but such a use as comes from entwinement with the preacher's own thought. It would almost appear as if many preachers knew the Scriptures by heart.

In some cases, however, this admirable use was marred by an exaggerated mystical interpretation, which originated in the East and was much sought after by the Jews. Secondly, power on the part of the preachers of adapting their discourses to the wants of the poor and ignorant. Thirdly, simplicity, the aim being to impress a single striking idea. Fourthly, use of familiar maxims, examples, and illustrations from life—their minds must have been much in touch with nature. And, fifthly, intense realization, which necessarily resulted in a certain dramatic effect—they saw with their eyes, heard with their ears, and the past became present.

Scholastic philosophy supplied an almost inexhaustible store of information; it trained the mind in analysis and precision; whilst, at the same time, it supplied a lucidity of order and cogency of arrangement such as we look for in vain in even the great orations of Chrysostom.

Philosophy regards man only as an intellectual being, without considering his emotions, and makes its appeal solely to his intellectual side. And, even in this appeal, philosophy, while, like algebra, speaking the formal language of intellect, is likely to be wanting from the view-point of persuasiveness, inasmuch as, from its nature, it makes for condensation rather than for amplification. The latter is the most important thing in oratory -- "Summa laus eloquentiæ amplificare rem ornando." Fénelon (Second Dialogue) describes it as portrayal; De Quincey, as a holding of the thought until the mind gets time to eddy about it; Newman gives a masterly analysis of it; his own sermons are remarkable for this quality of amplification as are those of Bourdaloue on the intellectual, and those of Massillon on the intellectual-emotional side, v. g. the latter's sermon on the Prodigal Son. Philosophy, indeed, is necessary for oratory; philosophy alone does not constitute oratory, and, if too one-sided, may have an injurious effect -- "Logic, therefore, so much as is useful, is to be referred to this one place with all her well-couched heads and topics, until it be time to open her contracted palm into a graceful and ornate rhetoric". What has been here stated refers to philosophy as a system, not to individual philosophers. It is scarcely necessary to say that many Scholastics, such as Sts. Thomas and Bonaventure, were noted preachers.

In a discussion of the history of preaching, a reference to the mystics is called for. The tendency of mysticism is, in the main, the opposite to that of philosophy. Mysticism makes for warmth; philosophy, for coldness -- "Cold as a mountain in its star-pitched tent stood high philosophy." The next noted period in the history of preaching is the Renaissance. This period, too, is treated in its proper place. As to preaching, Humanism contributed more to oratorical display than to piety in the pulpit. The motto of its two representative types, Reuchlin and Erasmus, was: "Back to Cicero and Quintilian." Erasmus on visiting Rome exclaimed: "Quam mellitas eruditorum hominum confabulationes, quot mundi lumina." Pierre Batiffol says: "One Good Friday, preaching before the pope, the most famous orator of the Roman Court considered that he could not better praise the Sacrifice of Calvary than by relating the self-devotion of Decius and the sacrifice of Iphigenia." Fortunately, this period did not last long; the good sense of ecclesiastics rebelled against it, and the religious upheaval that soon followed gave them something else to think of. In the Reformation and post-Reformation period the air was too charged with controversy to favour high-class preaching. The Council of Trent recommended preachers to turn aside from polemics; it also pronounced that the primary duty of preaching devolved on bishops, unless they were hindered by a legitimate impediment; and ordered that they were to preach in person in their own church, or, if impeded, through others; and, in other churches, through pastors or other representatives.

Notable French Preachers

The French preachers of the classical seventeenth-century period were, according to Voltaire, probably the greatest in pulpit oratory of all time. The best known were Bossuet, Bourdaloue, and Massillon; Fénelon burnt his sermons. The first was considered to be the most majestic; the second, the most logical and intellectually compelling; the third, the greatest searcher of hearts, the most like Chrysostom, and, taken all in all, the greatest of the three. We are told that Voltaire kept a copy of his *Grand Carême* on his table, side by side with the "Athalie" of Racine. In this age

Chrysostom was the great model for imitation; but it was Chrysostom the orator, not Chrysostom the homilist. Their style, with its grand exordium and its sublime peroration, became the fashion in the following age. The "Dialogues" of Fénelon, however, remained as a check. Of these "Dialogues" Bishop Dupanloup said: "If the precepts of Fénelon had been well understood, they would have long since fixed the character of sacred eloquence among us." Other principles were laid down by Blaise Gisbert in his *L'Eloquence chrétienne dans l'idée et dans la pratique*, by Amadeus Bajocensis in *Paulus Ecclesiastes, seu Eloquentia Christiana*, and by Guido Angelis in *De Verbi Dei Prædicatione*, all of which sounded a return to the simplicity of style of the Church Fathers.

Jacques-Bénigne Bossuet

Conférences in Notre Dame

The next important era is the so-called *conférences* in Notre-Dame in Paris, following the Revolution of 1830. The most prominent name identified with this new style of preaching was that of the Dominican Lacordaire, who, for a time, with Montalembert, was associate editor with de Lamennais of "L'Avenir". This new style of preaching discarded the form, the division, and analysis of the scholastic method. The power of Lacordaire as an orator was beyond question; but the *conférences*, as they have come down to us, while possessing much merit, are an additional proof that oratory is too elusive to be committed to the pages of a book. The Jesuit Père de Ravignan shared with Lacordaire the pulpit of Notre-Dame. Less eloquent men followed, and the semi-religious, semi-philosophic style was beginning to grow tiresome, when Jacques-Marie-Louis Monsabré, a disciple of Lacordaire, set it aside, and confined himself to an explanation of the Creed; whereupon it was sententiously remarked that the bell had been ringing long enough.

Present Day

As to preaching at the present day, we can clearly trace the influence, in many respects, of Scholasticism, both as to matter and form. In matter a sermon may be either moral, dogmatic, historical, or liturgical—by moral and dogmatic it is meant that one element will predominate, without, however, excluding the other. As to form, a discourse may be either a formal, or set, sermon; a homily; or a catechetical instruction. In the formal, or set, sermon the influence of Scholasticism is most strikingly seen in the analytic method, resulting in divisions and subdivisions. This is the thirteenth-century method, which, however, had its beginnings in the sermons of Sts. Bernard and Anthony. The underlying syllogism, too, in every well-thought-out sermon is due to Scholasticism; how far it should appear is a question that belongs to a treatise on homiletics. As to the catechetical discourse, it has been so much favoured by Pope Pius X that it might be regarded as one of the characteristics of preaching at the present day. It is, however, a very old form of preaching. It was used by Christ Himself, by St. Paul, by St. Cyril of Jerusalem, by St. Clement and Origen at Alexandria, by St. Augustine, who wrote a special treatise thereon (De catechizandis rudibus), also, in later times, by Gerson, chancellor of the University of Paris, who wrote "De parvulis ad Christum trahendis"; Clement XI and Benedict XIV gave to it all the weight of their authority, and one of the greatest of all catechists was St. Charles Borromeo. There is the danger, however, from the very nature of the subject, of this form of preaching becoming too dry and purely didactic, a mere catechesis, or doctrinism, to the exclusion of the moral element and of Sacred Scripture. In recent days, organized missionary preaching to non-Catholics has received a new stimulus. In the United States, particularly, this form of religious activity has flourished; and the Paulists, amongst whom the name of Father Hecker is deserving of special mention, are to be mainly identified with the revival. Special facilities are afforded at the central institute of the organization for the training of those who are to impart catechetical instruction, and the non-controversial principles of the association are calculated to commend it to all earnestly seeking after truth.

In the Roman Catholic Church, the Holy See, through the Congregation for Divine Worship and the Discipline of the Sacraments (headed as of February 2015 by Cardinal Prefect Robert Sarah), publishes an official guide and directory for use by bishops, priests, and deacons, who are charged with the ministry of preaching by virtue of their ordination, and for those studying the subject, among others seminarians and those in diaconal formation, called the Homiletic Directory.

St. John Chrysostom and St. Augustine

Practice preceded theory. Certain ideas are to be found in the Church Fathers, and these have been collected by Paniel in the introduction to his work "Geschichte der christlich. Beredsamkeit". The first to treat of the theory of preaching was St. John Chrysostom, in his work "On the Priesthood" (*peri Hierosynes*). Inasmuch as this contains only reflections on preaching, St. Augustine's *De doctrina christiana* might be regarded as the first manual on the subject; its first three books deal with collecting the materials for preaching, "modus inveniendi quæ intelligenda sunt", and the last with the presentation thereof, "modus proferendi quæ intellecta sunt". He goes to the Roman pagan orator Cicero for rules in the latter. He makes a distinction, in which he evidently follows Cicero, between *sapientia* (wisdom) and *eloquentia*(the best expression of it). Sapientia without eloquentia will do no good; neither will eloquentia without sapientia, and it may do harm; the ideal is sapientia with eloquentia. He adapts Cicero's *ut doceat, ut delectet, ut flectat*, changing them to *ut veritas pateat, ut placeat, ut moveat*; and lays down these as the rules by which a sermon is to be judged. This work of Augustine was the classic one in homiletics.

He describes it practically in relation to the classical theory of oratory, which has five parts: *inventio* (the choice of the subject and decision of the order), *dispositio* (the structure of the oration), *elocutio* (the arrangement of words and figure of speech), *memoria*(learning by heart), and *pronuntiatio* (the delivery). He constructed this theory in four parts: the basic principles of rhetoric, a study on the rhetoric of Scriptural texts, an analysis of styles, and some peculiar rules of rhetoric for sermons. The essential part of Book IV deals with three styles of sermons (*genera tenue/ docere*; *genera medium / delectare*; *genera grande / flectere*), which was influenced by Cicero's Orator 1.3.

Augustine stresses the importance of principle and discipline at the same time. Preachers need to practice again and again so that they can use these styles in any situation of preaching. But they should pay attention to the priority of order. Continuous and diligent study of the Bible is more important than mere memorization, that is to say, they should pursue wisdom more than knowledge. The best is the combination of wisdom and eloquence as seen in the Pauline letters and prophetic writings. Yet, he does not praise eloquence itself; rather he prefers a concrete proclamation than a showing off of rhetorical technique. It is truth, not rhetoric, that preachers try to deliver.

The most significant practice and discipline is prayer. Augustine advises to be a prayer before being a preacher. Preachers should pray before and after his sermon. Augustine himself was a good model of this practice. Before the preaching, he invited the congregation to pray. After the sermon he also prayed. For Augustine's homiletics, the time of prayer is the most precious time, because that time is a time when all the audience meets God the Truth, and through that time they can understand the truth of God more fully. Prayer is a major means of grace in knowing God. Augustine says that love is the most important discipline in Christian life in his sermon, *De disciplina christiana*. If one adds another to Christian discipline besides love, prayer will come first.

The preacher should be a good example of all sermons. The manner of life can be an eloquent sermon. In most of the cases, it seems to be true that the sermon of a preacher cannot be better than his or her life, but vice versa seems also to be true: the sermon cannot be worse than the preacher's life. The more a preacher endeavors after humility, discipline, and love, the better his or her sermon becomes. And now these three are always necessary for all Christian teachers: humility, discipline, and love. But the greatest of these is love. For "the goal of this command is love".

Hugh of St. Victor

Hugh of St. Victor in the Middle Ages laid down three conditions for a sermon: that it should be "holy, prudent and noble", for which, respectively, he required sanctity, knowledge and eloquence in the preacher. François Fénelonstipulated "must prove, must portray, must impress".

St. Augustine's work "De rudibus catechizandis". St. Gregory the Great's "Liber regulæ pastoralis" is still extant, but is inferior to St. Augustine's; it is rather a treatise on pastoral theology than on homiletics.

Hincmar says that a copy used to be given to bishops at their consecration.

In the ninth century Rabanus Maurus, Archbishop of Mainz, wrote a treatise *De institutione clericorum*, in which he depends much on St. Augustine.

In the twelfth century Guibert, Abbot of Nogent, wrote a famous work on preaching entitled "Quo ordine sermo fieri debet". This is one of the historical landmarks in preaching. It is replete with judicious instruction; it recommends that preaching should be preceded by prayer; it says that it is more important to preach about morals than on faith, that for moral sermons the human heart must be studied, and that the best way of doing so is (as Massillon recommended in later times) to look into one's own. It is more original and more independent than the work of Rabanus Maurus, who, as has been said, drew largely from St. Augustine.

Guibert's work was recommended by Pope Alexander as a model to all preachers. St. Francis gave to his friars the same directions as are herein contained.

Alain de Lille

To the same period belongs the "Summa de arte prædicatoriâ" by Alain de Lille, which defines preaching: "Manifesta et publica instructio morum et fidei, informationi hominum deserviens, ex rationum semitâ et auctoritatum fonte proveniens". He lays stress on explanation and use of Scripture and recommends the preacher to insert verba commotiva. The remarks of Cæsarius of Heisterbach have been collected by Cruel; his sermons display skill in construction and considerable oratorical power. Conrad of Brundelsheim, whose sermons have come down to us under his cognomen of "Brother Sock", was one of the most interesting preachers at this time in Germany. Humbert of Romans, General superior of the Dominicans, in the second book of his work, "De eruditione prædicatorum", claims that he can teach "a way of promptly producing a sermon for any set of men, and for all variety of circumstances". Linsenmayer, in his history of preaching, gives information about Humbert, who was a severe critic of the sermons of his time. Trithemius quotes a work by Albertus Magnus, "De arte prædicandi", which is lost. St. Bonaventure wrote "De arte concionandi", in which he treats of *divisio, distinctio, dilatatio*, but deals extensively only with the first.

Thomas Aquinas

Thomas Aquinas's claim rests chiefly on the "Summa", which, of course, has principally influenced preaching since, both in matter and form. He insists very strongly on the importance of preaching, and says that it belongs principally to bishops, and baptizing to priests, the latter of whom he regards as holding the place of the seventy disciples. There is a treatise entitled *De arte et vero modo prædicandi* attributed to him, but it is simply a compilation of his ideas about preaching that was made by another. Henry of Hesse is credited with a treatise, "De arte prædicandi", which is probably not due to him. There is a monograph quoted by Hartwig which is interesting for the classification of the forms of sermon: *modus antiquissimus*, i. e. postillatio, which is purely the exegetic homily; modus modernus, the thematic style; *modus antiquus*, a sermon on the Biblical text; and *modus subalternus*, a mixture of homiletic and text sermon. Jerome Dungersheym wrote a tract *De modo discendi et docendi ad populum sacra seu de modo prædicandi*. He treats of his subject on three points: the preacher, the sermon, the listeners. He lays stress on Scripture as the book of the preacher. Ulrich Surgant wrote a "Manuale Curatorum" , in which he also recommends Scripture. His first book gives for material of preaching the usual order -- *credenda, facienda, fugienda, timenda, appetenda* and ends by saying: "Congrua materia prædicationis est Sacra Scriptura." He uses the figure of a tree in laying stress on the necessity of an organic structure.

Humanist Writings

In the works of the two humanists, Johannes Reuchlin (*Liber congestorum de arte prædicandi*) and Desiderius Erasmus (*Ecclesiastes seu de ratione concionandi*), the return is marked to Cicero and Quintilian. A masterwork on the art of preaching is the "Rhetorica Sacra" of Luis de Granada, for modern use rather old. The work shows an easy grasp of rhetoric, founded on the principles of Aristotle, Demetrius and Cicero. He treats the usual subjects of invention, arrangement, style and delivery in easy and polished Latin. Of the same class is Didacus Stella in his "Liberdemodo concionandi". Valerio, in Italy, also wrote on the art of preaching. Another landmark on preaching are the "Instructiones Pastorum" by Charles Borromeo. At his request Valerio, Bishop of Verona, wrote a systematic treatise on homiletics entitled "Rhetorica Ecclesiastica", in which he points out the difference between profane and sacred eloquence and emphasizes the two principal objects of the preacher, to teach and to move (*docere et commovere*).

Laurentius a Villavicentio, in his work "De formandis sacris concionibus" , disapproves of transferring the ancient modes of speaking to preaching. He would treat the truths of the Gospel according to I Tim., iii, 16. He also recommended moderation in fighting heresy. The same was the view of St. Francis Borgia, whose contribution to homiletics is the small but practical work: "Libellus de ratione concionandi". Claudius Acquaviva, General of the Jesuits, wrote in 163, "Instructio pro superioribus". They were principally ascetic, and in them he regulated the spiritual training necessary for the preacher. Carolus Regius, S.J., deals in his "Orator Christianus" with the whole field of homiletics under the grouping: "De concionatore"; "De concione"; "De concionantis prudentiâ et industriâ". Much is to be found in the writings of St. Vincent de Paul, St. Alphonsus Liguori and St. Francis de Sales, especially in his celebrated letter to André Fremiot, Archbishop of Bourges.

Among the Dominicans, Alexander Natalis wrote "Institutio concionantium tripartita".

In the "Rhetorica ecclesiastica" of Jacobus de Graffiis is contained a symposium of the instructions on preaching by the Franciscan Francis Panigarola, the Jesuit Francis Borgia and the Carmelite Johannes a Jesu.

The "Dialogues" of Fénelon, the works of Père Blaise Gisbert, Amadeus Bajocensis and Guido ab Angelis have already been referred to. In the nineteenth century homiletics took its place as a branch of pastoral theology, and many manuals have been written thereon, for instance in German compendia by Brand, Laberenz, Zarbl, Fluck and Schüch; in Italian by Gotti and Guglielmo Audisio; and many in French and English.

Relation to Profane Rhetoric

Some assert the independent character of homiletics and say that it is independent in origin, matter and purpose. The upholders of this view point to passages in Scripture and in the Fathers, notably to the words of Paul; and to the testimony of Cyprian, Arnobius, Lactantius, and to Gregory of Nazianzus, Augustine of Hippo, Jerome and John Chrysostom. The last-named says that the great difference may be summed up in this: that the orator seeks personal glory, the preacher practical good.

Paul's own sermons are in many cases replete with oratory, *e.g.*, his sermon on the Areopagus; and the oratorical element generally enters largely into Scripture. Lactantius regretted that there were so few trained preachers, and Gregory, as well as Chrysostom and Augustine, made use of rhetoric in preaching. Gregory censured the use in the pulpit of the eloquence and pronunciation of the theatre. Demetrius, *On Style*, uses many of the tricks of speech.

Steps for Effective Homiletics

1. Claiming a Personal Theology of Preaching

The foundational principle of all preaching rests on developing an integrated theology. Why preach? When teaching seminarians studying for the priesthood, it is not unusual to hear that the initial call to ministry had little to do with a call to preach the Gospel, but centered more generally on sacramental and pastoral engagement. Fair enough. Yet the USCCB underlines the importance of a theology in *Fulfilled in Your Hearing* and *Preaching the Mystery of Faith.* Pope Francis's Post Synodal Apostolic Exhortation *Evangelii Gaudium* or *The Joy of the Gospel* gives the liturgical homily pride of place as an essential pastoral and biblical encounter with the People of God. "The mediator of meaning." If the preacher intends to name grace by proclaiming God's Word, how can such gifts be disclosed to the liturgical assembly unless the preacher is a personal witness to God's saving action in the Bible and the world? Preaching is an integrating discipline, inviting the homilist to draw together the fruits of theological reflection, pastoral care, and biblical study into a public testimony of faith. Committing to a personal spirituality of preaching focuses a vocational call in the light of the New Evangelization and the Church's mission to spread the Gospel.

2. Preaching from the Table of the Word and Sacrament

St. Jerome says, "Ignorance of scripture is ignorance of Christ." It is worth the time and effort on the part of everyone who preaches to develop a learning plan with the Bible, which would include prayerful meditation in *lectio divina*, as well as reference to ancient and contemporary commentaries. One of the more challenging aspects of ministry in the Christian tradition these days remains articulating a unified story of salvation history. Scripture acknowledges a God who loved creation into being, and who will one day set it "free from slavery to corruption and share in the glorious freedom of the children of God". But in a Western culture which promotes largely episodic lives—untethered to historical memory—preaching faces intense competition with Instagram, YouTube, Twitter, and other social media platforms which thrive only in the disposable present. In addition to Scripture, there are enormous resources available to the preacher in the rich Catholic historical and liturgical tradition which continues to remember the saving work of God in Christ. A familiarity with the liturgical texts in the Roman Missal is a remarkable thesaurus for the liturgical homily, drawing from the language of the collects, proper prayers, and prefaces. Preaching inside the Church's memory in the language of Word and Sacrament repositions the liturgical assembly from the chaos of a busy world into God's sacred narrative of salvation. That mission is the preacher's unique call.

3. Crafting a Unified Homily

There is one underdeveloped aspect of the Sunday homily which drives listeners to distraction and often right out the doors: too many ideas. That may seem odd, since it appears counterintuitive that in a world craving information the hearer would resist more ideas. But this misstep on the ladder of preaching remains close to fatal. Preachers write for collective human ears which require a center of gravity. Much of the craft of preaching is linked not to pulling out themes in the text, but developing a single focus sentence, which finds its way to the listener through artfully positioned tactics driving that focus home. Good preachers deploy what the late Bishop Ken Untener referred to as a single "pearl" to carry the homiletic event through to the end—which is the listener. And as *FIYH* reminds us, the purpose of the Sunday homily is to "deepen the faith of the baptized," not to dole out scattered observations.

4. Finding a Homiletic Method

Creating unity comes from finding a kind of armature on which to hang the homiletic text. Too many unarranged ideas without a focus yield confusion and frustration in the hearer and a lack of unity in the text. In his *Poetics*, Aristotle observed that plotting in narrative depends crucially on the arrangement of the material. As it has been developed over the last several years by pioneers such as Fred Craddock, David Buttrick, and Eugene Lowry, narrative homiletics follows Aristotelian methodology in which preachers re-present the action of the biblical text in a kind of plot for the hearer to unpack through stages. These methods, then, allow for the hearer to become silent dialogue partners, as they would when they engage any narrative, such as a novel, film, or play. Using an appropriate form, homilies are plotted inductively with narrative tension and then are gradually resolved by the hearer. Paul Scott Wilson's method, for instance, includes a four-part paradigm: *Trouble in the Tex /Trouble in the World/God's Action in the Text/God's Action in the World.* Overall, these homiletic methods help the preacher to create the unity identified in the previous (third) step by an effective arrangement of the text.

Benefits of Homiletics

1) Homiletics helps us to make more economical use of our time

One of the questions that we often receive is: "how can we plan our sermons when we don't have enough time to prepare sermons?" What the questioner doesn't realize is that in the grand scheme of things, Homiletics helps us to make greater use of our time.

A good sermon plan first of all allows preachers to prepare at all times. When you are in the grocery checkout line, you can think about either the next sermon or any sermon that you have in your plan. Illustrations come to mind at any time. You can capture them rather than simply forcing them to fit at the last minute or attempting to find a sermon illustration from books. Yes, good Homiletics allows the preacher to make greater use of her or his time.

2) Homiletics allows the preacher to more easily address the people's real needs

This is true because Homiletics allows us first of all to find the people's real needs. We no longer make assumptions about what is needed in the congregation, we analyze the congregation to determine them.

When you construct a sermon plan, you give yourself a chance to plan in the people's needs in a much greater way than when you are preaching week to week without a sermon plan. You can plan for a sermon series to address a weakness in your congregation or perhaps throw in a few sermons to strengthen the strengths of the congregation. When you plan, you and the Spirit decide what will be the larger direction of your pulpit ministry more than what would happen if you preached week to week without engaging in sermon planning.

3) Homiletics allows us to see our "blind spots"

All preachers have "blind spots" in their preaching ministry. These are areas where we either don't preach or don't spend enough time preaching. When we have such issues we deprive our congregation of certain themes that may be needed by the congregation.

Homiletics will help us see these blind spots. Just seeing them is helpful. An adequate sermon plan also will helps us determine how much we need to preach on some of these issues in our particular congregation. When you plan, you can put in sermons that address these places that we would normally ignore if we did not go through the effort of planning our sermon ministry.

4) Homiletics allows us to preach a more broad message

Related to that, those who preach sermons derived from week to week preaching (without a plan) can preach a limited message. The sermons address the same themes. They often exhibit a limited theology. "Ain't God Good" might be the only theme addressed. Or other preachers may end up with a "You Need to Live Right" message. Both of these themes are true and valuable in and of themselves, but they are not the full counsel of God. The full counsel would include both of these themes and more. A good way to broaden our message is to engage in sermon planning.

5) Homiletics allows us to spend more time on exegesis and sermon construction

One of the great things that Homiletics does is that it removes the frantic search for an "idea" or "thought" or "text." The text and a basic direction are taken care of in the plan

References

- Public-speaking, skills-and-tools: cleverism.com, Retrieved 10 March 2018
- Valenzano III, Joseph M.; Braden, Stephen W. (2012). The Speaker The Tradition and practice of public speaking. United States of America: Fountainhead press. p. 221. ISBN 978-1-59871-522-4
- 6-reasons-why-public-speaking-skills-are-important-to-career-and-finances: squirrelers.com, Retrieved 19 June 2018
- Woo, B. Hoon (2013). "Augustine's Hermeneutics and Homiletics in De doctrina christiana". Journal of Christian Philosophy. 17: 110–112
- 10-tips-improving-your-public-speaking-skills, professional-development: extension.harvard.edu, Retrieved 27 July 2018
- Advantages-and-disadvantages-of-speech: thebusinesscommunication.com, Retrieved 27 April 2018
- Wernicke K. (1995). "The aphasia symptom-complex: A psychological study on an anatomical basis (1875)". In Paul Eling. Reader in the History of Aphasia: From sasi(Franz Gall to). 4. Amsterdam: John Benjamins Pub Co. pp. 69–89. ISBN 90-272-1893-5
- Create-a-keynote-speech: examples.com, Retrieved 10 March 2018
- Plunkett, Kim; Juola, Patrick (1999). "A connectionist model of english past tense and plural morphology". Cognitive Science. 23 (4): 463–490. doi:10.1207/s15516709cog2304_4
- What-is-eloquence-1690642: thoughtco.com, Retrieved 16 May 2018
- 9-speaking-habits-that-make-you-sound-smarter: inc.com, Retrieved 10 June 2018
- Types-debates-2476: classroom.synonym.com, Retrieved 24 May 2018
- Levelt, Willem J. M. (1999). "Models of word production". Trends in Cognitive Sciences. 3(6): 223–232. doi:10.1016/s1364-6613(99)01319-4.
- Five-benefits-of-sermon-planning: soulpreaching.com, Retrieved 14 June 2018

2

Basic Elements of Public Speaking

The most important requirements in public speaking are the message to be conveyed, the medium of communications and the audience for whom the message is intended. Lasswell's model of communication describes the five elements of public speaking. The aim of this chapter is to give an overview of the basic elements of public speaking and includes vital topics related to medium of public speaking, the targeted audience, effect of the speech delivery, etc.

- Overcoming Your Fear

  Public speaking is an overwhelming affair. In fact, it is the number one fear in North America. Overcoming this takes a number of steps. Begin by identifying what it is you are afraid of and finding a way to face it. Also ensure adequate preparation and practice, either in front of a mirror or with increasing frequency of the speeches you give. Tearing down your fear for public speaking is a gradual process but it is important as it affects your level of confidence with an audience.

- Knowing Your Audience

  Your audience will have certain expectations of you, and in order to fulfill them, you need to know certain details about them. Aside from knowing how many there are, you should have a good idea what their age-group is and how much they understand the subject or topic you'll be presenting. Whether they are experienced or novices in the subject, your delivery should be holistic enough to let them learn something new and emphasize on obvious points without undermining their intelligence.

- Researching Your Topic

  An essential part of your presentation is in the knowledge you convey. For this reason, research should entail much of your preparation. Knowing your topic works well in your delivery and ability to answer questions from participants. In-depth knowledge of a topic keeps you from making sweeping statements and from having awkward moments in the middle of your speech or when questions come up, all of which can make your audience lose confidence in your capability to talk about the subject at hand.

- Having a Personality

  You need to be relatable and impressionable to your audience. Personality is conveyed through your tone, body language and the general sense of expression. Find ways to squeeze in some personal opinions on the subject you're delivering. You could illustrate points in your speech with stories drawn from personal experience so that your audience is also able to apply the knowledge you're imparting to them in their own lives. Your tone should be clear and friendly, even in professional circumstances. Move up and down the stage to keep yourself from being stale in your delivery.

- Encouraging Audience Participation

  Depending on the kind of speech you're delivering, you might consider finding a way to engage with your audience. Small groups could be given room to ask questions or a platform to make brief statements that are moderated. If you're dealing with a large group of attendees, you could have a catch word that they chant in response to points you make, to keep them alert and to emphasize the message of the talk you're giving. Your speech then becomes less monotonous and focus shifts from you towards the people you're addressing.

Communicator

Public Speaker:

- Puts the Message Before the People
- Asks: What Do I Have
- Emphasizes Techniques
- Focus is on Content of the Words
- Polished (Image Conscious)
- Goal: Complete the Message

Communicator:

- Puts the People Before the Message
- Asks: What Do They Need
- Emphasizes Atmosphere
- Focus is Change in the Listeners
- Personal (Impact Conscious)
- Goal: Complete the People

Despite the many ways to communicate, good communicators share in common important principles and techniques that enable them to communicate effectively. The characteristics of good communicators cut across all languages and cultures. Becoming a good communicator has many benefits and advantages in nearly all careers, the home, and in commerce.

Ten Qualities of Great Communicators

No Conversation Stoppers

There are eight conversational responses that are highly likely to stop your partner from continuing to share his or her more vulnerable thoughts and feelings. All of us have used these phrases and behaviors at times, often without realizing how badly they can make our partners feel.

Once you recognize them, you will hopefully not use them again. You can express these responses in effective ways at other times if your partner is interested, but never when your partner needs to be heard.

- Minimizing: Making the problem seem trivial.
- Taking the Other Person's Side: Not supporting your partner's experience.
- Blaming: Criticizing your partner for feeling or acting the way he or she does.
- Fixing: Offering to solve the situation without being asked.
- Giving Unsolicited Advice: Telling your partner how to act or feel.
- Shock: Expressing upset or outrage at what your partner is saying.
- Holier than Thou: Don't say how you could have handled the situation better.
- Negativity: Keep impatience, irritation, sarcasm, or sounding burdened out of your response.

Full Support Independent of Agreement

Many people believe that if they support the way their partners think or feel that they will automatically have to agree with them. Support and agreement do not have to be the same response. Even if you don't see things the same way, you can still be empathetic and understanding of how your speaker thinks and feels.

Too often listeners are so concerned that if they don't immediately argue for a different point of view, that there will be no way for them to disagree later, so they preempt their partner's conclusions to share how they may see the situation differently.

If you and your partner have agreed that emotional and psychological support do not automatically mean agreement, you are free to totally validate the thoughts and feelings of the other. Once your partner feels heard and understood, you can ask him or her if feedback is wanted.

Tracking

Your speaker will be far more likely to continue sharing if he or she feels that you are paying attention to all that's been said. That not only includes the present, but anything that might also reference the past. Take notes, if it helps you to do that as you are listening.

Many times when speakers are emotionally distressed, they repeat themselves or skip logical sequencing. It is very helpful to them if you can help them stay on track. Caringly ask the kind of questions or make comments that help them put their ideas together. It's like holding each important statement as an emotional puzzle piece, ever-ready to help your partner eventually see better how they can go together.

Presence

Anyone trying to share something painful or scary knows instantly if you are preoccupied or not really present. You'll know if you are "drifting" because your answers will sound patronizing, impatient, or matter-of-fact. Your speaker will soon feel he or she is boring you and will automatically shorten the conversation or push harder to be heard.

It's sometimes hard to stay focused listening to your partner, especially when he or she is angry, upset, or too repetitive. That's even truer if the object of the distress is you. If you feel defensive at any point and you can't be present anymore because of your own reactivity, ask for some time out to re-stabilize before you go on.

Rhythm

Good listeners get the cadence and urgency of their speaker's communication style and present need. They don't try to suppress emotions or change their rhythm or the way the words are being expressed. Some people get worked up as they get deeper into their emotions or change from one rhythm to another according to the subject they are unearthing.

If you can be flexible enough to flow with them at the same time as holding on to your own internal rhythm, you may be able to help them find a more comfortable pace that better enables both of you as close to the core truths as possible.

Emotional Anthropology

It is very tempting to impose one's own thoughts and feelings on another person, especially when he or she is vulnerable or needy. When your partner is trying to explore a deeper thought or feeling, he or she may seem unsteady or in need of direction, and that can feel like an invitation to redirect.

At those times, it is particularly important to just stay authentically interested, curious about those reflections and conclusions, and wanting to truly understand how that person came to feel the way he or she does in that moment.

Anthropologists know how important it is to respect and support another culture, even if they don't see the world in the same way. Every human being is a culture unto themselves and intimate partners need to remember that their partner's view of reality must be viewed with the same sacredness.

Timing

Even good listeners can make the mistake of answering too quickly, saying too much, interrupting, or pulling away and shutting down too quickly. It can be very hard to stay on track and not push your own timing agenda when you are on the other end of an emotionally upset person or have your own priorities.

In any conversation, you are absolutely allowed to tell your partner that you are overwhelmed or beginning to feel defensive, especially if your own emotions do not allow you to stay in the moment. You cannot continue to be a good listener when you're impatient, and it's always better to reconnect when you can be authentically present. If you do have to disconnect, make a time soon when you can continue so your partner doesn't feel abandoned.

Non-judgmental Feedback

When your partner feels safe, heard, and ready, you can offer non-judgmental feedback after asking if he or she is ready to listen to it. Using any notes you have taken, share your summary of what you thought was said, what your partner seemed to have needed, and where you agree or see things differently. Even if your experience is not positive, you can still deliver your feelings in a caring way.

Tell your partner how you feel about what you heard and what your responses are. Ask for feedback as to how you were as a listener and any differences he or she might have wished for. Where were you accurate and where might you have misunderstood? Did your partner feel cared for, understood, and supported, and in what ways? Does he or she have any good feedback for you?

Patience

Patience is not just "waiting." Patience is being so involved that you don't notice the passage of time. When you are listening deeply to another, with no other thought than to be there doing what you are doing, you feel emotionally weightless and unconnected to the past or future. Your only desire is to be there fully for the one you love.

Emotional patience feels to the other like chivalry. There is no resentment, impatience, martyrdom, or boredom in the gift of listening as long and to whatever your partner needs from you at the time. You feel absolutely willing to put your own needs aside, and feeling honored to do so at the time.

This may seem idealistic, but most people sharing something vulnerable or painful know exactly what it feels like to be on the other end of someone who truly wants to listen. You may not be able to do it for long periods of time, but the rewards for the listener are as great as for the speaker.

Weaving

This capability is the true art of a great communicator. People in pain or trying to express negative or hurt feelings often cannot keep track of what they've said or make sense of their presentation while they are in that emotional state.

A great listener weaves statements of the past, relates them to the present, and takes them forward into the future. To do that, he or she must take cues from the past and combine them with what listener already knows about that person. Using a combination of emotional support, accurate listening, tracking, rhythm, presence, and care, an effective listener helps his or her partner to continue getting closer to the true message offered.

Weaving helps a person remember his or her past and how it is affecting the present. It also helps point out repetitive patterns that have not yielded good results, and makes them less likely to continue into the future. It is crucial that weaving is not done in a way that makes the sharing partner feel trapped or labeled, just known more deeply as to whom he or she behaves in the relationship.

Message

The word "message" actually comes from the word "to send." The message is fundamental to communication.

With regard to public speaking and speech communication, your speech is your message. But you may have other intentions for your speech as well: the message behind the message. Perhaps you have a singular goal, point or emotion you want your audience to feel and understand. Every single word that you use to craft your speech then, works to achieve that singular goal, point or emotion.

As the sender, the speech writer and speech giver, you may also be getting messages back from your receivers: your audience. This is what's known as feedback, when the receiver sends a message of response *back* to the sender. In this way, messaging becomes a dynamic conversation of feedback as the sender sends his or her message to his or her audience, receives feedback from the audience, and then adjusts the message accordingly based on said feedback.

Messages can be sent both verbally and non-verbally. You can say one thing with your words, but depending on how you say it and the non-verbal cues such as posture and eye contact, you may send an entirely different message to your audience. That said, it's important to consider all aspects of your overall message, from verbal to non-verbal to the meaning and message behind the message, when crafting your speech.

Ways to Clarify your Message as a Public Speaker

- Clarify To Whom You Are Speaking

  If you don't know your audience, they will at best inadvertently detach themselves from your message. At worst, they will intentionally "check-out" emotionally, psychologically and mentally from your message.

  Is this really what we want as speakers? Do we really think that we will have any impact if we don't internalize a profound knowledge of those to whom we communicate?

- Clarify the Precise Message You Want Everyone to Hear

  Clarity sounds simple, but most leaders struggle to speak with simplicity.

  Think to the future for a minute. Imagine your audience walking out of the room. They have listened to you. They desire to make a change. They desire to take action on your words.

  What did you say that motivated them? What was the core message they heard?

  They certainly heard hundreds of words. They may have taken notes. They noticed your gestures. But can they articulate in 1-2 sentences the message they heard? Was this message something you repeated two, three, or four times? If so, what was it?. It is *vital* to clarify your message.

  Take a minute (or more than a minute) and clarify your message. What primary message do you want your audience to take away?

You must take the time to clarify your message in *your mind* if you have any hope of your audience hearing that central message:

- Clarify your message in your mind.
- Clarify your message on paper.
- Clarify your message in your presentation software, slides, handouts, etc.
- Clarify your message to an extreme, and then relate everything else to your unifying point or message.

- Clarify the Action You Want People to Take

  The key message you communicate will create little impact if it isn't fleshed out in the life of the listener.

  Examples:

  - Use words that relate your message to potential audience action steps.
  - Paint a picture of your message in the day-to-day life of your audience.
  - Bring your message to life in their lives.
  - Clarify for yourself and for your audience what success will look like if they move your message into their life.

- Clarify Why You Plan to Cover Your Given Topic

  You could make a strong argument that the "why" must precede all else. If you and others don't know why you speak on a given topic, motivation for change and action will decrease.

  Help your audience to see the negative impact on their life if they neglect to apply your message. Captivate them with how application of the message will impact their business, career, family, marriage, or community.

- Clarify Your Biases and Preferences

  These may cause you to stumble. In your mind, these are obvious. Unless you identify these ideas, thoughts, or biases, they will generate confusion. They are always clearer to the speaker's mind than the listener.

  We all have blind spots about what we know the most about. That's convicting.

  You likely will need to get outside input to identify these areas. In our mind, they are clear as day. To our audience, they are unclear, questionable, or outright mistaken.

- Clarify What You Will Not Say

  Most of the time we hyper focus on what we *will* say. We want to "get it right." We want to say those perfect words that will invigorate our audience.

But what about the words we will not say? You may have never thought of this step. No problem.

Effective speech eliminates distractions from the core message. Ask yourself what stories or rabbit trails you tend to discuss. Do any of these distract from your core message?

Perhaps just as effective, ask a colleague, close friend, or family member where you tend to lose focus when speaking. Ask one of these people to listen to your speech in advance and identify 2-3 things that provide neutral benefit or weren't clearly related to your primary message. Trust me. Those closest to you can identify the distractions more effectively than you can.

By doing this exercise it will allow you to clarify your message and make that message loud and clear without the distracting rabbit trails.

Beware of the temptation to trust your intuition: As a speaker, nearly all the information you've considered clearly relates to the main topic. You can't hear your unclear messages nearly as well as your audience can. This is why having someone else read or listen to your message first can help avoid being unclear.

When you and those around you clarify what you will not say, you give yourself freedom to set those things aside. You block out those potential points that might confuse your audience. You clarify not only what matters, but you also eradicate what distracts from the important message. This is a vital step when you are trying to clarify your message.

- Clarify What You Will Repeat

Clarification always involves repetition and repetition nearly always yields clarification.

Clarify your message. Repeat the core message. Say it again in a different way. Then, circle the wagon back to the core message.

But how do you integrate repetition without coming across as redundant?

After you repeat your core message, seek out ways to repeat the meaning, to illustrate the message in real life, and to further support your central message. You can do this with quotes, statistics, or other evidence. These things will serve to support, endorse, bolster, or otherwise clarify your message in the hearts and minds of the listeners.

- Clarify The Illustrations that Will Support Your Main Point (and how you'll communicate the illustrations)

The illustrations you use should bring the main message to life, connect with the heart of the listener, or give people something to help remember your speech. Do your illustrations and metaphors do that?

Illustrations put flesh on the ideas you communicate. *Choose them wisely.*

All too often I've heard public speakers communicate multiple illustrations in a row. Many times they didn't even sound connected to one another. Using illustrations in this way distracts the listener from your core message. It leaves them thinking about a distantly related illustration rather than what you were trying to communicate.

Once you decide on your illustration, practice the way in which you will communicate it. We often share illustrations that resonate with us as speakers. Make sure that you take the time to plan how you will communicate the illustration and use gestures so that it resonates with the audience as well.

The best illustrations tend to be obvious and self-explanatory. But exercise caution sharing an illustration without some type of explanation. If you don't explain it, you leave the door open to confusion and miscommunication rather than clarity.

- Clarify How You'll Follow-Up

What steps will you take to reinforce your message? I don't hear many unforgettable messages. You likely don't either.

If the average speech is not unforgettable, I'd say it's unwise if you don't design follow-up material to reinforce it. But even if you deliver a memorable speech, why wouldn't you want to make sure it "sticks" and results in life change?

- Clarify How You'll Evaluate Your Effectiveness

Design measures that provide a barometer of your persuasive precision and communication clarity.

When you evaluate your communication, you learn from it. You repeat what works. You demonstrate teachability to your audience. You never stop growing.

Evaluation also prioritizes your audience. If you don't evaluate your communication, either the audience you just spoke to or future audiences will know. People remember the best public speakers not for their consistent mistakes, but their ability to repeat success.

When it comes to communication, we either commit to clarity or confusion. Don't risk assuming that people receive your communication more clearly than is actually the case. Own it and be intentionally clear.

Medium

The venue of your speech should suggest the appropriate selection of presentation aids. In your classroom, you have several choices, including some that omit technology. If you are speaking in a large auditorium, you will almost certainly need to use technology to project text and images on a large screen.

Many students feel that they lack the artistic skills to render their own graphics, so they opt to use copyright-free graphics on their presentation aids. You may do this as long as you use images that are created in a consistent style. For instance, you should not combine realistic renderings with cartoons unless there is a clear and compelling reason to do so. Being selective in this way will result in a sequence of presentation aids that look like a coherent set, thereby enhancing your professionalism.

Computer-Based Media

In most careers in business, industry, and other professions for which students are preparing themselves, computer-based presentation aids are the norm today. Whether the context is a weekly department meeting in a small conference room or an annual convention in a huge amphitheater, speakers are expected to be comfortable with using PowerPoint or other similar software to create and display presentation aids.

If your public speaking course meets in a smart classroom, you have probably had the opportunity to see the computer system in action. Many such systems today are nimble and easy to use. Still, "easy" is a relative term. Don't take for granted someone else's advice that "it's really self-explanatory"—instead, make sure to practice ahead of time. It is also wise to be prepared for technical problems, which can happen to even the most sophisticated computer users. When Steve Jobs, CEO of Apple and cofounder of Pixar, introduced a new iPhone 4 in June, 2010, his own visual presentation froze. The irony of a high-tech guru's technology not working at a public presentation did not escape the notice of news organizations.

In addition to presentation software such as PowerPoint, speakers sometimes have access to interactive computer-based presentation aids. These are often called "clickers"—handheld units that audience members hold and that are connected to a monitor to which the speaker has access. These interactive aids are useful for tracking audience responses to questions, and they have the advantage over asking for a show of hands in that they can be anonymous. A number of instructors in various courses use "clickers" in their classrooms.

Using computer-based aids in a speech brings up a few logistical considerations. In some venues, you may need to stand behind a high-tech console to operate the computer. You need to be aware that this will physically isolate you from the audience you with whom you are trying to establish a relationship in your speech. When you stand behind presentation equipment, you may feel really comfortable, but you end up limiting your nonverbal interaction with your audience.

Audiovisual Media

Although audio and video clips are often computer-based, they can be (and, in past decades, always were) used without a computer.

Audio presentation aids are useful for illustrating musical themes. For instance, if you're speaking about how the Polish composer Frederick Chopin was inspired by the sounds of nature, you can convey that meaning only through playing an example. If you have a smart classroom, you may be able to use it to play an MP3. Alternatively, you may need to bring your music player. In that case, be sure the speakers in the room are up to the job. The people in the back of the room must be able to hear it, and the speakers must not sound distorted when you turn the volume up.

Video that clarifies, explains, amplifies, emphasizes, or illustrates a key concept in your speech is appropriate, as long as you do not rely on it to do your presentation for you. There are several things you must do. First, identify a specific section of video that delivers meaning. Second, "cue up" the video so that you can just pop it into the player, and it will begin at the right place. Third, tell your audience where the footage comes from. You can tell your audience, for instance, that you are showing them an example from the 1985 BBC documentary titled "In Search of the Trojan War." Fourth, tell your audience why you're showing the footage. For instance, you can tell them, "This is an example of storytelling in the Bardic tradition." You can interrupt or mute the video to make a comment about it, but your total footage should not use more than 20 percent of the time for your speech.

Low-Tech Media

In some speaking situations, of course, computer technology is not available. Even if you have ready access to technology, there will be contexts where computer-based presentation aids are unnecessary or even counterproductive. And in still other contexts, computer-based media may be accompanied by low-tech presentation aids. One of the advantages of low-tech media is that they are very predictable. There's little that can interfere with using them. Additionally, they can be inexpensive to produce. However, unlike digital media, they can be prone to physical damage in the form of smudges, scratches, dents, and rips. It can be difficult to keep them professional looking if you have to carry them through a rainstorm or blizzard, so you will need to take steps to protect them as you transport them to the speech location. Let's examine some of the low-tech media that you might use with a speech.

Chalk or Dry-Erase Board

If you use a chalkboard or dry-erase board you are not using a prepared presentation aid. Your failure to prepare visuals ahead of time can be interpreted in several ways, mostly negative. If other speakers carefully design, produce, and use attractive visual aids, yours will stand out by contrast. You will be seen as the speaker who does not take the time to prepare even a simple aid. Do not use a chalkboard or marker board and pretend it's a prepared presentation aid.

However, numerous speakers do utilize chalk and dry-erase boards effectively. Typically, these speakers use the chalk or dry-erase board for interactive components of a speech. For example, maybe you're giving a speech in front of a group of executives. You may have a PowerPoint all prepared, but at various points in your speech you want to get your audience's responses. Chalk or dry-erase boards are very useful when you want to visually show information that you are receiving from your audience. If you ever use a chalk or dry-erase board, follow these three simple rules:

1. Write large enough so that everyone in the room can see.
2. Print legibly; don't write in cursive script.
3. Write short phrases; don't take time to write complete sentences.

It is also worth mentioning that some classrooms and business conference rooms are equipped with smartboards, or digitally enhanced whiteboards. On a smartboard you can bring up prepared visuals and then modify them as you would a chalk or dry-erase board. The advantage is that you can keep a digital record of what was written for future reference. However, as with other technology-based media, smartboards may be prone to unexpected technical problems, and they require training and practice to be used properly.

Flipchart

A flipchart is useful when you're trying to convey change over a number of steps. For instance, you could use a prepared flipchart to show dramatic population shifts on maps. In such a case, you should prepare highly visible, identical maps on three of the pages so that only the data will change from page to page. Each page should be neatly titled, and you should actively point out the areas of change on each page. You could also use a flip chart to show stages in the growth and development of the malaria-bearing mosquito. Again, you should label each page, making an effort to give the pages a consistent look.

Organize your flip chart in such a way that you flip pages in one direction only, front to back. It will be difficult to flip large pages without damaging them, and if you also have to "back up" and "skip forward," your presentation will look awkward and disorganized. Pages will get damaged, and your audience will be able to hear each rip.

In addition, most flip charts need to be propped up on an easel of some sort. If you arrive for your speech only to find that the easel in the classroom has disappeared, you will need to rig up another system that allows you to flip the pages.

Poster Board or Foam Board

Foam board consists of a thin sheet of Styrofoam with heavy paper bonded to both surfaces. It is a lightweight, inexpensive foundation for information, and it will stand on its own when placed in an easel without curling under at the bottom edge. Poster board tends to be cheaper than foam board, but it is flimsier, more vulnerable to damage, and can't stand on its own.

If you plan to paste labels or paragraphs of text to foam or poster board, for a professional look you should make sure the color of the poster board matches the color of the paper you will paste on. You will also want to choose a color that allows for easy visual contrast so your audience can see it, and it must be a color that's appropriate for the topic. For instance, hot pink would be the wrong color on a poster for a speech about the Protestant Reformation.

Avoid producing a presentation aid that looks like you simply cut pictures out of magazines and pasted them on. Slapping some text and images on a board looks unprofessional and will not be viewed as credible or effective. Instead, when creating a poster you need to take the time to think about how you are going to lay out your aid and make it look professional. You do not have to spend lots of money to make a very sleek and professional-looking poster.

Some schools also have access to expensive, full-color poster printers where you can create large poster for pasting on a foam board. In the real world of public speaking, most speakers rely on the creation of professional posters using a full-color poster printer. Typically, posters are sketched out and then designed on a computer using a program like Microsoft PowerPoint or Publisher (these both have the option of selecting the size of the printed area).

Handouts

Handouts are appropriate for delivering information that audience members can take away with them. As we will see, handouts require a great deal of management if they are to contribute to your credibility as a speaker.

First, make sure to bring enough copies of the handout for each audience member to get one. Having to share or look on with one's neighbor does not contribute to a professional image. Under no circumstances should you ever provide a single copy of a handout to pass around. There are several reasons this is a bad idea. You will have no control over the speed at which it circulates, or the direction it goes. Moreover, only one listener will be holding it while you're making your point about it and by the time most people see it they will have forgotten why they need to see it. In some case, it might not even reach everybody by the end of your speech. Finally, listeners could still be passing your handout around during the next speaker's speech.

There are three possible times to distribute handouts: before you begin your speech, during the speech, and after your speech is over. Naturally, if you need your listeners to follow along in a handout, you will need to distribute it before your speech begins. If you have access to the room ahead of time, place a copy of the handout on each seat in the audience. If not, ask a volunteer to distribute them as quickly as possible while you prepare to begin speaking. If the handout is a "takeaway," leave it on a table near the door so that those audience members who are interested can take one on their way out; in this case, don't forget to tell them to do so as you conclude your speech. It is almost never appropriate to distribute handouts during your speech, as it is distracting and interrupts the pace of your presentation.

Like other presentation aids, handouts should include only the necessary information to support your points, and that information should be organized in such a way that listeners will be able to understand it. For example, in a speech about how new health care legislation will affect small business owners in your state, a good handout might summarize key effects of the legislation and include the names of state agencies with their web addresses where audience members can request more detailed information.

If your handout is designed for your audience to follow along, you should tell them so. State that you will be referring to specific information during the speech. Then, as you're presenting your speech, ask your audience to look, for example, at the second line in the first cluster of information. Read that line out loud and then go on to explain its meaning.

As with any presentation aid, handouts are not a substitute for a well-prepared speech. Ask yourself what information your audience really needs to be able to take with them and how it can be presented on the page in the most useful and engaging way possible.

Key Points

- Speakers in professional contexts are expected to be familiar with presentation software, such as PowerPoint.
- Computer-based media can produce very professional-looking presentation aids, but as with any other media, the universal principles of good design apply.
- Speakers using computer-based media need to practice ahead of time with the computer they intend to use in the speech.
- Each presentation aid vehicle has advantages and disadvantages. As such, speakers need to think through the use of visual aids and select the most appropriate ones for their individual speeches.

- Every presentation aid should be created with careful attention to content and appearance.

Audience

An audience is a group of people who come together to listen to the speaker. The audience may be face to face with the speaker or they may be connected by communication technology such as computers or other media. The audience may be small or it may be a large public audience. A key characteristic of the audience in public speaking situations is the unequal distribution of speaking time. What does this mean? The speaker talks much more and the audience listens, often without asking questions or responding with any feedback. In some situations the audience may ask questions or respond overtly by clapping or making comments.

Audience Centered Approach to Speaking

Since there is usually limited communication between the speaker and the audience, there is limited opportunity to go back to explain your meaning. In order to prepare, it is important to know about the audience and adapt the message to the audience. You want to prepare your speech with a focus on the audience, not just you, the speaker, or your message. We call this approach audience-centered.

In public speaking, you are speaking for and to your audience; thus, understanding the audience is a major part of the speech making process. In audience-centered speaking, getting to know your target audience is one of the most important tasks that you face. You want to learn about the major demographics of the audience such as age, gender, sexual orientation, education, religion, what culture, ethnic group or race as well as to what groups the audience members belong. Additionally, learning about the values, attitudes and beliefs of the members of your audience will allow you to anticipate and plan your message.

Finding Common Ground by Taking Perspective

You want to analyze your audience prior to your speech so you can create a link between you, the speaker and the audience during the speech. You want to be able to step inside the minds of the audience to understand the world from their perspective. Through this process you can find common ground with the audience, which allows you to align your message with what the audience already knows or believes.

Key Points

- Knowing your audience: Their general age, gender, education level, religion, language, culture, and group membership—is the single most important aspect of developing your speech.
- Analyzing your audience will help you discover information that you can use to build common ground between you and the members of your audience.

- A key characteristic in public speaking situations is the unequal distribution of speaking time between the speaker and the audience. This means that the speaker talks more and the audience listens, often without asking questions or responding with any feedback.

Key Terms

- Audience: One or more people within hearing range of some message; for example, a group of people listening to a performance or speech; the crowd attending a stage performance.
- Audience analysis: A study of the pertinent elements defining the makeup and characteristics of an audience.
- Audience-centered: Tailored to an audience. When preparing a message, the speaker analyzes the audience in order to adapt the content and language usage to the level of the listeners.

Benefits of Understanding Audiences

When you are speaking, you want listeners to understand and respond favorably to what you are saying. An audience is one or more people who come together to listen to the speaker. Audience members may be face to face with the speaker or they may be connected by communication technology such as computers or other media. The audience may be small and private or it may be large and public. A key characteristic of public speaking situations is the unequal distribution of speaking time between speaker and audience. As an example, the speaker usually talks more while the audience listens, often without asking questions or responding with any feedback.

Know the Size of your Audience

Will you be speaking to just a few people or to dozens or even hundreds of people? Clearly, the audience size determines the physical setting and, in turn, guides the type of visuals you should use. What's more, for a large audience, you may need to use a lectern and a microphone. If so, that will enter into your planning and preparation as well.

Know the Attitudes and Biases of your Audience

This may be easy to do if you're presenting to a small number of colleagues, in contrast to an audience you haven't met before. Easy or not, it's important nonetheless. What does your audience think about your topic? What do they think about you? Are they likely to be skeptical - even hostile? Or are they likely to respond favorably? If your goal is to persuade or motivate your audience, what biases, concerns or fears must you first overcome to achieve your goal? You may decide in the end that you cannot completely satisfy everyone's concerns. But at least you can present your position strategically, while taking those concerns into account and through that, showing your own awareness and sensitivity.

As much as Possible, Know what Motivates your Audience

Your audience may have strongly held views about your topic. They may also have certain expectations. What are these, and what can you do to help meet them? There may be issues that trigger strong emotions in your audience. Find out what these are, and prepare to deal with them.

How much does your Audience Already Know

Good communicators never talk down to their audience. If your audience already knows a good deal about your topic, your presentation should build on what your audience knows, and not simply repeat what is already known. Good communicators also don't talk over the head of others. If your audience knows little about your topic, tell them what they need to know to respond as you want them to.

Talk to their Interests, not yours

You should talk to the specific interests of your audience. Again, those interests are easy enough to know if you're presenting to an intimate group of colleagues. With other audiences, however, it may take some digging. Don't assume or guess what those interests are: ask, instead. An audience of senior-level managers, for example, may well have different interests than an audience of entry-level professionals. Factors such as educational and job background, professional interest, even recent work or personal experiences your listeners might have had, are also important. You may also want to know the relationship of your audience members to one another. Do they have common interests, or do their interests conflict with one another? Again, the more you know about these, the more likely you are to connect with your listeners from *their* point of view.

The "What's- in-it-for me?" Rule

This is also known as the "Why- should-I-listen-to-you?" rule. It applies especially to business audiences. When preparing your presentation, embed the answers to these questions early in your remarks, so that your listeners know what they're going to get out of your presentation.

Audience is where it all Starts

It follows that this part of your preparation - the phase known as audience analysis - is essential in determining how you will build your presentation. The more you know about your audience, the better you can target your remarks to reflect their specific interests and concerns. And the more likely you are to succeed as a presenter.

Effect

Public speaking skills allow people to influence the world through public leadership in society, including roles in commercial organizations, the volunteer sector, groups, and clubs. They can also enhance one's personal development and self-confidence.

Public Leadership as Influence

Public speakers have the opportunity to influence others; they can use their knowledge of persuasion to motivate others to take collective action to achieve desired goals. There is a strong correlation between leadership and communication skills. Leadership has been described as "a process of social influence in which one person can enlist the aid and support of others in the accomplishment of a common task." Public speaking skills can be used to influence multiple people simultaneously, such as in a meeting or when addressing a large group. Speaking skills can help when setting and agreeing to a motivating vision or future for a group or organization to ensure unity of purpose; creating positive peer pressure towards shared, high performance standards and an atmosphere of trust and team spirit; and driving successful collective action and results.

Martin Luther King, Jr. Winston Churchill, and Nelson Mendela are notable examples of effective orators who used oratory to have a significant impact on society. The influence of the great leaders may have been initially limited to moving an audience in person with written copies of their speeches distributed. With the invention of radio and television, listeners who could not attend in person were still influenced by the words of the speaker.

Global Leadership as Influence

Today, the reach of technology is pervasive and global. In the past, influencing others involved speaking directly to an audience face-to-face or having expensive equipment for broadcasting. Today, modern communication technology coupled with the internet means that speakers can share messages and thoughts with audiences anyplace in the world for the cost of an internet connection and a camera, or simply a smart phone recorder.

How Influence Works in Daily Life

Public speaking skills are not reserved for global leaders; anyone can use the same skills in his or her daily life to speak with confidence. Aristotle defined rhetoric as the "faculty of discovering the possible means of persuasion in reference to any subject whatever."

For example, imagine someone who wants to persuade his or her parents for money. Chances are that this person will work through strategies for persuading them why he or she needs the money and why the parents should provide it. He or she will reflect on what has and has not worked in the past, including previous successful and unsuccessful strategies. From this analysis, he or she constructs a message that fits the occasion and audience.

Now, imagine that the same person wants to persuade his or her roommate to go out to get Mexican food for dinner. He or she is not going to use the same message or approach that he or she used with the parents. The same logic exists in public speaking situations. Aristotle highlighted the importance of finding the appropriate message and strategy for the audience and occasion in order to persuade.

By training in public speaking and actually speaking in front of an audience, one develops a sense of self-confidence. Public speakers learn to overcome fear of failure and lack of confidence in order to deliver a message to an audience. They learn to think about ideas, evaluate their truthfulness, and then organize them into a message to share with others.

The flip side of public speaking is listening; people can learn how to influence by learning how to listen. Trained speakers know how to recognize sound logic, reasoning, and ethical appeals. A critical listener is less likely to be persuaded by unsound logic and fallacies or to take action that is not in his or her best interest.

Lasswell's Model of Communication

Lasswell's communication model was developed by communication theorist Harold D. Lasswell in

1948. Lasswell's model of communication (also known as action model or linear model or one way model of communication) is regarded as one the most influential communication models.

Components of Lasswell's Communication Model

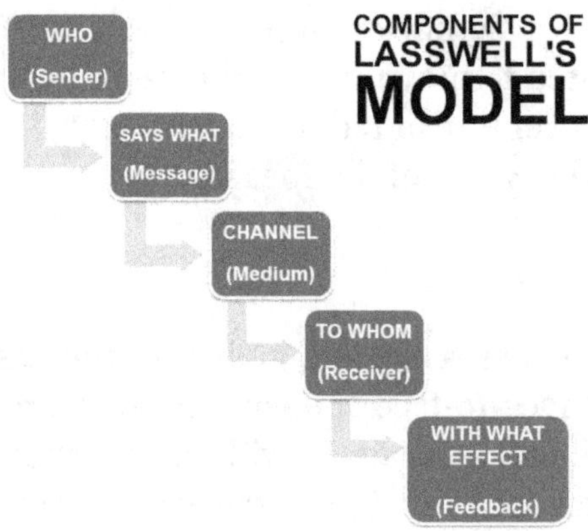

Lasswell's communication model has 5 components which is used as an analysis tool for evaluating the communication process and components. The components are the questions to be asked to get the answers and keep communication going.

Components	Meaning	Analysis
Who	the communicator or sender or source of message	Control Analysis
Says What	the content of the message	Content Analysis
In Which Channel	the medium or media	Media Analysis
To Whom	the receiver of the message or an audience	Audience Analysis
With What Effect	the feedback of the receiver to the sender	Effect Analysis

Components of Lasswell's Model

- Control analysis: It helps the sender to have all the power.
- Content analysis: It is associated to stereotyping and representation of different groups politically. It is also related to the purpose or the ulterior motives of the message.
- Media analysis: It represents which medium should be used to exercise maximum power against the receivers.
- Audience analysis: Shows who are the target population to be manipulated or brain-washed.
- Effect analysis: It is done before the process starts. It is used to predict the effect of message over the target population to be exploited.

Lasswell's Communication Model

Though Lasswell's model was developed to analyze mass communication, this model is used for interpersonal communication or group communication to be disseminated message to various groups in various situations.

Lasswell's model was developed to study the media propaganda of countries and businesses at that time. Only rich people used to have communication mediums such as televisions and radios back them. It was made to show the mass media culture.

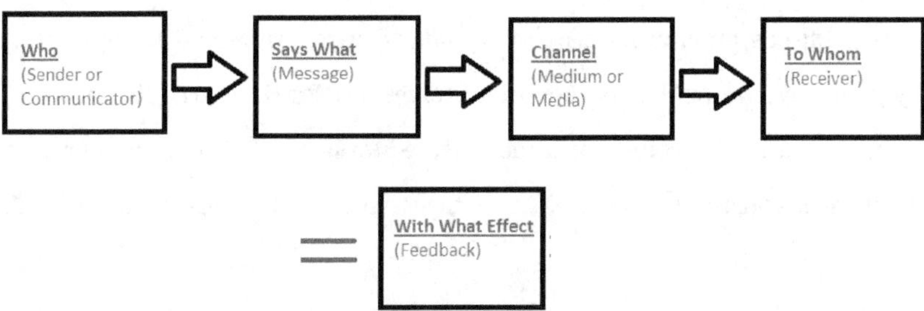

Lasswell also brought the concept of Effective Communication Process. He talked about the relation between presentation of facts and how it generates different effects. The use of the concept of effect makes Lasswell's model non-linear unlike it's name. It's because effect can also be taken as feedback.

Though, generally, the component of effect was made to be more about outcome of the message, the model is applied in different medias and fields despite being developed specifically for mass communication.

Advantages and Disadvantages of the Model

This model of the study of communication has been one of the most used since it was first raised, but has also received a lot of criticism. Next we will see some of its most important advantages and disadvantages.

Advantage

- It is a simple and easy to understand model, since it does not recharge the communication process and focuses on its most basic elements.
- It is valid for practically any type of communication, regardless of the type of medium by which it occurs, who the sender and receiver are, or what type of message is transmitted.
- It was the first model to focus on the effect produced by a certain type of communication and to study its effects.

Disadvantages

- No feedback is mentioned by the receiver, which has been included in more modern and complex communication models.
- No mention is made of noise, which is any element of communication (usually part of the channel) that can hinder the process of transmitting information.
- It is a linear model of communication, which can be a problem to study information exchanges in which the receiver and the issuer exchange roles continuously.

References

- 5-essential-elements-in-successful-public-speaking: careeraddict.com, Retrieved 20 March 2018
- Are-you-a-communicator-or-a-public-speaker: presentationxpert.com, Retrieved 24 April 2018
- The-ten-qualities-great-communicators: psychologytoday.com, Retrieved 28 June 2018
- 10-ways-clarify-your-message-public-speaker: bradbridges.net, Retrieved 11 July 2018
- Lasswell-communication-model, communication: businesstopia.net, Retrieved 24 May 2018
- Lasswell-model-what-it-consists-in-elements-advantages-and-disadvantages: lifepersona.com, Retrieved 30 June 2018

3

Public Speaking Skills

Public speaking can serve the purpose of motivating people, telling a story or transmitting information. Some of the public speaking skills required to be an expert orator are self-confidence, strategic planning, good body language and ability to engage an audience, which have been discussed in great detail in this chapter.

Every public speaker should be able to:

- Research a topic: Good speakers stick to what they know. Great speakers research what they need to convey their message.
- Focus: Help your audience grasp your message by focusing on your message. Stories, humour or other "sidebars" should connect to the core idea. Anything that doesn't needs to be edited out.
- Organize ideas logically: A well-organized presentation can be absorbed with minimal mental strain. Bridging is key.
- Employ quotations, facts and statistics: Don't include these for the sake of including them, but do use them appropriately to complement your ideas.
- Master metaphors: Metaphors enhance the understandability of the message in a way that direct language often cannot.
- Tell a story: Everyone loves a story. Points wrapped up in a story are more memorable.
- Start strong and close stronger: The body of your presentation should be strong too, but your audience will remember your first and last words (if, indeed, they remember anything at all).
- Incorporate humour: Knowing when to use humour is essential. So is developing the comedic timing to deliver it with greatest effect.
- Vary vocal pace, tone, and volume: A monotone voice is like fingernails on the chalkboard.
- Punctuate words with gestures: Gestures should complement your words in harmony. Tell them how big the fish was, and show them with your arms.
- Utilize 3-dimensional space: Chaining yourself to the lectern limits the energy and passion you can exhibit. Lose the notes, and lose the chain.
- Complement words with visual aids: Visual aids should *aid* the message; they should not *be* the message.
- Analyze your audience: Deliver the message they want (or need) to hear.
- Connect with the audience: Eye contact is only the first step. Aim to have the audience conclude "This speaker is just like me." The sooner, the better.

- Interact with the audience: Ask questions (and care about the answers). Solicit volunteers. Make your presentation a dialogue.
- Conduct a Q&A session: Not every speaking opportunity affords a Q&A session, but understand how to lead one productively. Use the Q&A to solidify the impression that you are an expert, not (just) a speaker.
- Lead a discussion: Again, not every speaking opportunity affords time for a discussion, but know how to engage the audience productively.
- Obey time constraints: Maybe you have 2 minutes. Maybe you have 45. Either way, customize your presentation to fit the time allowed, and respect your audience by not going over time.
- Craft an introduction: Set the context and make sure the audience is ready to go, whether the introduction is for you or for someone else.
- Exhibit confidence and poise: These qualities are sometimes difficult for a speaker to attain, but easy for an audience to sense.
- Handle unexpected issues smoothly: Maybe the lights will go out. Maybe the projector is dead. Have a plan to handle every situation.
- Be coherent when speaking off the cuff: Impromptu speaking (before, after, or during a presentation) leaves a lasting impression too. Doing it well tells the audience that you are personable, and that you are an expert who knows their stuff beyond the slides and prepared speech.
- Seek and utilize feedback: Understand that no presentation or presenter (yes, even you.) is perfect. Aim for continuous improvement, and understand that the best way to improve is to solicit candid feedback from as many people as you can.
- Listen critically and analyze other speakers: Study the strengths and weakness of other speakers.
- Act and speak ethically: Since public speaking fears are so common, realize the tremendous power of influence that you hold.

Self-confidence

Self-confidence is one's ability to judge his own social and personal standing with respect to his environment and be able to derive satisfaction out of it.

Self-confidence is influenced by factors like upbringing, work environment, and levels of dedication towards pursuing a cause. High self-confidence is an important factor in improving business ties and balancing personal life.

Being confident about your strengths helps you draw courage and resolution when the going gets tough in life. It helps you to keep things in perspective and back yourself when everyone else says that the task ahead is nearly impossible to complete in the stipulated time.

A confident person has enough ability to understand his limitations and knows how to make up for that with his resolve and strengths.

Now that we have understood how self-confidence depends on your perceived ability to manage an action, let's discuss the actions that help cultivating a sense of self-confidence.

Action that help Cultivating Sense of Self-confidence

Self-confidence thrives in an atmosphere where the person is provided constructive feedback and the focus is always on the positive.

In such a working environment, a confident person will be able to practice his skills and talent beyond expectations, as he will get an opportunity to setting goals, forget his own past mistakes, and learn new things.

On the other hand, a person's self-confidence can be seriously hampered in an environment where there is constant comparison with others and where expectations are unrealistic. People are pitted against each other as per their performance in the numbers game.

In these conditions, a person will be forced to nurture an unhealthy competitive mentality by resorting to unfair means for success, listening to unworthy role models, being too harsh in judging his own performances, and underestimating his own capabilities.

Such an environment breeds an unhealthy workplace where the stress is more on beating one another's performances, as opposed to coming together as a team in helping one another. Such companies might peak for some time, but they ultimately crash.

People with High Self-confidence

People with high self-confidence approach their problems differently as compared to others. They know the importance of building relationships and hence, they love meeting new people to get and share new ideas. It is this quality of theirs that makes them likeable, as they are always willing to be in a conversation that gives equal importance and respect to all those who have participated in it.

Confident people love expressing their ideas in front of others, as they are emotionally secure enough to take constructive criticisms and reject emotional ones. That doesn't mean that they are arrogant; on the contrary, they give everyone the opportunity to put their points forth. However, they have the courage to stick to their decision in spite of a lot of opposition to their ideas, if they are convinced what they are doing is right.

There are two outcomes to any decision taken either it turns out to be the correct one, or you fail. However, what sets a confident person apart is that he doesn't boss around on detractors when he succeeds.

In addition, a self-confident person has the humility to acknowledge his mistakes and learn from them when he fails. This objective approach towards both success and failure is what makes a confident person a lovable and respectable personality.

People with Low Self-confidence

When compared to people with high self-confidence, people with low self-confidence have a very harsh and critical view of themselves. They are prone to taking emotional decisions, as opposed to thinking rationally. They tend to be in their "caves" instead of meeting new people. They try to shun new company and avoid meeting new people.

An under-confident person tend to feel that he has nothing consequential or constructive to add to any process. This feeling of low self-worth, combined with a complete denial towards any change, makes an under-confident person extremely susceptive to mistreatment and undervaluation.

People with low confidence hesitate in sharing their thoughts and opinions, as they think their views will be ridiculed in public. In addition to this, their past experiences and interactions with people have not done anything to enhance their self-worth and change their views about their productivity and importance.

This is where a productive atmosphere comes in play. Every person learns from his surroundings and your self-confidence depends directly on the kind of people you meet and the type of discussions you have with them. While self-confident people interact with people whom they have something to learn from, under confident people are convinced that they cannot change and are going to be undervalued in spite of what they do.

Effects of Low Self-confidence

Every person needs someone who he can idolize and follow so that he gauges his own talents, achievements, and progress in comparison to that person and constantly improves. This is exactly what self-confident people do. While interacting with others, reading about others, and putting their ideas in public to gain perspective, they constantly improve their skills and knowledge.

But what happens when people stop doing that? They tend to lose focus, as they don't have any anchor left in their life who can stabilize them when they are getting adrift. When interaction with society is stopped, a person tends to think about himself and that reflects in the way he accepts criticism. Even constructive criticism for his work will appear personal criticism for him, as his approach would have become extremely self-centered by then.

People with low self-confidence tend to think they have no talent or skill to complete a given task and be appreciated. In fact, genuine praise for a good effort comes to them as a surprise and they perceive that as fake appreciation.

Theories and Correlations with other Variables and Factors

Self-confidence as an Intra-psychological Variable

Social psychologists have found self-confidence to be correlated with other psychological variables within individuals, including saving money, how individuals exercise influence over others, and being a responsible student. Marketing researchers have found that general self-confidence of a person is negatively correlated with their level of anxiety.

Some studies suggest various factors within and beyond an individual's control that affect their self-confidence. Hippel and Trivers propose that people will deceive themselves about their own positive qualities and negative qualities of others so that they can display greater self-confidence than they might otherwise feel, thereby enabling them to advance socially and materially. Others have found that new information about an individual's performance interacts with an individual's prior self-confidence about their ability to perform. If that particular information is negative feedback, this may interact with a negative affective state (low self-confidence) causing the individual to become demoralized, which in turn induces a self-defeating attitude that increases the likelihood of failure in the future more than if they did not lack self-confidence. On the other hand, some also find that self-confidence increases a person's general well-being and one's motivation and therefore often performance. It also increases one's ability to deal with stress and mental health.

A meta-analysis of 12 articles found that generally when individuals attribute their success to a stable cause (a matter under their control) they are less likely to be confident about being successful in the future. If an individual attributes their failure to an unstable cause (a factor beyond their control, like a sudden and unexpected storm) they are less likely to be confident about succeeding in the future. Therefore, if an individual believes he/she and/or others failed to achieve a goal (e.g. give up smoking) because of a factor that was beyond their control, he or she is more likely to be more self-confident that he or she can achieve the goal in the future. Whether a person in making a decision seeks out additional sources of information depends on their level of self-confidence specific to that area. As the complexity of a decision increases, a person is more likely to be influenced by another person and seek out additional information. However, people can also be relatively self-confident about what they believe if they consult sources of information that agree with their world views (e.g. New York Times for liberals, Fox News for conservatives), even if they do not know what will happen tomorrow. Several psychologists suggest that people who are self-confident are more willing to examine evidence that both supports and contradicts their attitudes. Meanwhile, people who are less self-confident about their perspective and are more defensive about them may prefer proattitudinal information over materials that challenge their perspectives.

Relationship to Social Influences

An individual's self-confidence can vary in different environments, such as at home or in school, and with respect to different types of relationships and situations. In relation to general society, some have found that the more self-confident an individual is, the less likely they are to conform to the judgments of others. Leon Festinger found that self-confidence in an individual's ability may only rise or fall where that individual is able to compare themselves to others who are roughly similar in a competitive environment. Furthermore, when individuals with low self-confidence receive feedback from others, they are averse to receiving information about their relative ability and negative informative feedback, and not averse to receiving positive feedback.

People with high self-confidence can easily impress others, as others perceive them as more knowledgeable and more likely to make correct judgments, despite the fact that often a negative correlation is sometimes found between the level of their self-confidence and accuracy of their claims. When people are uncertain and unknowledgeable about a topic, they are more likely to believe the testimony, and follow the advice of those that seem self-confident. However, expert psychological testimony on the factors that influence eyewitness memory appears to reduce juror reliance on self-confidence.

People are more likely to choose leaders with greater self-confidence than those with less self-confidence. Heterosexual men who exhibit greater self-confidence than other men are more likely to attract single and partnered women. Salespeople who are high in self-confidence are more likely to set higher goals for themselves and therefore more likely to stay employed. yield higher revenues and customer service satisfaction In relation to leadership, leaders with high self-confidence are more likely to influence others through persuasion rather than coercive means. Individuals low in power and thus in self-confidence are more likely to use coercive methods of influence and to become personally involved while those low in self-confidence are more likely to refer problem to someone else or resort to bureaucratic procedures to influence others (e.g. appeal to organizational policies or regulations). Others suggest that self-confidence does not affect style of leadership but is only correlated with years of supervisory experience and self-perceptions of power.

Variation between different Categorical Groups

Social scientists have found ways in which self-confidence seems to operate differently within various groups in society.

Children

In children, self-confidence emerges differently than adults. For example, Fenton suggested that only children as a group are more self-confident than other children. Zimmerman claimed that if children are self-confident they can learn they are more likely to sacrifice immediate recreational time for possible rewards in the future enhancing their self-regulative capability. By adolescence, youth that have little contact with friends tend to have low self-confidence. Successful performance of children in music also increases feelings of self-confidence, increasing motivation for study.

Students

Many studies focus on students in school. In general, students who perform well have increased confidence which likely in turn encourages students to take greater responsibility to successfully complete tasks. Students who perform better receive more positive evaluations report and greater self-confidence. Low achieving students report less confidence and high performing students report higher self-confidence. Teachers can greatly affect the self-confidence of their students depending on how they treat them. In particular, Steele and Aronson established that black students perform more poorly on exams (relative to white students) if they must reveal their racial identities before the exam, a phenomenon known as "stereotype threat." Keller and Dauenheimer find a similar phenomena in relation to female student's performance (relative to male student's) on math tests Sociologists of education Zhou and Lee have observed the reverse phenomena occurring amongst Asian-Americans, whose confidence becomes tied up in expectations that they will succeed by both parents and teachers and who claim others perceive them as excelling academically more than they in fact are.

In one study of UCLA students, males (compared to females) and adolescents with more siblings (compared to those with less) were more self-confident. Individuals who were self-confident specifically in the academic domain were more likely to be happy but higher general self-confidence was not correlated with happiness. With greater anxiety, shyness and depression, emotionally vulnerable students feel more lonely due to a lack of general self-confidence. Another study of first year college students found men to be much more self-confident than women in athletic and academic activities. In regards to inter-ethnic interaction and language learning, studies show that those who engage more with people of a different ethnicity and language become more self-confident in interacting with them.

Men Versus Women

In the aftermath of the first wave of feminism and women's role in the labor force during the World War, Maslow argued that some women who possessed a more "dominant" personality were more self-confident and therefore would aspire to and achieve more intellectually than those that had a less "dominant" personality—even if they had the same level of intelligence as the "less dominant" women. However, Phillip Eisenberg later found the same dynamic among men.

Another common finding is that males who have low generalized self-confidence are more easily persuaded than males of high generalized self-confidence. Some have found that women who are either high or low in general self-confidence are more likely to be persuaded to change their opinion than women with medium self-confidence. However, when specific high confidence (self-efficacy) is high, generalized confidence plays less of a role in affecting their ability to carry out the task. Research finds that females report self-confidence levels in supervising subordinates proportionate to their experience level, while males report being able to supervise subordinates well regardless of experience. Women tend to respond less to negative feedback and be more averse to negative feedback than men. Barber and Odean find that male common stock investors trade 45% more than their female counterparts, which they attribute greater self-confidence (though also recklessness) of men, reducing men's net returns by 2.65 percentage points per year versus women's 1.72 percentage points. Niederle and Westerlund found that men are much more competitive and obtain higher compensation than women and that this difference is due to differences in self-confidence, while risk and feedback-aversion play a negligible role. Some scholars partly attribute the fact to women being less likely to persist in engineering college than men to women's diminished sense of self-confidence.

Evidence also has suggested that women who are more self-confident may receive high performance evaluations but not be as well liked as men that engage in the same behavior. However confident women were considered a better job candidates than both men and women who behaved modestly This may be related to gender roles, as a study found that after women who viewed commercials with women in traditional gender roles, they appeared less self-confident in giving a speech than after viewing commercials with women taking on more masculine roles. Such self-confidence may also be related to body image, as one study found a sample of overweight people in Australia and the US are less self-confident about their body's performance than people of average weight, and the difference is even greater for women than for men. Others have found that if a baby child is separated from their mother at birth the mother is less self-confident in their ability to raise that child than those mothers who are not separated from their children, even if the two mothers did not differ much in their care-taking skills. Furthermore, women who initially had low self-confidence are likely to experience a larger drop of self-confidence after separation from their children than women with relatively higher self-confidence.

Self-confidence in different Cultures

Some have suggested that self-confidence is more adaptive in cultures where people are not very concerned about maintaining harmonious relationships. But in cultures that value positive feelings and self-confidence less, maintenance of smooth interpersonal relationships are more important, and therefore self-criticism and a concern to save face is more adaptive. For example, Suh argue that East Asians are not as concerned as maintaining self-confidence as Americans and many even find Asians perform better when they *lack* confidence.

Athletes

Many sports psychologists have noted the importance of self-confidence in winning athletic competitions. Amongst athletes, gymnasts who tend to talk to themselves in an instructional format tended to be more self-confident than gymnasts that did not.Researchers have found that self-confidence is also one of the most influential factors in how well an athlete performs in a competition. In particular, "robust self-confidence beliefs" are correlated with aspects of "mental toughness," or the ability to cope better than your opponents with many demands and remain determined, focused and in control under pressure. In particular, Bull et al. (2005) make the distinction between "robust confidence" which leads to tough thinking, and "resilient confidence" which involves over-coming self doubts and maintaining self-focus and generates "tough thinking." These traits enable athletes to "bounce back from adversity." When athletes confront stress while playing sports, their self-confidence decreases. However feedback from their team members in the form of emotional and informational support reduces the extent to which stresses in sports reduces their self-confidence. At high levels of support, performance related stress does not affect self-confidence.

Measures

One of the earliest measures of self-confidence used a 12-point scale centered on zero, ranging from a minimum score characterizing someone who is "timid and self-distrustful, Shy, never makes decisions, self effacing" to an upper extreme score representing someone who is "able to make decisions, absolutely confident and sure of his own decisions and opinions."

Some have measured self-confidence as a simple construct divided into affective and cognitive components: anxiety as an affective aspect and self-evaluations of proficiency as a cognitive component.

The more context-based Personal Evaluation Inventory (PEI), developed by Shrauger measures specific self-esteem and self-confidence in different aspects (speaking in public spaces, academic performance, physical appearance, romantic relationships, social interactions, athletic ability, and general self-confidence score. Other surveys have also measured self-confidence in a similar way by evoking examples of more concrete activities (e.g. making new friends, keeping up with course demands, managing time wisely, etc.). The Competitive State Anxiety Inventory-2 (CSAI-2) measures on a scale of 1 to 4 how confident athletes feel about winning an upcoming match. Likewise, the Trait Robustness of Sports-Confidence Inventory (TROSCI) requires respondents to provide numerical answers on a nine-point scale answering such questions about how much one's self-confidence goes up and down, and how sensitive one's self-confidence is to performance and negative feedback.

Others, skeptical about the reliability of such self-report indices, have measured self-confidence by having examiners assess non-verbal cues of subjects, measuring on a scale of 1 to 5 whether the individual:

(1) Maintains frequent eye contact or almost completely avoids eye contact,

(2) Engages in little or no fidgeting, or, a lot of fidgeting,

(3) Seldom or frequently uses self-comforting gestures (e.g. stroking hair or chin, arms around self),

(4) Sits up straight facing the experimenter or sits hunched over or rigidly without facing the experimenter,

(5) Has a natural facial expression, or, grimaces,

(6) Does not twiddle hands or frequently twiddles something in their hand,

(7) Uses body and hand gestures to emphasize a point, or, never uses hand or body gestures to emphasize a point or makes inappropriate gestures.

Wheel of Wellness

The Wheel of Wellness was the first theoretical model of Wellness based in counseling theory. It is a model based on Adler's individual psychology and cross-disciplinary research on characteristics of healthy people who live longer and with a higher quality of life. The Wheel of Wellness includes five life tasks that relate to each other: spirituality, self-direction, work and leisure, friendship, and love. There are 15 subtasks of self-direction areas: sense of worth, sense of control, realistic beliefs, emotional awareness and coping, problem solving and creativity, sense of humor, nutrition, exercise, self-care, stress management, gender identity, and cultural identity. There are also five second-order factors, the Creative Self, Coping Self, Social Self, Essential Self, and Physical Self, which allow exploration of the meaning of wellness within the total self. In order to achieve a high self-esteem, it is essential to focus on identifying strengths, positive assets, and resources related to each component of the Wellness model and using these strengths to cope with life challenges.

Developing Confidence in Public Speaking

Positive Mental Imagery

Psychologists have found that deeply confident public speakers actually *see* themselves that way in their mental imagery. If your mental imagery is constantly reinforcing your lack of confidence, this is what will show up in your speaking. To unpick your mental imagery, you can do the following:

- Picture yourself speaking. What senses are stimulated? What do you see or smell or hear? Do you feel confident or nervous? What in your mental imagery makes it that way?
- Now play with this mental image, picture yourself looking out from your body. Change the colors in the room and see what happens to your confidence. How do you see your audience? Sitting or standing? Are they close or far? Now adjust the audience in your mental image until you feel powerful.

- Are there any "scary" people in the audience? Snipers or unreceptive audience members? Picture them with a clown nose and see if it makes you feel more confident. Do it. Yes it seems silly but do it anyway.
- Do you hear laughter or silence? Try both and see which reaction "feels" confident.
- Is your body heavy or light? Is the floor soft and inviting or hard and firm beneath your feet? Usually a firm grounding with the floor in your mental imagery will make you feel more confident.
- Practice these shifts in your mental image every time you think about giving your speech - this will help you to rewire the nervous habits of your brain to access your confidence (Especially the clown nose part.)

Visualizing Public Speaking Success

Create that positive affirmative space by literally *seeing* yourself presenting with confidence. Think your own inner movie no subtitles necessary:

- Close your eyes and imagine yourself breathing in confidence as a color and exhaling fear as a different color. Breathe in and out. Now imagine yourself walking confidently into a room.
- See all around you. Notice the look and feel of the place. Enjoy the audience.
- As you begin speaking, suddenly you're in the mind of the audience, amazed at how well informed and entertaining you are. Go through your entire speech this way.
- As you begin to conclude your speech, go back to your own self and revel in your powerful and confident public speaking. Look at your smiling audience who are thanking you for your words.
- This is your public speaking power. Take it with you out of your visualization. Remember this feeling in the place where your confidence lives. In your "gut" or stomach or your heart.

Demon Slaying

The inner critic or 'inner demon' is the negative inner dialogue that can surround your speaking. Most of us have some kind of inner dialogue that diminishes our confidence as a speaker, if we chose to believe it.

So get aware of negative 'thoughts inside the head' and overcome them by:

- Giving it space to 'burn itself out' - sometimes when you listen to an inner demon you just know it isn't true.
- Show it all the reasons why you should be confident by focusing on all your past successes in communication. Even if you're not an experienced speaker, look at all the other communication scenarios where you have succeeded.
- Make friends with the demon. After all, it just wants you to be safe, so it's really your friend. But, like any other friend who's trying to hold you back, if you give it a bit of love and patience, it will eventually calm down.

- If the demon is *still* not on your side, try banishing it. Imagine pushing it off a cliff, throwing it in the trash, or sending it up on a space craft. You don't need him anymore.

Juicy Stage Persona

Confident public speaking is *not* about putting on an act, but it can help to adopt a stage persona that helps you stretch into the full and fearless parts of your character. This key is that this *is* you - it's just a fuller version of you unleashed on stage.

To develop a fearless stage persona, ask yourself the following questions:

- What are your best qualities as a speaker? Are you cool or compassionate or gruff and focused? Are you a powerful peacemaker or a wizard of change?
- What might your 'trademark' features be? What are your hands doing? Are you slow and calculated with your movements or energetic and moving about the stage? Develop these internal traits and utilize them to make confident public speaking second nature.
- What's a name you could give your stage persona? Names are fun. Play with this (I used to be 'Energizer Bunny' and now I'm, well, 'Ginger').

If this doesn't come easily, give yourself permission to use a persona. Some actors call this "turning the lights on". The lights were there all time, you just need a spark of electricity.

Self-confidence is only an umbrella term for a lot of things. Emotional constraint, humor, empathy, resilience, string relationships, all go into creating the personality that exudes self-confidence.

A self-confident person would know how to say things that are honest without hurting others sentiments. A self-confident man also knows how to be heard with dignity, when there is a difference of opinion. All this takes practice, but the most important thing is the belief that you can be better. This is the cornerstone for any improvement in the world.

Planning

Planing is the fundamental management function, which involves deciding beforehand, what is to be done, when is it to be done, how it is to be done and who is going to do it. It is anintellectual process which lays down organisation's objectives and develops various courses of action, by which the organisation can achieve those objectives. It chalks out exactly, how to attain a specific goal.

Planning is nothing but thinking before the action takes place. It helps us to take a peep into the future and decide in advance the way to deal with the situations, which we are going to encounter in future. It involves logical thinking and rational decision making.

Importance of Planning

1. First and foremost managerial function: Planning provides the base for other functions of

the management, i.e. organising, staffing, directing and controlling, as they are performed within the periphery of the plans made.

2. Goal oriented: It focuses on defining the goals of the organisation, identifying alternative courses of action and deciding the appropriate action plan, which is to be undertaken for reaching the goals.
3. Pervasive: It is pervasive in the sense that it is present in all the segments and is required at all the levels of the organisation. Although the scope of planning varies at different levels and departments.
4. Continuous Process: Plans are made for a specific term, say for a month, quarter, year and so on. Once that period is over, new plans are drawn, considering organisation's present and future requirements and conditions. Therefore, it is an ongoing process, as the plans are framed, executed and followed by another plan.
5. Intellectual Process: It is a mental exercise at it involves the application of mind, to think, forecast, imagine intelligently and innovate etc.
6. Futuristic: In the process of planning we take a sneak peek of future. It encompasses looking into future, to analyse and predict it, so that the organisation can face the future challenges effectively.
7. Decision making: Decisions are made regarding the choice of alternative courses of action that can be undertaken to reach the goal. The alternative chosen should be best among all, with least number of negative and highest number of positive outcomes.

Planning is concerned with setting objectives, targets, and formulating plan to accomplish them. The activity helps managers analyse the present condition to identify the ways of attaining the desired position in future. It is both, the need of the organisation and the responsibility of managers.

Importance of Planning

- It helps managers to improve future performance, by establishing objectives and selecting a course of action, for the benefit of the organisation.
- It minimises risk and uncertainty, by looking ahead into future.
- It facilitates coordination of activities. Thus, reduces overlapping among activities and eliminates unproductive work.
- It states in advance, what should be done in future, so it provides direction for action.
- It uncovers and identifies future opportunities and threats.
- It sets out standards for controlling. It compares actual performance with the standard performance and efforts are made to correct the same.

The best speeches and presentations – the ones that are delivered effortlessly; the ones that we remember; the ones that make an impact – are usually the result of thorough and careful preparation.

An iceberg is an excellent metaphor for a good speech or presentation. Most of an iceberg lies under water. Thus, we have the expression, "the tip of the iceberg". The speech or presentation is like the tip of an iceberg because that is what the audience sees. What the audience doesn't see – the preparation – is like part of the iceberg beneath the water.

In an ideal world, we would have days or even weeks to focus on an important speech or presentation. But we live in the real world. Time is often short and we have many obligations. Nevertheless, you owe it to your audience to give a speech or presentation that is worthy of their time.

Before you Begin

Before you begin the exercise, you have to do something that might seem counterintuitive: turn off the computer. The computer is a tool, and like any tool, it has to be used for the right job at the right time in the right way.

Too many people make the mistake of firing up PowerPoint or Keynote or Prezi and adding slide after slide full of details. You have to resist that temptation and take a step backwards to get some perspective on your speech or presentation.

Alan Kay, the renowned American computer scientist said it well:

If you have the ideas, you can do a lot without machinery. Once you have those ideas, the machinery starts working for you, most ideas you can do pretty darn well with a stick in the sand.

This exercise is all about getting the ideas right. So put away the computer and get some good old-fashioned paper and a pencil or pen.

Step 1. Have Eagle Vision

An eagle's eye is a marvel of nature, up to eight times more powerful than a human eye. As it flies, an eagle can survey a large amount of territory. It can spot a rabbit or fish at a distance of up to three kilometres and when it does, it can keep that prey in perfect focus as it swoops in to catch it.

As a speaker, you can do the same thing – metaphorically – as you prepare for your talk.

There are three cornerstones to any speech or presentation: the speaker; the subject; and the audience. On a sheet of paper, make a large triangle (Δ). At the top, write your name; at the bottom left, the name of the audience; and at the bottom right, the subject of your speech or presentation.

Now, think about the relationships between the three cornerstones and write a few notes along the sides of the triangle about each. For example:

- Speaker – Subject: What do you know about the subject? Why are you speaking about it? What expertise do you have? What insights can you share with the audience?
- Audience – Subject: What does the audience know about the subject? Do they like the subject? Are they afraid of it? Are they bored by it? How is the subject relevant for the audience?

- Speaker – Audience: What do you know about the audience? What do they know about you? Do you have authority over them? Do they have authority over you?

Once you have made your notes, you need to need to think about the speaking situation and how it might affect your analysis above. Just as the weather can change from day to day, so too the speaking situation can change for a speaker or an audience.

For example, imagine a CEO who has to give a speech at the company's annual shareholders meeting. In Year 1, the company has had a great year. Profits are up, the company is gaining market share and the stock price has doubled. In Year 2, the company has had a terrible year. The new product was a disaster, the company has lost market share and the stock prices has tumbled. Same speaker, same audience, same subject. Very different situations.

Here are some questions to ask when thinking about the speaking situation:

- Are these good times? Tough times? How does the situation affect the subject of the presentation, if at all? Will the situation affect your delivery? What will happen – for you and the audience – if the presentation goes well? What will happen if it goes poorly?
- As you think about these questions, review the notes that you made and add or amend them as necessary.
- The purpose of this first step is to get as clear a picture as possible of the key components of your talk. Like an eagle, you want a broad vision of the landscape before narrowing your focus on your target.

Step 2. Define your Objective

At the end of your speech or presentation, the audience should be changed in some way. What is your objective for the talk? What do you want the audience to do when your talk is over?

Some possible objectives for a business presentation:

(a) You want people to invest in a project;

(b) You want people to take some action;

(c) You want people to be aware of certain information;

(d) You want to bring about a change in the company.

Sometimes speakers just want the audience to know something and that is fine. But the most powerful speeches and presentations are the ones that move people to action. If you can get your audience to take some concrete action, you will have made an impact.

When thinking about what you want the audience to do, be specific. Write out the objective as follows: "At the end of the presentation, I want the audience to."

There are countless objectives that a speech or presentation might have. Give it some thought. Just remember that the objective should be clear and realistic. Audiences need to know what, precisely, they have to do, and they have to be able to do it.

Step 3. What is your Key Message

A speech or presentation should be built around a key message. It is fine to have more than one key message, but I would only have two or three at most. The more messages you have, the more complicated your talk will be; the more complicated the talk, the less likely it is that people will remember it.

Too often, a presentation rambles along, leaving the audience confused as to what the point was. Very often, this is because the speaker has not thought clearly about the message and so did not construct a coherent talk.

Think about what you want the audience to remember even if they forget everything else that you have said. Then, write your entire presentation in one or two complete sentences. Not bullet points, the purpose of this step is to help you get to the heart of what you want to say.

When you can condense your speech or presentation into a single sentence or two, the message is clear in your mind. Then, when it comes to building your talk, as you think about adding a slide, a statistic, a story, a chart, a graph, etc., ask yourself whether it supports the key message. If it does, it can stay. If it doesn't, you might want to save it for another talk.

Step 4. Why Should the Audience Care

A speech or presentation is never about the speaker or her product or service or company. It is always about the audience. When speakers put the audience first, that's when great things can happen with a speech or presentation.

The final step of the exercise is to be clear about why your audience should care about your key message? Why is it important for them? List the reasons. If you can't think of any, you have a problem. Either you are giving the wrong talk to this audience or you are speaking to the wrong audience. But if you know the reasons why the audience should care, you have the basis for a meaningful speech or presentation.

In this regard, it's worth remembering the humorous, but insightful, comment of the late Ken Haemer, former Manager of Presentation Research at AT&T:

Designing a presentation without an audience in mind is like writing a love letter and addressing it: "To Whom It May Concern."

Even if you do not have a lot of time to prepare a speech or presentation, the foregoing exercise will help you clarify your ideas about your talk. Ultimately, this will save you time as you design it and will help you deliver a message that is clear, memorable and relevant for your audience.

Audience Engagement

An effective public speaker should be able to utilize devices that will be able to capture the attention of the audience. One effective way of hooking your audience is to get them on stage. Make them participate. When someone is on stage and he or she happens to be a member of the audience, the rest will almost always stay attentive. Why? Because they would like to see what you will be doing to one of them. Also, because they are thinking they could be up there themselves and so to save their egos from embarrassment they at least need to know what is going on.

Steps to Engage the Audience

Observe

Start by putting the spotlight on your audience. What do the objects of your attention look like today? What's the vibe in the audience? Is it just after lunch? End of the day? Are they tired, bored, or snoring?

Activate

Get active, utilize activities that promote audience engagement:

- Make your points into an audience debate. Nothing arouses interest more than controversy.
- Small groups activities will not only keep your audience awake but they'll get excited about their "part".
- Give them a task and have the small groups report to the whole group.

Change it up

Make sure you embrace many changes throughout your presentation. There is a 10 minute limit to the average attention span, so change it up often:

- Moving around the room if possible will provide a fresh perspective to both you and your message.
- Change your tone of voice and speaking volume, remember no one likes a robot.
- Introduce an astonishing video or powerful story to add texture to your talk. Find more than one way to "speak" your message.

Believe

You provide more of an impact than you realize.

- You are the expert at your topic.
- You can keep a speech interesting if you just put a little enthusiasm into the preparation and delivery.
- Doing something to engage your audience helps them to learn so don't be embarrassed, try something unexpected.
- An audience *loves* to connect with their speaker, so give them the chance by being open to them.

Body Language

Body language is another means of communication. Sometimes it can send signals stronger than words. Body language is controlled by your subconscious mind, so a reader can actually understand if there's a difference in what you are saying and thinking. In order to ensure that your words and body language compliment each other, you need to read and practice a bit.

Impact of Body Language

Body language often has great impact in transmitting messages to the listener. Facial expression and eye movements are very important while conveying your feelings. Smile on the face reflects confidence. If you are in meeting and you are not moving your eyes over all the participants, you will fail to add impact. You need to maintain intensity of voice to match the heat of the topic. Good posture coordinates your verbal language. If you have right body posture, you can easily control your voice. Your body weight needs to be equally balanced on the feet to have correct posture. Try to notice your body posture when you are happy and confident. You will find that your body is equally balanced and consequently, you are taking full breath at ease and body is moving synchronously with your voice.

Body language plays an essential role in communicating with people. Body language comprises of the gestures and movements we make of the different parts of our body when communicating with people. Many a times, body language speaks more than words. Certainly, the body language must be in synch with the words.

Points to Remember

- Never be up tied or stiff while making movements.
- Avoid body language that may be misunderstood or look unprofessional. E.g. Winking.
- A consistent eye contact is a positive sign and must be used.
- Avoid fiddling with things around. It may distract the attention.
- Each body part movement signifies something and helps in interpreting. e.g. Standing with hands on hips signifies aggressions, nodding signifies agreement and active listening, biting nails signifies nervousness.
- Unlike emails, body language does not give time to think. Hence they must be used appropriately.

Benefits of using Body Language while Communicating

- Body language can instantly help to evaluate the interest of people.
- It is a personal way of expressing emotions when words don't help.
- It can make communication interesting and non monotonous.

Positive Body Gestures

Positive body gestures are a sign of confidence and security. They are a sign of active participation and leave a good impression. Positive gestures include:

- Walking upright.
- Shaking hands confidently.
- Having a pleasant face.
- Nodding head is a positive gesture.
- A steady eye contact.

Negative Body Gestures

Following negative gestures are a sign of insecurity and restlessness. Such gestures show a lack of confidence. Such gestures should be avoided in interviews or meetings:

- Being uptight.
- Biting nails.
- Getting distracted.
- Faking a smile.
- Looking at something else while talking instead of the speaker.
- Proper etiquettes should be followed.

Physical Expressions

Facial Expression

Facial expression is integral when expressing emotions through the body. Combinations of eyes, eyebrow, LIPS, nose, and cheek movements help form different moods of an individual (example happy, sad, depressed, angry, etc.).

A few studies show that facial expression and bodily expression (body language) are congruent when interpreting emotions. Behavioral experiments have also shown that recognition of facial expression is influenced by perceived bodily expression. This means that the brain processes the other's facial and bodily expressions simultaneously.Subjects in these studies showed accuracy in judging emotions based on facial expression. This is because the face and the body are normally seen together in their natural proportions and the emotional signals from the face and body are well integrated.

For example, a lack of crinkles around the eyes suggests a potentially fake smile. At one point, researchers believed that making a genuine smile was nearly impossible to do on command. When you're smiling joyfully, they crinkle. When you're faking it, they don't. If someone's trying to look happy but really isn't, you won't see the wrinkles. More recently, a study from Northeastern University researchers found that people could do a pretty good job of faking a Duchenne smile, even when they weren't feeling especially happy.

Body Postures

Emotions can also be detected through body postures. Research has shown that body postures are more accurately recognized when an emotion is compared with a different or neutral emotion. For example, a person feeling angry would portray dominance over the other, and their posture would display approach tendencies. Comparing this to a person feeling fearful: they would feel weak, submissive and their posture would display avoidance tendencies, the opposite of an angry person.

Sitting or standing postures also indicate one's emotions. A person sitting till the back of their chair, leans forward with their head nodding along with the discussion implies that they are open, relaxed and generally ready to listen. On the other hand, a person who has their legs and arms crossed with the foot kicking slightly implies that they are feeling impatient and emotionally detached from the discussion.

In a standing discussion, a person stands with arms akimbo with feet pointed towards the speaker could suggest that they are attentive and is interested in the conversation. However, a small difference in this posture could mean a lot. Standing with arms akimbo is considered rude in Bali.

Gestures

Gestures are movements made with body parts (example hands, arms, fingers, head, legs) and they may be voluntary or involuntary. Arm gestures can be interpreted in several ways. In a discussion, when one stands, sits or even walks with folded arms, it is normally not a welcoming gesture. It could mean that they have a closed mind and are most likely unwilling to listen to the speaker's viewpoint. Another type of arm gesture also includes an arm crossed over the other, demonstrating insecurity and a lack of confidence.

Everybody does shoulder shrug. The shrug is a good example of a universal gesture that is used to show that a person doesn't understand what you are saying. "It's a multiple gesture that has three main parts," "Exposed palms to show nothing is being concealed in the hands, hunched shoulders to protect the throat from attack, and raised brow, which is a universal, submissive greeting."

Hand gestures often signify the state of well-being of the person making them. Relaxed hands indicate confidence and self-assurance, while clenched hands may be interpreted as signs of stress or anger. If a person is wringing their hands, this demonstrates nervousness and anxiety.

Finger gestures are also commonly used to exemplify one's speech as well as denote the state of well-being of the person making them. In certain cultures, pointing using one's index finger is deemed acceptable. However, pointing at a person may be viewed as aggressive in other cultures—for example, people who share Hindu beliefs consider finger pointing offensive. Instead, they point with their thumbs. Likewise, the thumbs up gesture could show "OK" or "good" in countries like the US, France and Germany. But this same gesture is insulting in other countries like Iran, Bangladesh and Thailand, where it is the equivalent of showing the middle finger in the US.

In most cultures the Head Nod is used to signify 'Yes' or agreement. It's a stunted form of bowing - the person symbolically goes to bow but stops short, resulting in a nod. Bowing is a submissive gesture so the Head Nod shows we are going along with the other person's point of view. Research conducted with people who were born deaf, dumb and blind shows that they also use this gesture to signify 'Yes', so it appears to be an inborn gesture of submission.

Handshakes

Handshakes are regular greeting rituals and commonly done on meeting, greeting, offering congratulations or after the completion of an agreement. They usually indicate the level of confidence and emotion level in people. Studies have also categorized several handshake styles, e.g. the finger squeeze, the bonc crusher (shaking hands too strongly), the limp fish (shaking hands too weakly), etc. Handshakes are popular in the US and are appropriate for use between men and women. However, in Muslim cultures, men may not shake hands or touch women in any way and vice versa. Likewise, in Hindu cultures, Hindu men may never shake hands with women. Instead, they greet women by placing their hands as if praying.

A firm, friendly handshake has long been recommended in the business world as a way to make a good first impression, and the greeting is thought to date to ancient times as a way of showing a stranger you had no weapons.

Breathing

Body language related to breathing and patterns of breathing can be indicative of a person's mood and state of mind; because of this, the relationship between body language and breathing is often considered in contexts such as business meetings and presentations. Generally, deeper breathing which uses the diaphragm and abdomen more is interpreted as conveying a relaxed and confident impression; by contrast, shallow, excessively rapid breathing is often interpreted as conveying a more nervous or anxious impression.

Some business advisers, such as those who promote neuro-linguistic programming, recommend mirroring a person's breathing pattern in order to convey an impression of mutual understanding.

Different Physical Movements

Covering one's mouth suggests suppression of feeling and perhaps uncertainty. This could also mean that they are thinking hard and may be unsure of what to say next. What you communicate through your body language and nonverbal signals affects how others see you, how well they like and respect you, and whether or not they trust you.

Unfortunately, many people send confusing or negative nonverbal signals without even knowing it. When this happens, both connection and trust are damaged.

Other Subcategories

Oculesics

Oculesics, a subcategory of body language, is the study of eye movement, eye behavior, gaze, and eye-related nonverbal communication. As a social or behavioral science, oculesics is a form of nonverbal communication focusing on deriving meaning from eye behavior. It is also crucial to note that Oculesics is culturally dependent. For example, in traditional Anglo-Saxon culture, avoiding eye contact usually portrays a lack of confidence, certainty, or truthfulness. However, in the Latino culture, direct or prolonged eye contact means that you are challenging the individual with whom you are speaking or that you have a romantic interest in the person.Also, in many Asian cultures, prolonged eye contact may be a sign of anger or aggression.

Haptics

Haptics, a subcategory of Body Language, is the study of touching and how it is used in communication. As such, handshakes, holding hands, back slapping, high fives, brushing up against someone or patting someone all have meaning.

Based on the Body Language Project, touching is the most developed sense at birth and formulates our initial views of the world. Touching can be used to sooth, for amusement during play, to flirt, to express power and maintain bonds between people, such as with baby and mother. Touching can carry distinct emotions and also show the intensity of those emotions. Touch absent of other cues can signal anger, fear, disgust, love, gratitude and sympathy depending on the length and type of touching that is performed. Many factors also contribute to the meaning of touching such as the length of the touch and location on the body in which the touching takes place.

Research has also shown that people can accurately decode distinct emotions by merely watching others communicate via touch.

Heslin outlines five haptic categories are follows:

- Functional/professional: Which expresses task-orientation

  Donald Walton stated in his book that touching is the ultimate expression of closeness or confidence between two people, but not seen often in business or formal relationships. Touching stresses how special the message is that is being sent by the initiator. "If a word of praise is accompanied by a touch on the shoulder, that's the gold star on the ribbon".

- Social/polite: Which expresses ritual interaction

  Communication with touch as the most intimate and involving form which helps people to keep good relationships with others. For example, strategic touching is a series of touching usually with an ulterior or hidden motive thus making them seem to be using touch as a game to get someone to do something for them.

- Friendship/warmth: Which expresses idiosyncratic relationship
- Love/intimacy: Which expresses emotional attachment

Public touch can serve as a 'tie sign' that shows others that your partner is "taken". When a couple is holding hands, putting their arms around each other, this is a 'tie sign' showing others that they are together. The use of 'tie signs' are used more often by couples in the dating and courtship stages than between their married counterparts according to Burgoon, Buller, and Woodall.

- Sexual/arousal: Which expresses sexual intent

  The amount of touching that occurs within a culture is also culturally dependent.

Proxemics

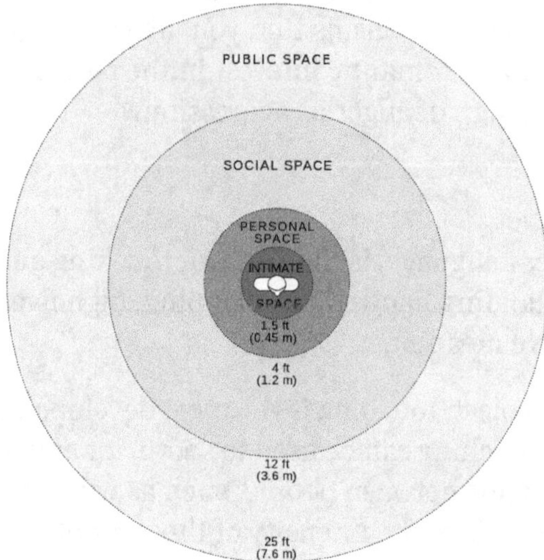

Another notable area in the nonverbal world of body language is that of spatial relationships, which is also known as Proxemics.

Four distinct zones in which most men operate are:

1. Intimate distance for embracing, touching or whispering

Close phase – less than 6 inches (15 cm)

Far phase – 6 to 18 inches (15 to 46 cm)

2. Personal distance for interactions among good friends or family members

Close phase – 1.5 to 2.5 feet (46 to 76 cm)

Far phase – 2.5 to 4 feet (76 to 122 cm)

3. Social distance for interactions among acquaintances

Close phase – 4 to 7 feet (1.2 to 2.1 m)

Far phase – 7 to 12 feet (2.1 to 3.7 m)

4. Public Distance used for public speaking

Close phase – 12 to 25 feet (3.7 to 7.6 m)

Far phase – 25 feet (7.6 m) or more.

In addition to physical distance, the level of intimacy between conversants can be determined by "socio-petal socio-fugal axis", or the "angle formed by the axis of the conversants' shoulders".

Changing the distance between two people can convey a desire for intimacy, declare a lack of interest, or increase/decrease domination. It can also influence the body language that is used. For example, when people talk they like to face each other. If forced to sit side by side, their body language will try to compensate for this lack of eye-to-eye contact by leaning in shoulder-to-shoulder.

It is important to note that as with other types of Body Language, proximity range varies with culture. "Physical contact between two people can be perfectly correct in one culture, and absolutely taboo in another". In Latin America, people who may be complete strangers may engage in very close contact. They often greet one another by kissing on the cheeks. North Americans, on the other hand, prefer to shake hands. While they have made some physical contact with the shaking of the hand, they still maintain a certain amount of physical space between the other person.

Tone of Voice

Tone of voice is a combination of spoken language and body language.

The manner in which something is said can affect how it should be interpreted. Shouting, smiling, irony and so on may add a layer of meaning which is neither pure body language nor speech.

Universal vs. Culture-specific

Scholars have long debated on whether body language, particularly facial expressions, are universally understood. In Darwin's (1872) evolutionary theory, he postulated that facial expressions of emotion are inherited. On the other hand, scholars have questioned if culture influences one's bodily expression of emotions. Broadly, the theories can be categorized into two models:

Cultural Equivalence Model

The cultural equivalence model predicts that "individuals should be equally accurate in understanding the emotions of ingroup and outgroup members". This model is rooted in Darwin's (1872) evolutionary theory, where he noted that both humans and animals share similar postural expressions of emotions such as anger/aggression, happiness, and fear. These similarities support the evolution argument that social animals (including humans) have a natural ability to relay emotional signals with one another, a notion shared by several academics. Where Darwin notes similarity in expression among animals and humans, the Cultural Equivalence Model notes similarity in expression across cultures in humans, even though they may be completely different.

One of the strongest pieces of evidence that supports this model was a study conducted by Ekman and Friesen (1971), where members of a preliterate tribe in Papua New Guinea reliably recognized the facial expressions of individuals from the United States. Culturally isolated and with no exposure to US media, there was no possibility of cross-cultural transmission to the Papuan tribesmen.

Cultural Advantage Model

On the other hand, the cultural advantage model predicts that individuals of the same race "process the visual characteristics more accurately and efficiently than other-race faces". Other factors that increase accurate interpretation include familiarity with nonverbal accents.

There are numerous studies that support both the cultural equivalence model and the cultural advantage model, but reviewing the literature indicates that there is a general consensus that seven emotions are universally recognized, regardless of cultural background: happiness, surprise, fear, anger, contempt, disgust, and sadness.

Recently, scholars have shown that the expressions of pride and shame are universal. Tracy and Robins concluded that the expression of pride includes an expanded posture of the body with the head tilted back, with a low-intensity face and a non Duchenne smile (raising the corner of the mouth). The expression of shame includes the hiding of the face, either by turning it down or covering it with the hands.

Applications

Fundamentally, body language is seemed as an involuntary and unconscious phenomena that adds to the process of communication. Despite that, there have been certain areas where the conscious harnessing of body language - both in action and comprehension - have been useful. The use of body language has also seen an increase in application and use commercially, with large volumes of books and guides published designed to teach people how to be conscious of body language, and how to use it to benefit them in certain scenarios.

The use of body language can be seen in a wide variety of fields. Body language has seen application in instructional teaching in areas such as second-language acquisition and also to enhance the teaching of subjects like mathematics. A related use of body language is as a substitution to verbal language to people who lack the ability to use that, be it because of deafness or aphasia. Body language has also been applied in the process of detecting deceit through micro-expressions, both in law enforcement and even in the world of poker.. Sometimes, Language Barrier could be such a problem to foreign people. Therefore, body language would be very beneficial to be used in communication.

Instructional Teaching

Second-language Acquisition

The importance of body language in second-language acquisition was inspired by the fact that to successfully learn a language is to achieve discourse, strategic, and sociolinguistic competencies. Sociolinguistic competence includes understanding the body language that aids the use of a particular language. This is usually also highly culturally influenced. As such, a conscious ability to recognize and even perform this sort of body language is necessary to achieve fluency in a language beyond the discourse level.

The importance of body language to verbal language use is the need to eliminate ambiguity and redundancy in comprehension. Pennycook (1985) suggests to limit the use of non-visual materials to facilitate the teaching of a second language to improve this aspect of communication. He calls this being not just bilingual but also 'bi-kinesic'.

Enhancing Teaching

Body language can be a useful aid not only in teaching a second language, but also in other areas. The idea behind using it is as a nonlinguistic input. It can be used to guide, hint, or urge a student towards the right answer. This is usually paired off with other verbal methods of guiding the student, be it through confirmation checks or modified language use.

- The intuitive feature of body language used in teaching is the exemplification of the language, especially individual words, through the use of matching body language. For example, when teaching about the word "cry", teachers can imitate a crying person. This enables a deeper impression which is able to lead to greater understanding of the particular word.
- The communicative feature is the ability of body language to create an environment and atmosphere that is able to facilitate effective learning. A holistic environment is more productive for learning and the acquisition for new knowledge.
- The suggestive feature of body language uses body language as a tool to create opportunities for the students to gain additional information about a particular concept or word through pairing it with the body language itself.

Detecting Deceit

Law Enforcement

Body language has seen use in the area of law enforcement. The relevance of body language in this area can be seen in the numerous Federal Bureau of Investigation (FBI) Law Enforcement Bulletinsthat have included it in their articles. The application of body language in law enforcement goes both ways. Members of law enforcement can use body language to catch unspoken clues by suspects or even victims, this enables a more calculated and more comprehensive judgement of people. The other side of body language is that of the investigators' themselves. The body language of the members of law enforcement might influence the accuracy of eyewitness accounts.

Poker

The game of poker involves not only an understanding of probability, but also the competence of reading and analyzing the body language of the opponents. A key component of poker is to be able to "cheat" the opponents. To spot these cheats, players must have the ability to spot the individual "ticks" of their opponents. Players also have to look out for signs that an opponent is doing well.

Kinesics

Kinesics is the study and interpretation of nonverbal communication related to the movement of any part of the body or the body as a whole; in layman's terms, it is the study of body language. However, Ray Birdwhistell, who is considered the founder of this area of study, never used the term *body language,* and did not consider it appropriate. He argued that what can be conveyed with the body does not meet the linguist's definition of language.

Birdwhistell pointed out that "human gestures differ from those of other animals in that they are polysemic, that they can be interpreted to have many different meanings depending on the communicative context in which they are produced". And, he "resisted the idea that 'body language' could be deciphered in some absolute fashion". He also indicated that "every body movement must be interpreted broadly and in conjunction with every other element in communication".

Body Language Tips to Empower Public Speaking

- To boost your confidence during your presentation, open your chest and and keep your back straight. This position will make you breathe better and you'll feel more relaxed.
- To make your audience comfortable, simply smile at them. Smiling is our most powerful weapon.
- To engage people, gesture with your arms and hands in a natural way. People tend to pay attention and to like people who look them in the eye.
- To demonstrate authority, keep calm and use small and stiff gestures. This way people will trust you and view you as a confident person.
- To bring movement to your speech, use the physical space you have available and walk it. For example, if you're presenting three points, talk about point A when you're at your first position; then move out 2 or 3 steps and talk about point B. This way, a movement that includes space will accompany your speech.
- To keep your audience's attention, vary your gestures throughout the presentation. Open gestures, small gestures. Gestures that involve your head, arms, and hands. Gestures that involve only your hands or only your head.
- To draw attention to a certain element of the presentation, point directly at it and look at it on the screen. At the same time, your audience will follow your eyes and finger.
- To encourage audience participation, use open gestures and if possible walk around and toward people. We tend to participate more when we have proximity to a speaker.
- To make a hard question seem easier, pause, breathe slowly (this will give you time to think) and then answer while looking the questioner in the eye.
- To make your audience buy your story, use positive gestures during the entire presentation; nodding, open gestures, mirroring, etc.

The most standard gesture, movement, posture and facial expression mistakes:

Gesture Issues

- Not using gestures at all: If you continue to keep your arms locked at your sides, you will seem anxious and your presentation will lack the visible component to accompany and enrich your words.
- Keeping your hand in your pockets: This situation prospects down the slippery slope to slouching and a sloppier posture. And you also may well unconsciously get started participating in with the keys or alter in your pocket.
- Fidgeting with your arms: Be knowledgeable of what your fingers are undertaking, such as "washing" every single other, grasping just about every other tightly, fiddling with your check out or jewelry etc. A single of my community speaking coaching consumers rolled and unrolled his shirt sleeves at the same time he introduced (we solved that issue by using him don limited sleeves). If you need to hold a thing, this kind of as your notes or the

PowerPoint remote, be acutely aware of how you are keeping it. Much too regularly the item gets a specific thing for you to play with unconsciously, or in the result in of notes, a crutch that stops you from wanting at the audience.

- Holding your fingers at the rear of your again: This gesture ordinarily resembles that of a little one reciting a poem at a faculty assembly. When not gesturing, your fingers may want to be in the "neutral place," hanging loosely at your sides.
- Pointing at the viewers: Yes, your mom was correct – it's not polite to point. Check out an open-handed gesture alternatively.
- Folding your arms across your chest: Even if you are only carrying out this for the reason that you experience chilly, this gesture will most likely be interpreted as your closing oneself off from the audience.
- Gripping the podium: This gesture is often accompanied by the "deer in the headlights" take a look. If you are working with a podium, put your hands lightly on the top notch of it or in a comfortable maintain on the edges.
- Using stilted gestures: Your gestures must be natural and flow smoothly fairly than trying compelled or robotic.

Movement Mistakes

- Moving without the need for goal: Most of the time you will want to stand confidently in just one position fairly than pacing again and forth or strolling aimlessly. If you do want to move, it really should have a goal. For example, walk confidently to the entrance of the home earlier than you get started talking and stroll with reason to the flipchart or to the laptop or computer.
- Shifting from your excess fat from 1 foot to the other: Quite a few individuals do this unconsciously and occasionally merely because their ft hurt. Alternatively, stand with your ft firmly planted on the ground, with your fat equally dispersed on equally toes.
- Hiding powering a desk, podium or flipchart: If the home configuration is set up so you are partly obscured driving a little something, then you have to count more intensely on your voice and facial expressions to convey that means. If you are nervous and truly feel exposed when there's absolutely nothing between you and the audience, follow, practice, follow – in front of the mirror, on video, in front of a pleasant team of colleagues. If you have to stand at the rear of a little something, do so with assurance and not as if you are shrinking from the viewers.

Posture Issues

- Standing far too stiffly: Yes, you should certainly stand up directly but it should really be pure, not like you are frozen at focus. Always keep your shoulders back again and keep your head up so you can make eye contact. This posture conveys self confidence and helps you breathe extra fully.

- Slouching and trying to keep your head down: Not only does it reduce you from shopping at the audience, but it also conveys nervousness and would make it more difficult for the audience to hear you.

Facial Expression Slipups

- Not smiling, ever: Until you are delivering horrible news, it is ideal for you to smile, even in a venture placing. Smiling will loosen up you and, in change, loosen up the viewers.
- Smiling too a great deal, certainly when delivering negative news: You could very well be smiling or even giggling considering that you are exceptionally anxious, but it undermines the seriousness of your concept and your sincerity. If you smile broadly or giggle even when announcing mass layoffs, for instance, your audience will interpret it as a sign of your lack of problem.

References

- Snyder, C. R.; Lopez, Shane J. (2009-01-01). Oxford Handbook of Positive Psychology. Oxford University Press. ISBN 9780195187243
- 25-skills-every-public-speaker-should-have: sixminutes.dlugan.com, Retrieved 06 July 2018
- Eisenberg, P.; Lazarsfeld, P. F. (1938-06-01). "The psychological effects of unemployment". Psychological Bulletin. 35 (6): 358–390. doi:10.1037/h0063426. ISSN 1939-1455
- Confident-public-speaking-how-to-become-fearless: gingerpublicspeaking.com, Retrieved 28 May 2018
- Jones, Stanley E. & A. Elaine Yarbrough; Yarbrough, A. Elaine (1985). "A naturalistic study of the meanings of touch". Communication Monographs. 52 (1): 19–56. doi:10.1080/03637758509376094. Retrieved 14 October 2014
- Importance-self-confidence-153023: iamwire.com, Retrieved 28 May 2018
- Tracy, Jessica L.; Robins, Richard W. (2008). "The nonverbal expression of pride: Evidence for cross-cultural recognition" (PDF). Journal of Personality and Social Psychology. 94 (3): 516–530. doi:10.1037/0022-3514.94.3.516
- The-importance-of-audience-participation-in-public-speaking: crowdink.com, Retrieved 18 March 2018
- Klima, Edward S.; & Bellugi, Ursula. (1979). The signs of language. Cambridge, MA: Harvard University Press. ISBN 0-674-80795-2
- Soft-Skills-Body-language: careerride.com, Retrieved 11 June 2018
- Maslow, A. H. (1943-07-01). "A theory of human motivation". Psychological Review. 50(4): 370–396. doi:10.1037/h0054346. ISSN 1939-1471
- 10-body-language-tips-to-empower-your-public-speaking: landit.com, Retrieved 12 March 2018
- Cruz, William. "Differences In Nonverbal Communication Styles between Cultures: The Latino-Anglo Perspective". Leadership and Management in Engineering. 1 (4): 51–53. doi:10.1061/(ASCE)1532-6748(2001)1:4(51). ISSN 1532-6748. Retrieved 14 October2014

4

Communication Tools for Public Speaking

Some of the tools of communication used in public speaking are public address system, microphone and loudspeaker, while in the modern age, video conferencing is a common and important tool of public communication. This chapter closely examines these tools to provide an insight into public speaking.

Inner Tools for Effective Public Speaking

Silence is the Answer

Every speech has one thing in common, there are points to be made. These could range from:

- Thoughts to consider
- New perspectives for understanding
- Questions that need to be answered

As a speaker, you have a duty to inform your audience of the points being addressed while on stage. Silence is one of the best ways to achieve this.

Whenever you make a point and keep quiet for a moment, this is what you have sent to your listeners: This is my point. Think about what I just said.

Silence is powerful. Having small pockets of silence after a certain sentence informs our listeners of their importance.

This is effective for questions as well. During a speech, when you ask a question to an audience: Why do we need to address this? Cue silence.

This emphasizes our questions. You want your audience to not only listen, but think as well. These are your markers, your ways to interact with them: This is my question. Can you answer it? Do you agree/disagree? What is the first thing that comes into your mind?

A moment of silence challenges your audience to think of the content they have just digested. It is similar to a conversation in that regard. We keep quiet to listen to others after all.

Do not underestimate the quiet ones. Silence is a core part of public speaking. The most powerful actions need not to be said, only experienced.

Intonation is Powerful

Have you ever been in a monotone conversation? Can you remember what was said?

It could be a talk with your least-favorite lecturer about a complex field. They could have no enthusiasm in their voice whatsoever. It can also be someone who has trouble speaking in large groups: their voices are small, and may not be taken seriously. In public speaking, intonation is essential.

It is generally known that the most compelling words are best told by the most strongest and energetic of voices. These are the ones who say with conviction what they want to say, and it doesn't matter if you agree with them or not. They are sure in their craft and opinion, and it leaves you with a good impression of them as an individual.

As a tool, the tone of our voice helps the audience recognize our intentions. It is a guide for the audience as they listen to what you say to understand the purpose of each word.

We can categorize our words by intention, or statement types:

- Is it a question? Raise your tone at the end of the sentence.
- It's a statement. Have a powerful ending to your sentence.
- It's a fact. Tone is slightly raised, with great clarity.
- An observation, a justification and a conclusion: Keeping it varied to distinguish between each section.

Tone allows you, the speaker, to influence the focus of your audience. Through your tone, you can tell your audience which sentences are questions, statements or observations. Making each intention clear helps them understand you better. When you are understood better, you have greater accountability.

Monotone speeches have very little emotion injected into them. They are then regarded as negative in terms of provocation and provide little engagement. It is akin to white noise – a constant pitch or sound. Without any change in tone, it would be the same as riding a train: a constant hum, which would inevitably bore us as an audience.

Keep your tone varied. Show them how enthusiastic you are.

Vocabulary must be Clear

To be clear, is to be concise. To make things simple is to make things easy to understand. To complicate things, is to show your inability to explain them.

This rings true for any audience. But, who is the right audience for you? Your vocabulary is the answer to that question.

Vocabulary is important when deciding what you want to say. It shows your ability to think from your audience's perspective.

Understand that the audience is willing to comprehend your speech from the very beginning. Complicating things will make it difficult for them to do so. Vocabulary is one way to counteract this. Some questions to ask ourselves included:

- Who is present? Age group, demographic?

- What is their language ability?
- Do you tailor your words to your audience?

Is your audience full of specialists? Are they experts in their field? If the vocabulary in your speeches consist mainly of technical terms, this would be a good fit.

Is it the general public? Depending on the demographic, they may have different levels of understanding. Little value can be obtained if you stick to complicated concepts and the like.

As public speakers, we need to make sure our speeches cater to the right audience. One way is to include and implement a wide variety of vocabulary. Though having technical vocab in your speech is optional and may depend on who is attending, clear concise vocab will always work.

Think of the Feynmann technique. This is a technique to ensure we keep the right perspective. This technique can be better explained as the 15-year-old Rule.

It's simple: Treat the audience like they are 15. It's not an insult, don't worry.

As the audience, we may not have much knowledge or understanding of what you're talking about. With that in mind, we may have more questions after listening to your explanation. we may want you to elaborate more, but without the expertise that you have (as the speaker).

As the speaker, your job is to dumb your speech down an easy-to-understand level, to allow all audiences to receive your points. This creates clarity and maximizes effectiveness.

Clear wording has less noise. People do not have to think so hard to understand what you say. This means that your other techniques could also be amplified: silence and tone for example. It is easier to include tonal techniques to short, clear points as opposed to long-winded theories.

For technical explanations, you need to define the purpose of each one. Some explanations can be a necessity, especially for an audience full of experts. As a public speaker, you need to define the following:

- What is the point of your explanation? Is it to have an idea of the situation being described?
- What can we, the audience, benefit from your explanation? Is this knowledge we can apply to our daily routine, for example?
- What are the main takeaways from using technical terms in my speech? Awareness? New perspective? A fun fact?
- How long is the explanation? Will it take a lot of time? Could we get bored as an audience member?

Clear vocab trumps all. Technical vocab is mainly used for specific audiences.

Make sure you use words with clear intended purposes.

Slides are not Always Important

Is there something that you need to show, or is there something very difficult to describe without a visual aid? An example would be ideas found in a field or a diagram that is very complex to explain.

Slides are a compliment. There is no defined context for them unless you, the speaker, are present to explain them for greater clarity. The presentation is not a primary source of information: you are the primary. Audience members can refer to the slides to stay on the topic, but they will refer to you as the expert.

There are cases where slides are beneficial or a necessity. But, you must be careful: make sure that there is a limit to detail concerning content on your slides. If you have too much, it may be daunting.

If your slides are too effective, why are you speaking? The point of you, the expert, being there diminishes. If your slides can talk for you, then it is not a public speaking event anymore. It can happen. Some people are visual learners as opposed to aural. They may ask to have a copy of the slides and leave it at that. You want to minimalize the chances of your audience losing their attention span, and resorting to other ways to learn the same content.

There are methods to mitigate this: speakers can benefit from ebooks or document links provided at the end of the talk as a refresher. This maintains you as the primary source of information during the public speech and serves to help your marketing/sales funnel if you have one. Very useful for an aspiring public speaker indeed.

In essence, most presentations can be done without slides. If slides are unavoidable however, try to avoid going more than 6 lines each slide. There is only so much information you can take from one slide, and trying to fill it up dense information can be detrimental to your audience.

Eye Contact is a Must

Maintaining eye contact maintains power. This is seen in everyday conversation. Timid individuals, or those from higher-context cultures, for example, tend to not focus on eye contact as a form of non-verbal communication.

Power is everything in a public speech. For those who are not so confident in public speaking, the ability to go on stage in the first place already gives a first impression. Maintaining that power requires you to hold your ground. One of the ways to do that is eye contact.

On the stage, if you make it clear that you are giving eye contact to your audience, this reaffirms your personal space on the stage. When you maintain this, these are the messages communicated:

- This is directed at you and is therefore relevant to you.
- I am the one on the stage, believe my word.
- I am giving you my full attention. Listen to me.

It also helps to maintain your eye contact across a large audience by scanning across the room. In your path to public speaking, there will be tons of people who want to hear what you say. You cannot neglect your audience, regardless of where they are in the hall.

Make them feel wanted with your eyes, and they will listen to what you say. You do not have to look directly into their eyes all the time: for large events, the act of it also works. Looking in their general direction shows that you are making an effort to create eye contact. This is done through your body language, and it does show weakness if you refuse to look your audience members in the eye. Maintaining eye contact (or 'faking' it), is a good way to show power when speaking. Use it often.

Pace Sets the Structure

Set the pace for everything that you do. Do you have a time limit for your speeches? A limited amount of slides to hold your content?

For the listening audience, they are there to learn and think. To achieve these two key objectives, having a structure in place is essential. Some may explain the outline of their presentation before starting, while others go straight into it.

Your pace defines structure. Generally, there is little value in telling your audience what they are about to see, as opposed to showing them said content. Instead, you can dive straight into the content and control your speed, to control the learning pace of everyone listening to you.

Examples include:

- Slowing down during a specific explanation informs your audience of its importance. It could be a point, or data, or a diagram. Whatever it is, it tells your audience that they must listen.
- Maintain a constant pace throughout a section of your presentation and people will assume that it is a standard explanation. It may be up to them to take notes, listen or ignore.
- Having a variety of speeds in a section helps with identifying different statement types. Important points can be stated slowly, but clearly (with proper tone.). Explanations after that add detail to reinforce the point, but it is complementary and can be mentioned at a regular pace.

Control the pace, and you will control your stage. If you are just blazing through your speech, you are letting the talk overwhelm you as an individual. That can result in mistakes or blunders, which are of little value to your audience. You have a responsibility to avoid this, and pace is one of the ways to do so. Remember that the stage is yours, so the pace is yours to manage. The stage is a wild animal: You control it, not the other way round.

Always Practice and become Better

- Reading advice helps, but nothing beats practice.
- Nothing beats going in front of a bear and checking your different aspects and apply them.
- Nothing beats being in front of an audience and seeing your feedback in real time.
- Nothing beats struggling under an intense environment.
- Nothing beats being in the field.
- Always practice and you will always improve. Just remember to make it a habit.

The external tools for communication in public speaking are: public address system, microphone, loudspeaker, video conferencing.

Public Address System

A public address system is an electronic sound amplification and distribution system with a microphone, amplifier and loudspeakers, used to allow a person to address a large public, for example for announcements of movements at large and noisy air and rail terminals. The term is also used for systems which may additionally have a mixing console, and amplifiers and loudspeakers suitable for music as well as speech, used to reinforce a sound source, such as recorded music or a person giving a speech or distributing the sound throughout a venue or building. Simple PA systems are often used in small venues such as school auditoriums, churches, and small bars. PA systems with many speakers are widely used to make announcements in public, institutional and commercial buildings and locations. Intercom systems, installed in many buildings, have microphones in many rooms allowing the occupants to respond to announcements. Sound reinforcement systems and PA systems may use some similar components, but with differing application, although the distinction between the two is not clear-cut. Sound reinforcement systems are for live music or performance, whereas PA systems are primarily for reproduction of speech.

Early Systems

Megaphone

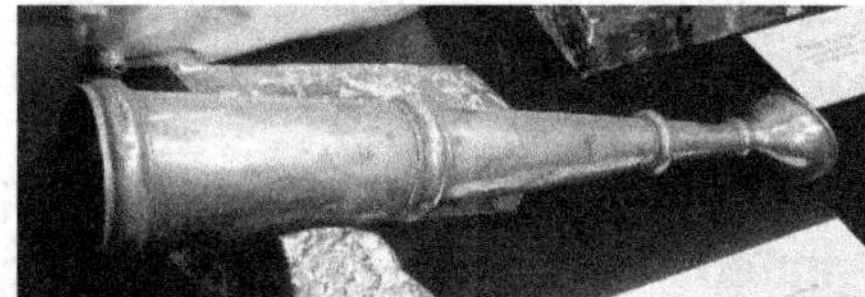

A late 19th-century speaking trumpet used by firefighters

A small sports megaphone for cheering at sporting events, next to a 3 in

From the Ancient Greek era to the nineteenth century, before the invention of electric loudspeakers and amplifiers, megaphone cones were used by people speaking to a large audience, to make their voice project more to a large space or group. Megaphones are typically portable, usually hand-held, cone-shaped acoustic horns used to amplify a person's voice or other sounds and direct it towards a given direction. The sound is introduced into the narrow end of the megaphone, by holding it up to the face and speaking into it. The sound projects out the wide end of the cone. The user can direct the sound by pointing the wide end of the cone in a specific direction. In the 2010s, cheerleading is one of the few fields where a nineteenth century-style cone is still used to project the voice. The device is also called "speaking-trumpet", "bullhorn" or "loud hailer".

Automatic Enunciator

In 1910, the Automatic Electric Company of Chicago, Illinois, already a major supplier of automatic telephone switchboards, announced it had developed a loudspeaker, which it marketed under the name of the *Automatic Enunciator*. Company president Joseph Harris foresaw multiple potential uses, and the original publicity stressed the value of the invention as a hotel public address system, allowing people in all public rooms to hear announcements. In June 1910, an initial "semi-public" demonstration was given to newspaper reporters at the Automatic Electric Company building, where a speaker's voice was transmitted to loudspeakers placed in a dozen locations "all over the building".

A short time later, the Automatic Enunciator Company formed in Chicago order to market the new device, and a series of promotional installations followed. In August 1912 a large outdoor installation was made at a water carnival held in Chicago by the Associated Yacht and Power Boat Clubs of America. Seventy-two loudspeakers were strung in pairs at forty-foot (12 meter) intervals along the docks, spanning a total of one-half mile (800 meters) of grandstands. The system was used to announce race reports and descriptions, carry a series of speeches about "The Chicago Plan", and provide music between races.

In 1913, multiple units were installed throughout the Comiskey Park baseball stadium in Chicago, both to make announcements and to provide musical interludes, with Charles A. Comiskey quoted as saying: "The day of the megaphone man has passed at our park." The company also set up an experimental service, called the Musolaphone, that was used to transmitted news and entertainment programming to home and business subscribers in south-side Chicago, but this effort was short-lived. The company continued to market the enunciators for making announcements in establishments such as hospitals, department stores, factories, and railroad stations.

Advertisements for automatic enunciator public address systems

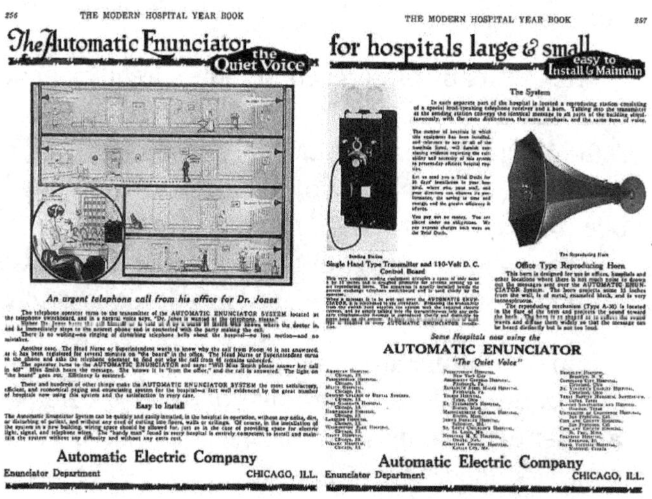

The Modern Hospital Yearbook

Magnavox

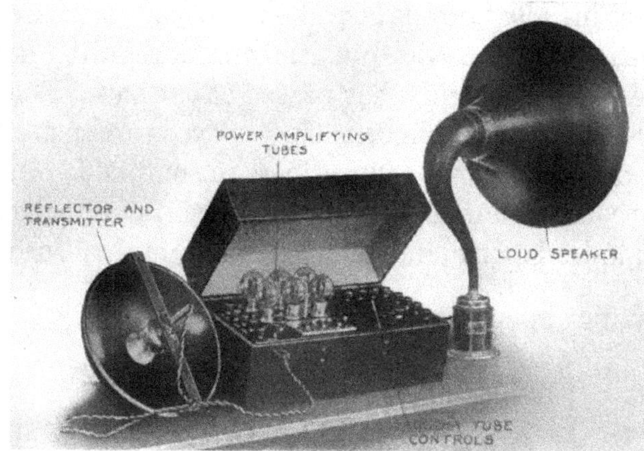

Early public-address system from around 1920 using a Magnavox speaker

The microphone had a metal reflector that concentrated the sound waves, allowing the speaker to stand back so it wouldn't obscure his or her face. The early vacuum tubes couldn't produce much gain, and even with six tubes the amplifier had low power. To produce enough volume, the system used a horn loudspeaker. The cylindrical driver unit under the horn contained the diaphragm, which the voice coil vibrated to produce sound through a flaring horn. It produced far more volume from a given amplifier than a cone speaker. Horns were used in virtually all early PA systems, and are still used in the 2010s in most systems, at least for the high-range tweeters.

Edwin Jensen and Peter Pridham of Magnavox began experimenting with sound reproduction in the 1910s. Working from a laboratory in Napa, California, they filed the first patent for a moving coil loudspeaker in 1911. Four years later, in 1915, they built a dynamic loudspeaker with a 1-inch (2.5 cm) voice coil, a 3-inch (7.6 cm) corrugated diaphragm and a horn measuring 34 inches (86 cm) with a 22-inch (56 cm) aperture. The electromagnet created a flux field of approximately 11,000 Gauss.

Their first experiment used a carbon microphone. When the 12 V battery was connected to the system, they experienced one of the first examples of acoustic feedback, a typically unwanted effect often characterized by high-pitched sounds. They then placed the loudspeaker on the laboratory's roof, and claims say that the amplified human voice could be heard 1 mile (1.6 km) away. Jensen and Pridham refined the system and connected a phonograph to the loudspeaker so it could broadcast recorded music. They did this on a number of occasions, including once at the Napa laboratory, at the Panama–Pacific International Exposition, and on December 24, 1915 at San Francisco City Hall alongside Mayor James Rolph. This demonstration was official presentation of the working system, and approximately 100,000 people gathered to hear Christmas music and speeches "with absolute distinctness".

The first outside broadcast was made one week later, again supervised by Jensen and Pridham. On December 30, when Governor of California Hiram Johnson was too ill to give a speech in person, loudspeakers were installed at the Civic Auditorium in San Francisco, connected to Johnson's house some miles away by cable and a microphone, from where he delivered his speech. Jensen oversaw the governor using the microphone while Pridham operated the loudspeaker.

The following year, Jensen and Pridham applied for a patent for what they called their "Sound Magnifying Phonograph". Over the next two years they developed their first valve amplifier. In 1919 this was standardized as a 3-stage 25 watt amplifier.

This system was used by former US president William Howard Taft at a speech in Grant Park, Chicago, and first used by a current president when Woodrow Wilson addressed 50,000 people in San Diego, California. Wilson's speech was part of his nationwide tour to promote the establishment of the League of Nations. It was held on September 9, 1919 at City Stadium. As with the San Francisco installation, Jensen supervised the microphone and Pridham the loudspeakers. Wilson spoke into two large horns mounted on his platform, which channelled his voice into the microphone.

Marconi

By the early 1920s, Marconi had established a department dedicated to public address and began producing loudspeakers and amplifiers to match a growing demand. In 1925, George V used such a system at the British Empire Exhibition, addressing 90,000 via six long-range loudspeakers. This public use of loudspeakers brought attention to the possibilities of such technology. The 1925 Royal Air Force Pageant at Hendon Aerodrome used a Marconi system to allow the announcer to address the crowds, as well as amplify the band. In 1929, the Schneider Trophy race at Calshot Spit used a public address system that had 200 horns, weighing a total of 20 tons.

Late 1920s-1930s

Engineers invented the first loud, powerful amplifier and speaker systems for public address systems and movie theaters. These large PA systems and movie theatre sound systems were very large and very expensive, and so they could not be used by most touring musicians. After 1927, smaller, portable AC mains-powered PA systems that could be plugged into a regular wall socket "quickly became popular with musicians"; indeed, "Leon McAuliffe (with Bob Wills) still used a carbon mic and a portable PA as late as 1935." During the late 1920s to mid-1930s, small portable PA systems and guitar combo amplifiers were fairly similar. These early amps had a "single volume control and one or two input jacks, field coil speakers" and thin wooden cabinets; remarkably, these early amps did not have tone controls or even an on-off switch. Portable PA systems you could plug into wall sockets appeared in the early 1930s when the introduction of electrolytic capacitors and rectifier tubes enabled economical built-in power supplies that could plug into wall outlets. Previously, amplifiers required heavy multiple battery packs.

Electric Megaphone

A woman using a small handheld electric megaphone at a demonstration in Portugal. Electric megaphones use a type of horn loudspeaker called a *reflex* or *reentrant horn*.

In the 1960s, an electric-amplified version of the megaphone, which used a loudspeaker, amplifier and a folded horn, largely replaced the basic cone-style megaphone. Small handheld, battery-powered electric megaphones are used by fire and rescue personnel, police, protesters, and people addressing outdoor audiences. With many small handheld models, the microphone is mounted at the back end of the device, and the user holds the megaphone in front of her/his mouth to use it, and presses a trigger to turn on the amplifier and loudspeaker. Larger electric megaphones may have a microphone attached by a cable, which enables a person to speak without having their face obscured by the flared horn.

Small Systems

Public address system in an old high school

The simplest, smallest PA systems consist of a microphone, an amplifier, and one or more loudspeakers. PA systems of this type, often providing 50 to 200 watts of power, are often used in small venues such as school auditoriums, churches, and coffeehouse stages. Small PA systems may extend to an entire building, such as a restaurant, store, elementary school or office building. A sound source such as a compact disc player or radio may be connected to a PA system so that music can be played through the system. Smaller, battery-powered 12 volt systems may be installed in vehicles such as tour buses or school buses, so that the tour guide and/or driver can speak to all the passengers. Portable systems may be battery powered and/or powered by plugging the system into an electric wall socket. These may also be used for by people addressing smaller groups such as information sessions or team meetings. Battery-powered systems can be used by guides who are speaking to clients on walking tours.

Public address systems consist of input sources (microphones, sound playback devices, etc.), amplifiers, control and monitoring equipment (e.g., LED indicator lights, VU meters, headphones), and loudspeakers. Usual input include microphones for speech or singing, direct inputs from musical instruments, and a recorded sound playback device. In non-performance applications, there may be a system that operators or automated equipment uses to select from a number of standard prerecorded messages. These input sources feed into preamplifiers and signal routers that direct the audio signal to selected zones of a facility (e.g., only to one section of a school). The pre-amplified signals then pass into the amplifiers. Depending on local practices, these amplifiers usually amplify the audio signals to 50V, 70V, or 100V speaker line level. Control equipment monitors the amplifiers and speaker lines for faults before it reaches the loudspeakers. This control equipment is also used to separate zones in a PA system. The loudspeaker converts electrical signals into sound.

Large Systems

Some PA systems have speakers that cover more than one building, extending to an entire campus of a college, office or industrial site, or an entire outdoor complex (e.g., an athletic stadium). A large PA system may also be used as an alert system during an emergency.

Public address system consisting of amplifiers, mixers, and routers for a major international airport

PA Systems by Size and Subwoofer Approach

PA system set-up	Venue size
Small system: 2 pole-mounted mid/high frequency PA speaker cabinets and 2 small subwoofer cabinets with 15" or 18" subwoofers (Note: this would be used in club where jazz, acoustic music, country music or soft rock is played)	Small club with capacity for up to 300 people
Small high amplifier power system: 2 high amplifier power-rated mid/high frequency PA speakers with 15" woofers and a large horn-loaded tweeter; two high amplifier power-rated subwoofer cabinets with one or two 18" subwoofer cabs (front-firing, also known as "front loaded", or manifold-loaded subwoofer cabinets)	Small club with capacity for up to 500 people
Mid-size PA system: 4 larger multi-woofer mid/high frequency PA speaker cabs (e.g., each with two 15" woofers) and four subwoofer cabinets, either front-firing, manifold loaded or a folded horn	Large clubs with capacity for 500+ people, small music festivals, fairs
Large-size PA system: Multiple mid/high frequency PA speakers, possibly "flown" up high in rigging, and a number of subwoofer cabinets (either front firing, manifold loaded or folded horn)	Large venues with capacity for 1000+ people, larger music festivals

Telephone Paging Systems

Some private branch exchange (PBX) telephone systems use a paging facility that acts as a liaison between the telephone and a PA amplifier. In other systems, paging equipment is not built into the telephone system. Instead the system includes a separate paging controller connected to a trunk port of the telephone system. The paging controller is accessed as either a designated directory number or central office line. In many modern systems, the paging function is integrated into the telephone system, so the system can send announcements to the phone speakers.

Many retailers and offices choose to use the telephone system as the sole access point for the paging system, because the features are integrated. Many schools and other larger institutions are no longer using the large, bulky microphone PA systems and have switched to telephone system paging, as it can be accessed from many different points in the school.

PA over IP

PA over IP refers to PA paging and intercom systems that use an Internet Protocol (IP) network, instead of a central amplifier, to distribute the audio signal to paging locations across a building or campus, or anywhere else in the reach of the IP network, including the Internet. Network-attached amplifiers and intercom units are used to provide the communication function. At the transmission end, a computer application transmits a digital audio stream via the local area network, using audio from the computer's sound card inputs or from stored audio recordings. At the receiving end, either specialized intercom modules (sometimes known as IP speakers) receive these network transmissions and reproduce the analog audio signal. These are small, specialized network appliances addressable by an IP address, just like any other computer on the network.

WMT PA Systems

Wireless Mobile Telephony PA Systems refers to PA paging and systems that use any form of

Wireless mobile telephony system such as GSM networks instead of a centralized amplifier to distribute the audio signal to paging locations across a building or campus, or other location. The GSM mobile Networks are used to provide the communication function. At the transmission end, a PSTN Telephone, mobile phone, VOIP phone or any other communication device that can access and make audio calls to a GSM based mobile SIM card can communicate with it. At the receiving end, a GSM transceiver receives these network transmissions and reproduce the analogue audio signal via a Power Amplifier and speaker. This was pioneered by Stephen Robert Pearson of Lancashire, England who was granted patents for the systems, which also incorporate control functionality. Using a WMT (GSM) network means that live announcements can be made to anywhere in the world where there is WMT connectivity. The patents cover all forms of WMT i.e., 2G, 3G, 4G xxG. A UK company called Remvox that has been appointed under license to develop and manufacture products based on the technology.

Long Line PA

London Underground employee making a Long Line Public Address system announcement using an RPA01 Radio Microphone at Bank Station

A Long-Line Public Address (LLPA) system is any public address system with a distributed architecture, normally across a wide geographic area. Systems of this type are commonly found in the rail, light rail, and metro industries, and let announcements be triggered from one or several locations to the rest of the network over low bandwidth legacy copper, normally PSTN lines using DSL modems, or media such as optical fiber, or GSM-R, or IP-based networks.

Rail systems typically have an interface with a passenger information system (PIS) server, at each station. These are linked to train describers, which state the location of rolling stock on the network from sensors on trackside signaling equipment. The PIS invokes a stored message to play from a local or remote digital voice announcement system, or a series of message fragments to assemble in the correct order, for example: " /the/23.30/First_Great_Western/Night_Riviera_sleeper_service/from/London_Paddington/to/ Penzance/ will depart from platform / one / this train is formed of / 12_carriages /." Messages are routed via an IP network and are played on local amplification equipment. Taken together, the PA, routing, DVA, passenger displays and PIS interface are referred to as the *customer information system (CIS)*, a term often used interchangeably with *passenger information system*.

Small Venue Systems

Small clubs, bars and coffeehouses use a fairly simple set-up, with front of house speaker cabinets (and subwoofers, in some cases) aimed at the audience, and monitor speaker cabinets aimed back at the performers so they can hear their vocals and instruments. In many cases, front of house speakers are elevated, either by mounting them on poles or by "flying" them from anchors in the ceiling. The Front of House speakers are elevated to prevent the sound from being absorbed by the first few rows of audience members. The subwoofers do not need to be elevated, because deep bass is omnidirectional. In the smallest coffeehouses and bars, the audio mixer may be onstage so that the performers can mix their own sound levels. In larger bars, the audio mixer may be located in or behind the audience seating area, so that an audio engineer can listen to the mix and adjust the sound levels. The adjustments to the monitor speaker mix may be made by a single audio engineer using the main mixing board, or they may be made by a second audio engineer who uses a separate mixing board.

This small venue's stage shows a typical PA system.

Large Venue Systems

For popular music concerts, a more powerful and more complicated PA System is used to provide live sound reproduction. In a concert setting, there are typically two complete PA systems: the "main" system and the "monitor" system. Each system consists of a mixing board, sound processing equipment, amplifiers, and speakers. The microphones that are used to pick up vocals and amplifier sounds are routed through both the main and monitor systems. Audio engineers can set different sound levels for each microphone on the main and monitor systems. For example, a backup vocalist whose voice has a low sound level in the main mix may ask for a much louder sound level through her monitor speaker, so she can hear her singing.

- The "main" system (also known as *Front of House*, commonly abbreviated FOH), which provides the amplified sound for the audience, typically uses a number of powerful amplifiers that drive a range of large, heavy-duty loudspeakers—including low-frequency speaker cabinets called subwoofers, full-range speaker cabinets, and high-range horns. A large club may use amplifiers to provide 3000 to 5000 watts of power to the "main" speakers. An outdoor concert may use 10,000 or more watts.

- The *monitor* system reproduces the sounds of the performance and directs them towards the onstage performers (typically using wedge-shaped monitor speaker cabinets), to help them to hear the instruments and vocals. In British English, the monitor system is referred to as the "foldback". The monitor system in a large club may provide 500 to 1000 watts of power to several foldback speakers; at an outdoor concert, there may be several thousand watts of power going to the monitor system.

At a concert using live sound reproduction, sound engineers and technicians control the mixing boards for the "main" and "monitor" systems, adjusting tone, levels, and overall volume.

A line array speaker system and subwoofer cabinets at a live music concert

Touring productions travel with relocatable large line-array PA systems, sometimes rented from an audio equipment hire company. The sound equipment moves from venue to venue along with various other equipment such as lighting and projection.

Acoustic Feedback

All PA systems have the potential for audio feedback, which occurs when a microphone picks up sound from the speakers, which is re-amplified and sent through the speakers again. It often sounds like a loud high-pitched squeal or screech, and can occur when the volume of the system is turned up too high. Feedback only occurs when the loop gain of the feedback loop is greater than one, so it can always be stopped by reducing the volume sufficiently.

Sound engineers take several steps to maximize gain before feedback, including keeping microphones at a distance from speakers, ensuring that directional microphones are not pointed towards speakers, keeping the onstage volume levels down, and lowering gain levels at frequencies where the feedback is occurring, using a graphic equalizer, a parametric equalizer, or a notch filter. Some 2010s-era mixing consoles and effects units have automatic feedback preventing circuits.

Feedback prevention devices detect the start of unwanted feedback and use a precise notch filter to lower the gain of the frequencies that are feeding back. Some automated feedback detectors require the user to "set" the feedback-prone frequencies by purposely increasing gain (during a sound check) until some feedback starts to occur. The device then retains these frequencies in its memory and it stands by ready to cut them. Some automated feedback prevention devices can detect and reduce new frequencies other than those found in the sound check.

A public address system gives you an immediate way to address everyone at a given location. Even though it's a more traditional form of communicating to large groups of people, it still offers advantages over modern formats:

1. Public address systems easily cut through background noise: Chatter, music, even loud local noises. Not only this, people tend to quiet down when they hear an announcement over a public address system. There's some peer pressure here. People perceive there's information that everyone next to them is about to hear, and they don't want to be left out. This means a public address system can quickly and effectively capture attention.

2. Whatever the speaker's voice, that effect of capturing attention is the same: Having a good voice over loudspeaker is a bonus, but it isn't crucial. This means that soft voices, shy voices, whatever it might be, will still come across to people as informational in nature. A stronger voice is a benefit, especially when announcing sales, but the public address system does the majority of the work when it comes to boosting voice and how your voice is perceived.

3. You can text blast an area with a notification, but this tends to annoy customers, guests, and attendees: It also feels like a violation of privacy. Many people maintain very private settings on their phones. This means they won't even get the text, and if they do, they'll feel angry that their mobile device has been used this way. This also assumes that people have their devices on them and turned on. A public address system feels informative instead of invasive, and people will much more readily accept it.

4. A public address system is relatively easy to maintain: The technology has become modernized and installation can be done with a minimal footprint. Maintenance is straightforward, and someone can be trained to operate the system with ease. We even help you and your employees learn PA system training when we do our installations. We know PA system training on the front end will make sure you get the most out of your equipment.

Microphone

As a public speaker you will be called upon to use a microphone as your career advances. This is included in the speaker skills as it is a skill that needs to be learned.

Like a pro ball player, actor, or any other high paid professional, mastering the microphone is essential to being on top of the public speaking game.

Do not use this information to try to impress the sound staff. Don't share this knowledge to make yourself look better. It can only get you in trouble. Rather, take this knowledge and put it to use as you grow in you skill.

Take notes of the brand of mic you speak with, the kind of problems you noticed or problems your coaches may note. Then armed with this you can talk to the AV staff and make requests that will help you have your best sound given the microphones you will have to speak into.

Types of Public Speaking Microphones

Take a look at the types of microphones, also called mics, and what they do.

- Condenser Microphones: A condenser mic can range from a karaoke mic to high-fidelity recording mic. These are the usual choice of both laboratory and studio recordings.
- Electric Condenser Mic: The application is varied from high-quality recording and lavaliere mics to built-in microphones in small sound recording devices and telephones.
- Dynamic Microphones: These mics are inexpensive, resistant to moisture and are most often used by singers.

Directionality in Public Speaking Microphones

- Omnidirectional Microphones: An omnidirectional mic picks up sound from all directions.
- Bi-directional: Receive sound from both the front and back of the element.
- Unidirectional Microphones: Sensitive to sounds from only one direction.
- Subcardioid, Cardioid, Supercardioid, Hypercardioid: The sensitivity is in the pattern of a heart shape. This is the most common speech or vocal mic used for sound systems where public speaking is preformed. Some mic's will have a tendency to pick up the popping P's. Awareness of this can help you be mindful to master the use of the microphone.

Problems Related to Mic

Another challenge in proper mic use is the pick up pattern. The mic you use can help or hinder your ability to communicate to the audience.

Speaking to an audience in a wide seating arrangement creates the biggest challenge.

As you look to the right and left, depending on the mic and if it is mounted, your voice could be picked up when facing the mic and not picked up as you look to the right and left.

Care of Public Speaking Microphones

There is one thing you can do that will set you apart from a hack and possibly keep you in the good graces of your sound professional. Never, ever blow into a mic to see if it works.

People do this because they see others doing this. It can directly damage the mic from the trauma of the human created micro cyclone entering the sensitive equipment. Secondary damage can come from spittle that comes out of your mouth. Both can ultimately damage the equipment.

Mistakes to Avoid while using a Microphone

If your asked to do a mic check, start talking. Quote a famous line or speech. Ad lib a famous speech. Read an appropriate magazine page. Just say testing, one, two, three and so on.

This allows the sound personnel to make adjustments to get the sound starting out at a reasonable level for an actual voice, which is what the mic is designed for.

Regardless of what you see on TV, never throw, drop or swing the mic if corded. All of these can damage the mic.

Never coil the coaxial microphone cable around your arm like a rope. It has a single copper wire inside and can be broken in time if not handled properly. If others do it and it is not yours, say nothing. But be aware that any problems in the system could be caused by a bad cable.

Never point a microphone at a speaker. The resulting noise (feedback) is annoying and distracting. It speaks of inexperience.

Some older mics if too close to each other can create another type of interference. If you note undesirable noises and your using two mics for two people, try separating the two a bit.

If you hear a ringing sound coming and going as you speak, the problem may not be the mic. It may just be you. The sound man may be giving you a que to hold the mic closer to your mouth.

He is turning up the sound as loud as he can and getting feedback. Then he backs it off a bit. The problem, he is having a hard time getting your voice to an adequate level for the audience. Putting the mic closer to your mouth will help.

Appropriate Distance of Microphone from your Mouth

Depending on the mic, most fixed mics can work adequately up to a foot away from your mouth. You will have better control if it is closer. Often times the speakers who dislike the mic in their face will be found looking down to read their speech rather than deliver it as if their own words.

If you have to read, pick up your notes and hold them to one side of the mic while not hiding your face from the audience.

Components

Electronic symbol for a microphone

The sensitive transducer element of a microphone is called its *element* or *capsule*. Sound is first converted to mechanical motion by means of a diaphragm, the motion of which is then converted to an electrical signal. A complete microphone also includes a housing, some means of bringing the signal from the element to other equipment, and often an electronic circuit to adapt the output of the capsule to the equipment being driven. A wireless microphone contains a radio transmitter.

Varieties

Microphones are categorized by their transducer principle, such as condenser, dynamic, etc., and by their directional characteristics. Sometimes other characteristics such as diaphragm size, intended use or orientation of the principal sound input to the principal axis (end- or side-address) of the microphone are used to describe the microphone.

Condenser

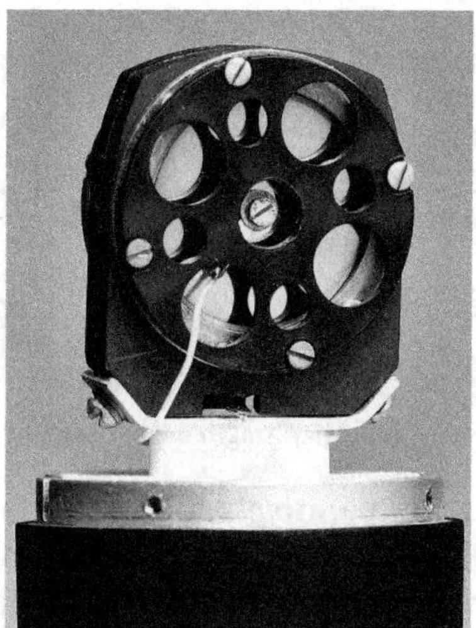

Inside the Oktava 319 condenser microphone

The condenser microphone, invented at Western Electric in 1916 by E. C. Wente, is also called a capacitor microphone or electrostatic microphone—capacitors were historically called condensers. Here, the diaphragm acts as one plate of a capacitor, and the vibrations produce changes in the distance between the plates. There are two types, depending on the method of extracting the audio signal from the transducer: DC-biased microphones, and radio frequency (RF) or high frequency (HF) condenser microphones. With a DC-biased microphone, the plates are biased with a fixed charge (*Q*).

The voltage maintained across the capacitor plates changes with the vibrations in the air, according to the capacitance equation:

$$(C = Q/V),$$

Where Q = charge in coulombs, C = capacitance in farads and V = potential difference in volts.

The capacitance of the plates is inversely proportional to the distance between them for a parallel-plate capacitor. The assembly of fixed and movable plates is called an "element" or "capsule".

A nearly constant charge is maintained on the capacitor. As the capacitance changes, the charge across the capacitor does change very slightly, but at audible frequencies it is sensibly constant.

The capacitance of the capsule (around 5 to 100 pF) and the value of the bias resistor (100 MΩ to tens of GΩ) form a filter that is high-pass for the audio signal, and low-pass for the bias voltage. Note that the time constant of an RC circuit equals the product of the resistance and capacitance.

Within the time-frame of the capacitance change (as much as 50 ms at 20 Hz audio signal), the charge is practically constant and the voltage across the capacitor changes instantaneously to reflect the change in capacitance. The voltage across the capacitor varies above and below the bias voltage. The voltage difference between the bias and the capacitor is seen across the series resistor. The voltage across the resistor is amplified for performance or recording. In most cases, the electronics in the microphone itself contribute no voltage gain as the voltage differential is quite significant, up to several volts for high sound levels. Since this is a very high impedance circuit, only current gain is usually needed, with the voltage remaining constant.

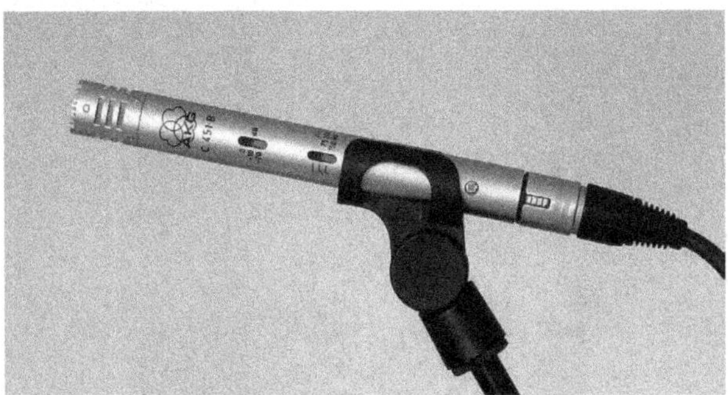

AKG C451B small-diaphragm condenser microphone

RF condenser microphones use a comparatively low RF voltage, generated by a low-noise oscillator. The signal from the oscillator may either be amplitude modulated by the capacitance changes produced by the sound waves moving the capsule diaphragm, or the capsule may be part of a resonant circuit that modulates the frequency of the oscillator signal. Demodulation yields a low-noise audio frequency signal with a very low source impedance. The absence of a high bias voltage permits the use of a diaphragm with looser tension, which may be used to achieve wider frequency response due to higher compliance. The RF biasing process results in a lower electrical impedance capsule, a useful by-product of which is that RF condenser microphones can be operated in damp weather conditions that could create problems in DC-biased microphones with contaminated insulating surfaces. The Sennheiser “MKH” series of microphones use the RF biasing technique.

Condenser microphones span the range from telephone transmitters through inexpensive karaoke microphones to high-fidelity recording microphones. They generally produce a high-quality audio signal and are now the popular choice in laboratory and recording studio applications. The inherent suitability of this technology is due to the very small mass that must be moved by the incident sound wave, unlike other microphone types that require the sound wave to do more work. They require a power source, provided either via microphone inputs on equipment as phantom power or from a small battery. Power is necessary for establishing the capacitor plate voltage and is also needed to power the microphone electronics (impedance conversion in the case of electret and DC-polarized microphones, demodulation or detection in the case of RF/HF microphones). Condenser microphones are also available with two diaphragms that can be electrically connected to provide a range of polar patterns, such as cardioid, omnidirectional, and figure-eight. It is also possible to vary the pattern continuously with some microphones, for example, the RødeNT2000 or CAD M179.

A valve microphone is a condenser microphone that uses a vacuum tube (valve) amplifier. They remain popular with enthusiasts of tube sound.

Electret Condenser

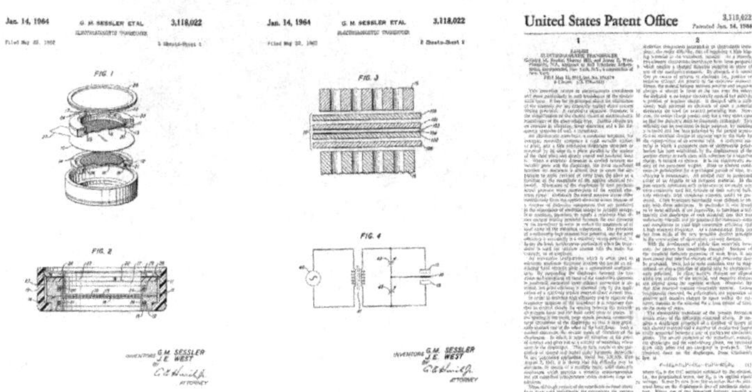

United States Patent Office

First patent on foil electret microphone by G.M. Sessler et al. (pages 1 to 3)

An electret microphone is a type of capacitor microphone invented by Gerhard Sesslerand Jim West at Bell laboratories in 1962. The externally applied charge described above under condenser microphones is replaced by a permanent charge in an electret material. An electret is a ferroelectric material that has been permanently electrically charged or *polarized*. The name comes from *elec*trostatic and magn*et*; a static charge is embedded in an electret by alignment of the static charges in the material, much the way a magnet is made by aligning the magnetic domains in a piece of iron.

Due to their good performance and ease of manufacture, hence low cost, the vast majority of microphones made today are electret microphones; a semiconductor manufacturer estimates annual production at over one billion units. Nearly all cell-phone, computer, PDA and headset microphones are electret types. They are used in many applications, from high-quality recording and lavalier use to built-in microphones in small sound recording devices and telephones. Though electret microphones were once considered low quality, the best ones can now rival traditional condenser microphones in every respect and can even offer the long-term stability and ultra-flat response needed for a measurement microphone. Unlike other capacitor microphones, they require no polarizing voltage, but often contain an integrated preamplifier that does require power (often incorrectly called polarizing power or bias). This preamplifier is frequently phantom powered in sound reinforcement and studio applications. Monophonic microphones designed for personal computer (PC) use, sometimes called multimedia microphones, use a 3.5 mm plug as usually used, without power, for stereo; the ring, instead of carrying the signal for a second channel, carries power via a resistor from (normally) a 5 V supply in the computer. Stereophonic microphones use the same connector; there is no obvious way to determine which standard is used by equipment and microphones.

Only the best electret microphones rival good DC-polarized units in terms of noise level and quality; electret microphones lend themselves to inexpensive mass-production, while inherently expensive non-electret condenser microphones are made to higher quality.

Dynamic

Patti Smith singing into a Shure SM58 (dynamic cardioid type) microphone

The dynamic microphone(also known as the moving-coil microphone) works via electromagnetic induction. They are robust, relatively inexpensive and resistant to moisture. This, coupled with their potentially high gain before feedback, makes them ideal for on-stage use.

Dynamic microphones use the same dynamic principle as in a loudspeaker, only reversed. A small movable induction coil, positioned in the magnetic field of a permanent magnet, is attached to the diaphragm. When sound enters through the windscreen of the microphone, the sound wave moves the diaphragm. When the diaphragm vibrates, the coil moves in the magnetic field, producing a varying current in the coil through electromagnetic induction. A single dynamic membrane does not respond linearly to all audio frequencies. For this reason, some microphones utilize multiple membranes for the different parts of the audio spectrum and then combine the resulting signals. Combining the multiple signals correctly is difficult; designs that do this are rare and tend to be expensive. On the other hand, there are several designs that are more specifically aimed towards isolated parts of the audio spectrum. The AKG D 112, for example, is designed for bass response rather than treble. In audio engineering several kinds of microphones are often used at the same time to get the best results.

Ribbon

Edmund Lowe using a ribbon microphone

Ribbon microphones use a thin, usually corrugated metal ribbon suspended in a magnetic field. The ribbon is electrically connected to the microphone's output, and its vibration within the magnetic field generates the electrical signal. Ribbon microphones are similar to moving coil microphones in the sense that both produce sound by means of magnetic induction. Basic ribbon microphones detect sound in a bi-directional pattern because the ribbon is open on both sides. Also, because the ribbon has much less mass it responds to the air velocity rather than the sound pressure. Though the symmetrical front and rear pickup can be a nuisance in normal stereo recording, the high side rejection can be used to advantage by positioning a ribbon microphone horizontally, for example above cymbals, so that the rear lobe picks up sound only from the cymbals. Crossed figure 8, or Blumlein pair, stereo recording is gaining in popularity, and the figure-eight response of a ribbon microphone is ideal for that application.

Other directional patterns are produced by enclosing one side of the ribbon in an acoustic trap or baffle, allowing sound to reach only one side. The classic RCA Type 77-DX microphone has several externally adjustable positions of the internal baffle, allowing the selection of several response patterns ranging from "figure-eight" to "unidirectional". Such older ribbon microphones, some of which still provide high-quality sound reproduction, were once valued for this reason, but a good low-frequency response could be obtained only when the ribbon was suspended very loosely, which made them relatively fragile. Modern ribbon materials, including new nano-materials, have now been introduced that eliminate those concerns and even improve the effective dynamic range of ribbon microphones at low frequencies. Protective wind screens can reduce the danger of damaging a vintage ribbon, and also reduce plosive artifacts in the recording. Properly designed wind screens produce negligible treble attenuation. In common with other classes of dynamic microphone, ribbon microphones don't require phantom power; in fact, this voltage can damage some older ribbon microphones. Some new modern ribbon microphone designs incorporate a preamplifier and, therefore, do require phantom power, and circuits of modern passive ribbon microphones, *i.e.*, those without the aforementioned preamplifier, are specifically designed to resist damage to the ribbon and transformer by phantom power. Also there are new ribbon materials available that are immune to wind blasts and phantom power.

Carbon

The carbon microphone was the earliest type of microphone. The carbon button microphone (or sometimes just a button microphone), uses a capsule or button containing carbon granules pressed between two metal plates like the Berliner and Edison microphones. A voltage is applied across the metal plates, causing a small current to flow through the carbon. One of the plates, the diaphragm, vibrates in sympathy with incident sound waves, applying a varying pressure to the carbon. The changing pressure deforms the granules, causing the contact area between each pair of adjacent granules to change, and this causes the electrical resistance of the mass of granules to change. The changes in resistance cause a corresponding change in the current flowing through the microphone, producing the electrical signal. Carbon microphones were once commonly used in telephones; they have extremely low-quality sound reproduction and a very limited frequency response range, but are very robust devices. The Boudet microphone, which used relatively large carbon balls, was similar to the granule carbon button microphones.

Unlike other microphone types, the carbon microphone can also be used as a type of amplifier, using a small amount of sound energy to control a larger amount of electrical energy. Carbon microphones found use as early telephone repeaters, making long distance phone calls possible in the era before vacuum tubes. These repeaters worked by mechanically coupling a magnetic telephone receiver to a carbon microphone: the faint signal from the receiver was transferred to the microphone, where it modulated a stronger electric current, producing a stronger electrical signal to send down the line. One illustration of this amplifier effect was the oscillation caused by feedback, resulting in an audible squeal from the old "candlestick" telephone if its earphone was placed near the carbon microphone.

Piezoelectric

A crystal microphone or piezo microphone uses the phenomenon of piezoelectricity—the ability of some materials to produce a voltage when subjected to pressure—to convert vibrations into an electrical signal. An example of this is potassium sodium tartrate, which is a piezoelectric crystal that works as a transducer, both as a microphone and as a slim line loudspeaker component. Crystal microphones were once commonly supplied with vacuum tube (valve) equipment, such as domestic tape recorders. Their high output impedance matched the high input impedance (typically about 10 megohms) of the vacuum tube input stage well. They were difficult to match to early transistor equipment and were quickly supplanted by dynamic microphones for a time, and later small electret condenser devices. The high impedance of the crystal microphone made it very susceptible to handling noise, both from the microphone itself and from the connecting cable.

Piezoelectric transducers are often used as contact microphones to amplify sound from acoustic musical instruments, to sense drum hits, for triggering electronic samples, and to record sound in challenging environments, such as underwater under high pressure. Saddle-mounted pickups on acoustic guitars are generally piezoelectric devices that contact the strings passing over the saddle. This type of microphone is different from magnetic coil pickups commonly visible on typical electric guitars, which use magnetic induction, rather than mechanical coupling, to pick up vibration.

Fiber Optic

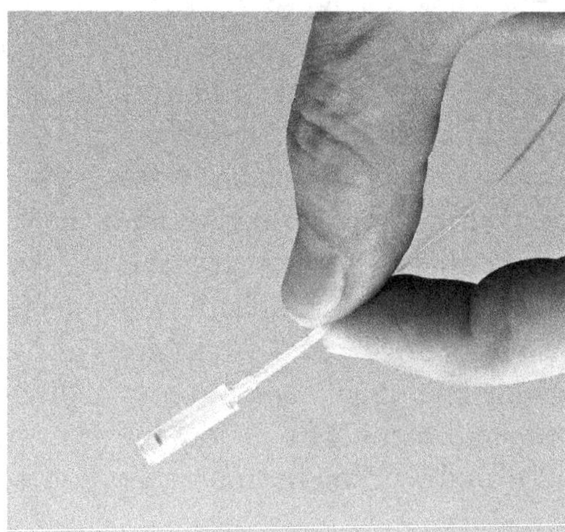

The Optoacoustics 1140 fiber optic microphone

A fiber optic microphone converts acoustic waves into electrical signals by sensing changes in light intensity, instead of sensing changes in capacitance or magnetic fields as with conventional microphones.

During operation, light from a laser source travels through an optical fiber to illuminate the surface of a reflective diaphragm. Sound vibrations of the diaphragm modulate the intensity of light reflecting off the diaphragm in a specific direction. The modulated light is then transmitted over a second optical fiber to a photo detector, which transforms the intensity-modulated light into analog or digital audio for transmission or recording. Fiber optic microphones possess high dynamic and frequency range, similar to the best high fidelity conventional microphones.

Fiber optic microphones do not react to or influence any electrical, magnetic, electrostatic or radioactive fields (this is called EMI/RFI immunity). The fiber optic microphone design is therefore ideal for use in areas where conventional microphones are ineffective or dangerous, such as inside industrial turbines or in magnetic resonance imaging(MRI) equipment environments.

Fiber optic microphones are robust, resistant to environmental changes in heat and moisture, and can be produced for any directionality or impedance matching. The distance between the microphone's light source and its photo detector may be up to several kilometers without need for any preamplifier or another electrical device, making fiber optic microphones suitable for industrial and surveillance acoustic monitoring.

Fiber optic microphones are used in very specific application areas such as for infrasound monitoring and noise-canceling. They have proven especially useful in medical applications, such as allowing radiologists, staff and patients within the powerful and noisy magnetic field to converse normally, inside the MRI suites as well as in remote control rooms. Other uses include industrial equipment monitoring and audio calibration and measurement, high-fidelity recording and law enforcement.

Laser

Laser microphones are often portrayed in movies as spy gadgets, because they can be used to pick up sound at a distance from the microphone equipment. A laser beam is aimed at the surface of a window or other plane surface that is affected by sound. The vibrations of this surface change the angle at which the beam is reflected, and the motion of the laser spot from the returning beam is detected and converted to an audio signal.

In a more robust and expensive implementation, the returned light is split and fed to an interferometer, which detects movement of the surface by changes in the optical path length of the reflected beam. The former implementation is a tabletop experiment; the latter requires an extremely stable laser and precise optics.

A new type of laser microphone is a device that uses a laser beam and smoke or vapor to detect sound vibrations in free air. This was issued for a Particulate Flow Detection Microphone based on a laser-photocell pair with a moving stream of smoke or vapor in the laser beam's path. Sound pressure waves cause disturbances in the smoke that in turn cause variations in the amount of laser light reaching the photo detector. A prototype of the device was demonstrated at the 127th Audio Engineering Society convention in New York City from 9 through.

Liquid

Early microphones did not produce intelligible speech, until Alexander Graham Bell made improvements including a variable-resistance microphone/transmitter. Bell's liquid transmitter consisted of a metal cup filled with water with a small amount of sulfuric acid added. A sound wave caused the diaphragm to move, forcing a needle to move up and down in the water. The electrical resistance between the wire and the cup was then inversely proportional to the size of the water meniscus around the submerged needle. Elisha Gray filed a caveat for a version using a brass rod instead of the needle. Other minor variations and improvements were made to the liquid microphone by Majoranna, Chambers, Vanni, Sykes, and Elisha Gray, and one version was patented by Reginald Fessenden in 1903. These were the first working microphones, but they were not practical for commercial application. The famous first phone conversation between Bell and Watson took place using a liquid microphone.

MEMS

The MEMS (Micro Electrical-Mechanical System) microphone is also called a microphone chip or silicon microphone. A pressure-sensitive diaphragm is etched directly into a silicon wafer by MEMS processing techniques, and is usually accompanied with integrated preamplifier. Most MEMS microphones are variants of the condenser microphone design. Digital MEMS microphones have built in analog-to-digital converter circuits on the same CMOS chip making the chip a digital microphone and so more readily integrated with modern digital products. Major manufacturers producing MEMS silicon microphones are Wolfson Microelectronics (WM7xxx) now Cirrus Logic,Inven Sense (product line sold by Analog Devices), Akustica (AKU200x), Infineon (SMM310 product), Knowles Electronics, Memstech (MSMx), NXP Semiconductors (division bought by Knowles), Sonion MEMS, Vesper, AAC Acoustic Technologies, and Omron.

There has been increased interest and research into making piezoelectric MEMS microphones which are a significant architectural and material change from existing condenser style MEMS designs.

Speakers as Microphones

A loudspeaker, a transducer that turns an electrical signal into sound waves, is the functional opposite of a microphone. Since a conventional speaker is constructed much like a dynamic microphone (with a diaphragm, coil and magnet), speakers can actually work "in reverse" as microphones. The resulting signal typically offers reduced quality including limited high-end frequency response and poor sensitivity. In practical use, speakers are sometimes used as microphones in applications where high quality and sensitivity are not needed such as intercoms, walkie-talkies or video game voice chat peripherals, or when conventional microphones are in short supply.

However, there is at least one practical application that exploits those weaknesses: the use of a medium-size woofer placed closely in front of a "kick drum" (bass drum) in a drum set to act as a microphone. A commercial product example is the Yamaha Subkick, a 6.5-inch (170 mm) woofer shock-mounted into a 10" drum shell used in front of kick drums. Since a relatively massive membrane is unable to transduce high frequencies while being capable of tolerating strong low-frequency transients, the speaker is often ideal for picking up the kick drum while reducing bleed from the nearby cymbals and snare drums.

Less commonly, microphones themselves can be used as speakers, but due to their low power handling and small transducer sizes, a tweeter is the most practical application. One instance of such an application was the STC microphone-derived 4001 super-tweeter, which was successfully used in a number of high quality loudspeaker systems from the late 1960s to the mid-70s.

Capsule Design and Directivity

The inner elements of a microphone are the primary source of differences in directivity. A pressure microphone uses a diaphragm between a fixed internal volume of air and the environment, and responds uniformly to pressure from all directions, so it is said to be omnidirectional. A pressure-gradient microphone uses a diaphragm that is at least partially open on both sides. The pressure difference between the two sides produces its directional characteristics. Other elements such as the external shape of the microphone and external devices such as interference tubes can also alter a microphone's directional response. A pure pressure-gradient microphone is equally sensitive to sounds arriving from front or back, but insensitive to sounds arriving from the side because sound arriving at the front and back at the same time creates no gradient between the two. The characteristic directional pattern of a pure pressure-gradient microphone is like a figure-8. Other polar patterns are derived by creating a capsule that combines these two effects in different ways. The cardioid, for instance, features a partially closed backside, so its response is a combination of pressure and pressure-gradient characteristics.

Polar Patterns

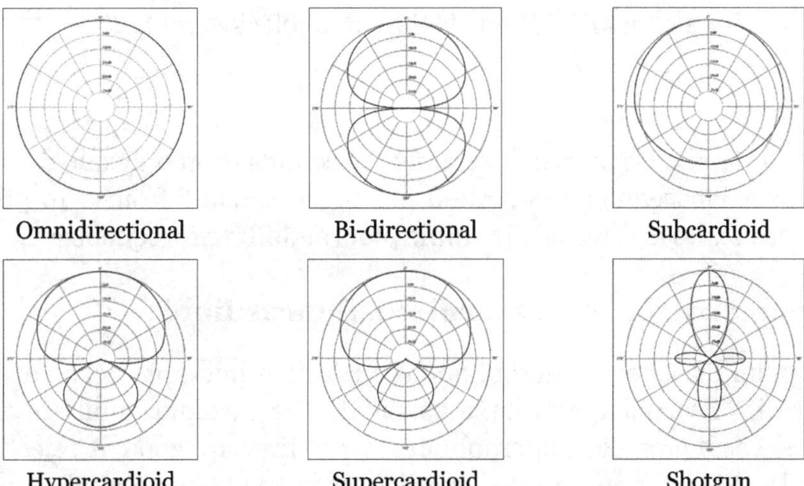

A microphone's directionality or polar pattern indicates how sensitive it is to sounds arriving at different angles about its central axis. The polar patterns illustrated above represent the locus of points that produce the same signal level output in the microphone if a given sound pressure level (SPL) is generated from that point. How the physical body of the microphone is oriented relative to the diagrams depends on the microphone design. For large-membrane microphones such as in the Oktava, the upward direction in the polar diagram is usually perpendicular to the microphone body, commonly known as "side fire" or "side address". For small diaphragm microphones such as the Shure, it usually extends from the axis of the microphone commonly known as "end fire" or "top/end address".

Some microphone designs combine several principles in creating the desired polar pattern. This ranges from shielding (meaning diffraction/dissipation/absorption) by the housing itself to electronically combining dual membranes.

Omnidirectional

An omnidirectional (or nondirectional) microphone's response is generally considered to be a perfect sphere in three dimensions. In the real world, this is not the case. As with directional microphones, the polar pattern for an "omnidirectional" microphone is a function of frequency. The body of the microphone is not infinitely small and, as a consequence, it tends to get in its own way with respect to sounds arriving from the rear, causing a slight flattening of the polar response. This flattening increases as the diameter of the microphone (assuming it's cylindrical) reaches the wavelength of the frequency in question. Therefore, the smallest diameter microphone gives the best omnidirectional characteristics at high frequencies.

The wavelength of sound at 10 kHz is 1.4" (3.5 cm). The smallest measuring microphones are often 1/4" (6 mm) in diameter, which practically eliminates directionality even up to the highest frequencies. Omnidirectional microphones, unlike cardioids, do not employ resonant cavities as delays, and so can be considered the "purest" microphones in terms of low coloration; they add very little to the original sound. Being pressure-sensitive they can also have a very flat low-frequency response down to 20 Hz or below. Pressure-sensitive microphones also respond much less to wind noise and plosives than directional (velocity sensitive) microphones.

An example of a nondirectional microphone is the round black *eight ball.*

Unidirectional

A unidirectional microphone is primarily sensitive to sounds from only one direction. The sound intensity for a particular frequency is plotted for angles radially from 0 to 360°. Professional diagrams show these scales and include multiple plots at different frequencies.

Cardioid, Hypercardioid, Supercardioid, Subcardioid

The most common unidirectional microphone is a cardioid microphone, so named because the sensitivity pattern is "heart-shaped", i.e. a cardioid. The cardioid family of microphones are commonly used as vocal or speech microphones, since they are good at rejecting sounds from other directions. In three dimensions, the cardioid is shaped like an apple centred around the microphone, which is the "stem" of the apple. The cardioid response reduces pickup from the side and rear, helping to avoid feedback from the monitors. Since these directional transducer microphones achieve their patterns by sensing pressure gradient, putting them very close to the sound source (at distances of a few centimeters) results in a bass boost due to the increased gradient. This is known as the proximity effect. The SM58 has been the most commonly used microphone for live vocals for more than 50 years demonstrating the importance and popularity of cardioid mics.

University Sound US664A dynamic supercardioid microphone

The cardioid is effectively a superposition of an omnidirectional (pressure) and a figure-8 (pressure gradient) microphone; for sound waves coming from the back, the negative signal from the figure-8 cancels the positive signal from the omnidirectional element, whereas for sound waves coming from the front, the two add to each other.

By combining the two components in different ratios, any pattern between omni and figure-8 can be achieved, which comprise the first-order cardioid family. Common shapes include:

- A hyper-cardioid microphone is similar to cardioid, but with a slightly larger figure-8 contribution, leading to a tighter area of front sensitivity and a smaller lobe of rear sensitivity. It is produced by combining the two components in a 3:1 ratio, producing nulls at 109.5°. This ratio maximizes the directivity factor (or directivity index).
- A super-cardioid microphone is similar to a hyper-cardioid, except there is more front pickup and less rear pickup. It is produced with about a 5:3 ratio, with nulls at 126.9°. This ratio maximizes the *front-back ratio*; the energy ratio between front and rear radiation.
- The sub-cardioid microphone has no null points. It is produced with about 7:3 ratio with 3-10 dB level between the front and back pickup.

Bi-directional

"Figure 8" or bi-directional microphones receive sound equally from both the front and back of the element. Most ribbon microphones are of this pattern. In principle they do not respond to sound pressure at all, only to the *change* in pressure between front and back; since sound arriving from the side reaches front and back equally there is no difference in pressure and therefore no sensitivity to sound from that direction. In more mathematical terms, while omnidirectional microphones are scalar transducers responding to pressure from any direction, bi-directional microphones are vector transducers responding to the gradient along an axis normal to the plane of the diaphragm. This also has the effect of inverting the output polarity for sounds arriving from the back side.

Shotgun and Parabolic

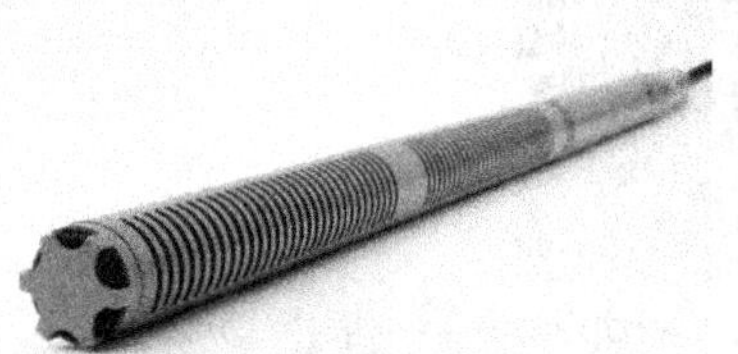

An Audio-Technica shotgun microphone

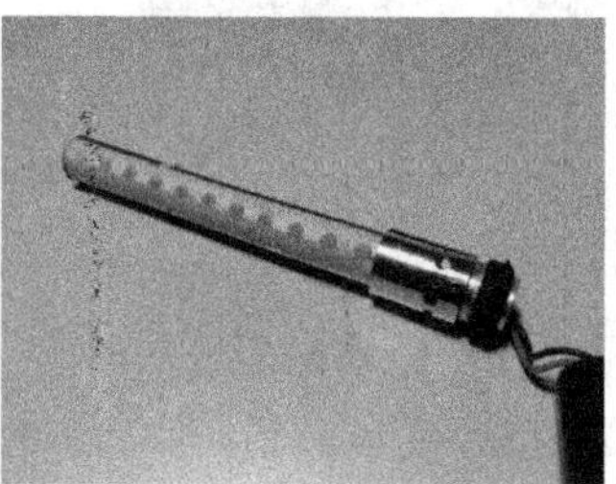

The interference tube of a shotgun microphone. The capsule is at the base of the tube.

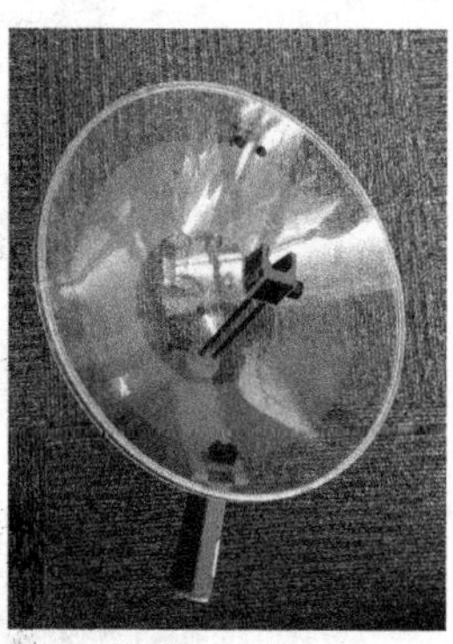

A Sony parabolic reflector, without a microphone. The microphone would face the reflector surface and sound captured by the reflector would bounce towards the microphone.

Shotgun microphones are the most highly directional of simple first-order unidirectional types. At low frequencies they have the classic polar response of a hypercardioid but at medium and higher frequencies an interference tube gives them an increased forward response. This is achieved by a process of cancellation of off-axis waves entering the longitudinal array of slots. A consequence of this technique is the presence of some rear lobes that vary in level and angle with frequency, and can cause some coloration effects. Due to the narrowness of their forward sensitivity, shotgun microphones are commonly used on television and film sets, in stadiums, and for field recording of wildlife.

Several approaches have been developed for effectively using a microphone in less-than-ideal acoustic spaces, which often suffer from excessive reflections from one or more of the surfaces (boundaries) that make up the space. If the microphone is placed in, or very close to, one of these boundaries, the reflections from that surface have the same timing as the direct sound, thus giving the microphone a hemispherical polar pattern and improved intelligibility. Initially this was done by placing an ordinary microphone adjacent to the surface, sometimes in a block of acoustically transparent foam. Sound engineers Ed Long and Ron Wickersham developed the concept of placing the diaphragm parallel to and facing the boundary. While the patent has expired, "Pressure Zone Microphone" and "PZM" are still active trademarks of Crown International, and the generic term boundary microphone is preferred. While a boundary microphone was initially implemented using an omnidirectional element, it is also possible to mount a directional microphone close enough to the surface to gain some of the benefits of this technique while retaining the directional properties of the element. Crown's trademark on this approach is "Phase Coherent Cardioid" or "PCC," but there are other makers who employ this technique as well.

Application-specific Designs

A lavalier microphone is made for hands-free operation. These small microphones are worn on the body. Originally, they were held in place with a lanyard worn around the neck, but more often they are fastened to clothing with a clip, pin, tape or magnet. The lavalier cord may be hidden by clothes and either run to an RF transmitter in a pocket or clipped to a belt (for mobile use), or run directly to the mixer (for stationary applications).

A wireless microphone transmits the audio as a radio or optical signal rather than via a cable. It usually sends its signal using a small FM radio transmitter to a nearby receiver connected to the sound system, but it can also use infrared waves if the transmitter and receiver are within sight of each other.

A contact microphone picks up vibrations directly from a solid surface or object, as opposed to sound vibrations carried through air. One use for this is to detect sounds of a very low level, such as those from small objects or insects. The microphone commonly consists of a magnetic (moving coil) transducer, contact plate and contact pin. The contact plate is placed directly on the vibrating part of a musical instrument or other surface, and the contact pin transfers vibrations to the coil. Contact microphones have been used to pick up the sound of a snail's heartbeat and the footsteps of ants. A portable version of this microphone has recently been developed. A throat microphone is a variant of the contact microphone that picks up speech directly from a person's throat, which it is strapped to. This lets the device be used in areas with ambient sounds that would otherwise make the speaker inaudible.

A parabolic microphone uses a parabolic reflector to collect and focus sound waves onto a microphone receiver, in much the same way that a parabolic antenna (e.g. satellite dish) does with radio waves. Typical uses of this microphone, which has unusually focused front sensitivity and can pick up sounds from many meters away, include nature recording, outdoor sporting events, eavesdropping, law enforcement, and even espionage. Parabolic microphones are not typically used for standard recording applications, because they tend to have poor low-frequency response as a side effect of their design.

A stereo microphone integrates two microphones in one unit to produce a stereophonic signal. A stereo microphone is often used for broadcast applications or field recording where it would be impractical to configure two separate condenser microphones in a classic X-Y configuration for stereophonic recording. Some such microphones have an adjustable angle of coverage between the two channels.

A noise-canceling microphone is a highly directional design intended for noisy environments. One such use is in aircraft cockpits where they are normally installed as boom microphones on headsets. Another use is in live event support on loud concert stages for vocalists involved with live performances. Many noise-canceling microphones combine signals received from two diaphragms that are in opposite electrical polarity or are processed electronically. In dual diaphragm designs, the main diaphragm is mounted closest to the intended source and the second is positioned farther away from the source so that it can pick up environmental sounds to be subtracted from the main diaphragm's signal. After the two signals have been combined, sounds other than the intended source are greatly reduced, substantially increasing intelligibility. Other noise-canceling designs use one diaphragm that is affected by ports open to the sides and rear of the microphone, with the sum being a 16 dB rejection of sounds that are farther away. One noise-canceling headset design using a single diaphragm has been used prominently by vocal artists such as Garth Brooks and Janet Jackson. A few noise-canceling microphones are throat microphones.

Stereo Microphone Techniques

Various standard techniques are used with microphones used in sound reinforcement at live performances, or for recording in a studio or on a motion picture set. By suitable arrangement of one or more microphones, desirable features of the sound to be collected can be kept, while rejecting unwanted sounds.

Powering

Microphones containing active circuitry, such as most condenser microphones, require power to operate the active components. The first of these used vacuum-tube circuits with a separate power supply unit, using a multi-pin cable and connector. With the advent of solid-state amplification, the power requirements were greatly reduced and it became practical to use the same cable conductors and connector for audio and power. During the 1960s several powering methods were developed, mainly in Europe. The two dominant methods were initially defined in German DIN 45595 as de:Tonaderspeisung or T-power and DIN 45596 for phantom power. Since the 1980s, phantom power has become much more common, because the same input may be used for both powered and unpowered microphones. In consumer electronics such as DSLRs and camcorders, "plug-in power" is more common, for microphones using a 3.5 mm phone plug connector. Phantom, T-power and plug-in power are described in international standard IEC 61938.

Connectors

A microphone with a USB connector

The most common connectors used by microphones are:

- Male XLR connector on professional microphones
- ¼ inch (sometimes referred to as 6.35 mm) phone connector on less expensive musician's microphones, using an unbalanced 1/4 inch (6.3 mm) TS phone connector. Harmonica microphones commonly use a high impedance 1/4 inch (6.3 mm) TS connection to be run through guitar amplifiers.
- 3.5 mm (sometimes referred to as 1/8 inch mini) stereo (and also come in varieties known as mono) mini phone plug on prosumer camera, recorder and computer microphones.
- USB allows direct connection to PCs. Electronics in these microphones powered over the USB connection performs pre amplification and AD conversion before the digital audio data is transferred via the USB interface.

Some microphones use other connectors, such as a 5-pin XLR, or mini XLR for connection to portable equipment. Some lavalier (or "lapel", from the days of attaching the microphone to the news reporters suit lapel) microphones use a proprietary connector for connection to a wireless transmitter, such as a radio pack. Since 2005, professional-quality microphones with USB connections have begun to appear, designed for direct recording into computer-based software.

Impedance-matching

Microphones have an electrical characteristic called impedance, measured in ohms (Ω), that depends on the design. In passive microphones, this value describes the electrical resistance of the magnet coil (or similar mechanism). In active microphones, this value describes the output resistance of the amplifier circuitry. Typically, the *rated impedance* is stated. Low impedance is considered under 600 Ω. Medium impedance is considered between 600 Ω and 10 kΩ. High impedance is above 10 kΩ. Owing to their built-in amplifier, condenser microphones typically have a output impedance between 50 and 200 Ω.

The output of a given microphone delivers the same power whether it is low or high impedance. If a microphone is made in high and low impedance versions, the high impedance version has a higher output voltage for a given sound pressure input, and is suitable for use with vacuum-tube guitar amplifiers, for instance, which have a high input impedance and require a relatively high signal input voltage to overcome the tubes' inherent noise. Most professional microphones are low impedance, about 200 Ω or lower. Professional vacuum-tube sound equipment incorporates a transformer that steps up the impedance of the microphone circuit to the high impedance and voltage needed to drive the input tube. External matching transformers are also available that can be used in-line between a low impedance microphone and a high impedance input.

Low-impedance microphones are preferred over high impedance for two reasons: one is that using a high-impedance microphone with a long cable results in high frequency signal loss due to cable capacitance, which forms a low-pass filter with the microphone output impedance. The other is that long high-impedance cables tend to pick up more hum (and possibly radio-frequency interference(RFI) as well). Nothing is damaged if the impedance between microphone and other equipment is mismatched; the worst that happens is a reduction in signal or change in frequency response.

Some microphones are designed *not* to have their impedance matched by the load they are connected to. Doing so can alter their frequency response and cause distortion, especially at high sound pressure levels. Certain ribbon and dynamic microphones are exceptions, due to the designers' assumption of a certain load impedance being part of the internal electro-acoustical damping circuit of the microphone.

Digital Microphone Interface

The AES42 standard, published by the Audio Engineering Society, defines a digital interface for microphones. Microphones conforming to this standard directly output a digital audio stream through an XLR or XLD male connector, rather than producing an analog output. Digital microphones may be used either with new equipment with appropriate input connections that conform to the AES42 standard, or else via a suitable interface box. Studio-quality microphones that operate in accordance with the AES42 standard are now available from a number of microphone manufacturers.

Neumann D-01 digital microphone and Neumann DMI-8 8-channel USB Digital Microphone Interface

Measurements and Specifications

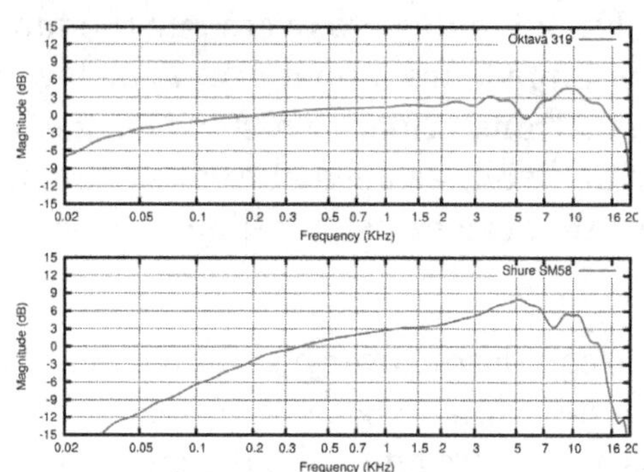

A comparison of the far field on-axis frequency response of the Oktava 319 and the Shure SM58

Because of differences in their construction, microphones have their own characteristic responses to sound. This difference in response produces non-uniform phase and frequency responses. In addition, microphones are not uniformly sensitive to sound pressure, and can accept differing levels without distorting. Although for scientific applications microphones with a more uniform response are desirable, this is often not the case for music recording, as the non-uniform response of a microphone can produce a desirable coloration of the sound. There is an international standard for microphone specifications, but few manufacturers adhere to it. As a result, comparison of published data from different manufacturers is difficult because different measurement techniques are used. The Microphone Data Website has collated the technical specifications complete with pictures, response curves and technical data from the microphone manufacturers for every currently listed microphone, and even a few obsolete models, and shows the data for them all in one common format for ease of comparison. Caution should be used in drawing any solid conclusions from this or any other published data, however, unless it is known that the manufacturer has supplied specifications in accordance with IEC 60268-4.

A frequency response diagram plots the microphone sensitivity in decibels over a range of frequencies (typically 20 Hz to 20 kHz), generally for perfectly on-axis sound (sound arriving at 0° to the capsule). Frequency response may be less informatively stated textually like so: "30 Hz–16 kHz ±3 dB". This is interpreted as meaning a nearly flat, linear, plot between the stated frequencies, with variations in amplitude of no more than plus or minus 3dB. However, one cannot determine from this information how *smooth* the variations are, nor in what parts of the spectrum they occur. Note that commonly made statements such as "20 Hz–20 kHz" are meaningless without a decibel measure of tolerance. Directional microphones' frequency response varies greatly with distance from the sound source, and with the geometry of the sound source. IEC 60268-4 specifies that frequency response should be measured in *plane progressive wave* conditions (very far away from the source) but this is seldom practical. *Close talking* microphones may be measured with different sound sources and distances, but there is no standard and therefore no way to compare data from different models unless the measurement technique is described.

The self-noise or equivalent input noise level is the sound level that creates the same output voltage as the microphone does in the absence of sound. This represents the lowest point of the microphone's dynamic range, and is particularly important should you wish to record sounds that are quiet. The measure is often stated in dB(A), which is the equivalent loudness of the noise on a decibel scale frequency-weighted for how the ear hears, for example: "15 dBA SPL" (SPL means sound pressure level relative to 20 micropascals). The lower the number the better. Some microphone manufacturers state the noise level using ITU-R 468 noise weighting, which more accurately represents the way we hear noise, but gives a figure some 11–14 dB higher. A quiet microphone typically measures 20dBA SPL or 32 dB SPL 468-weighted. Very quiet microphones have existed for years for special applications, such the Brüel & Kjaer 4179, with a noise level around 0 dB SPL. Recently some microphones with low noise specifications have been introduced in the studio/entertainment market, such as models from Neumann and Røde that advertise noise levels between 5–7dBA. Typically this is achieved by altering the frequency response of the capsule and electronics to result in lower noise within the A-weighting curve while broadband noise may be increased.

The maximum SPL the microphone can accept is measured for particular values of total harmonic distortion (THD), typically 0.5%. This amount of distortion is generally inaudible, so one can safely use the microphone at this SPL without harming the recording. Example: "142 dB SPL peak (at 0.5% THD)". The higher the value, the better, although microphones with a very high maximum SPL also have a higher self-noise.

The clipping level is an important indicator of maximum usable level, as the 1% THD figure usually quoted under max SPL is really a very mild level of distortion, quite inaudible especially on brief high peaks. Clipping is much more audible. For some microphones the clipping level may be much higher than the max SPL.

The dynamic range of a microphone is the difference in SPL between the noise floor and the maximum SPL. If stated on its own, for example "120 dB", it conveys significantly less information than having the self-noise and maximum SPL figures individually.

Sensitivity indicates how well the microphone converts acoustic pressure to output voltage. A high sensitivity microphone creates more voltage and so needs less amplification at the mixer or recording device. This is a practical concern but is not directly an indication of the microphone's quality, and in fact the term sensitivity is something of a misnomer, "transduction gain" being perhaps more meaningful, (or just "output level") because true sensitivity is generally set by the noise floor, and too much "sensitivity" in terms of output level compromises the clipping level. There are two common measures. The (preferred) international standard is made in millivolts per pascal at 1 kHz. A higher value indicates greater sensitivity. The older American method is referred to a 1 V/Pa standard and measured in plain decibels, resulting in a negative value. Again, a higher value indicates greater sensitivity, so −60dB is more sensitive than −70dB.

Measurement Microphones

An AKG C214 condenser microphone with shock mount

Some microphones are intended for testing speakers, measuring noise levels and otherwise quantifying an acoustic experience. These are calibrated transducers and are usually supplied with a calibration certificate that states absolute sensitivity against frequency. The quality of measurement microphones is often referred to using the designations "Class 1," "Type 2" etc., which are references not to microphone specifications but to sound level meters. A more comprehensive standard for the description of measurement microphone performance was recently adopted.

Measurement microphones are generally scalar sensors of pressure; they exhibit an omnidirectional response, limited only by the scattering profile of their physical dimensions. Sound intensity or sound power measurements require pressure-gradient measurements, which are typically made using arrays of at least two microphones, or with hot-wire anemometers.

Calibration

To take a scientific measurement with a microphone, its precise sensitivity must be known (in volts per pascal). Since this may change over the lifetime of the device, it is necessary to regularly calibrate measurement microphones. This service is offered by some microphone manufacturers and by independent certified testing labs. All microphone calibration is ultimately traceable to primary standard sat a national measurement institute such as NPL in the UK, PTB in Germany and NIST in the United States, which most commonly calibrate using the reciprocity primary standard. Measurement microphones calibrated using this method can then be used to calibrate other microphones using comparison calibration techniques.

Depending on the application, measurement microphones must be tested periodically (every year or several months, typically) and after any potentially damaging event, such as being dropped (most such microphones come in foam-padded cases to reduce this risk) or exposed to sounds beyond the acceptable level.

Arrays

A microphone array is any number of microphones operating in tandem. There are many applications:

- Systems for extracting voice input from ambient noise (notably telephones, speech recognition systems, hearing aids).
- Surround sound and related technologies.
- Locating objects by sound: acoustic source localization, *e.g.*, military use to locate the source(s) of artillery fire. Aircraft location and tracking.
- High fidelity original recordings.
- 3D spatial beam forming for localized acoustic detection of subcutaneous sounds.

Typically, an array is made up of omnidirectional microphones distributed about the perimeter of a space, linked to a computer that records and interprets the results into a coherent form.

Windscreens

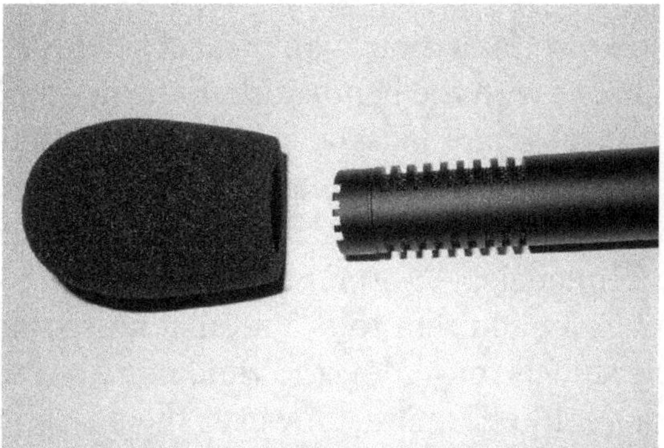

Microphone with its windscreen removed.

Windscreens (or windshields – the terms are interchangeable) provide a method of reducing the effect of wind on microphones. While pop-screens give protection from unidirectional blasts, foam "hats" shield wind into the grille from all directions, and blimps / zeppelins / baskets entirely enclose the microphone and protect its body as well. The latter is important because, given the extreme low frequency content of wind noise, vibration induced in the housing of the microphone can contribute substantially to the noise output.

The shielding material used – wire gauze, fabric or foam – is designed to have a significant acoustic impedance. The relatively low particle-velocity air pressure changes that constitute sound waves can pass through with minimal attenuation, but higher particle-velocity wind is impeded to a far greater extent. Increasing the thickness of the material improves wind attenuation but also begins to compromise high frequency audio content. This limits the practical size of simple foam screens. While foams and wire meshes can be partly or wholly self-supporting, soft fabrics and gauzes require stretching on frames, or laminating with coarser structural elements.

Since all wind noise is generated at the first surface the air hits, the greater the spacing between shield periphery and microphone capsule, the greater the noise attenuation. For an approximately spherical shield, attenuation increases by (approximately) the cube of that distance. Thus larger shields are always much more efficient than smaller ones. With full basket windshields there is an additional pressure chamber effect, first explained by Joerg Wuttke, which, for two-port (pressure gradient) microphones, allows the shield/microphone combination to act as a high-pass acoustic filter.

Since turbulence at a surface is the source of wind noise, reducing gross turbulence can add to noise reduction. Both aerodynamically smooth surfaces, and ones that prevent powerful vortices being generated, have been used successfully. Historically, artificial fur has proved very useful for this purpose since the fibres produce micro-turbulence and absorb energy silently. If not matted by wind and rain, the fur fibres are very transparent acoustically, but the woven or knitted backing can give significant attenuation. As a material it suffers from being difficult to manufacture with consistency, and to keep in pristine condition on location. Thus there is an interest (DPA 5100, Rycote Cyclone) to move away from its use.

In the studio and on stage, pop-screens and foam shields can be useful for reasons of hygiene, and protecting microphones from spittle and sweat. They can also be useful coloured idents. On location the basket shield can contain a suspension system to isolate the microphone from shock and handling noise.

Stating the efficiency of wind noise reduction is an inexact science, since the effect varies enormously with frequency, and hence with the bandwidth of the microphone and audio channel. At very low frequencies (10–100 Hz) where massive wind energy exists, reductions are important to avoid overloading of the audio chain – particularly the early stages. This can produce the typical "wumping" sound associated with wind, which is often syllabic muting of the audio due to LF peak limiting. At higher frequencies – 200 Hz to ~3 kHz – the aural sensitivity curve allows us to hear the effect of wind as an addition to the normal noise floor, even though it has a far lower energy content. Simple shields may allow the wind noise to be 10 dB less apparent; better ones can achieve nearer to a 50 dB reduction. However the acoustic transparency, particularly at HF, should also be indicated, since a very high level of wind attenuation could be associated with very muffled audio.

Advantages of a Microphone

Move without Restriction

By far the most obvious advantage of using a wireless microphone is the fact that the user can move unimpeded when performing. A singer or public speaker using this device will be able to wander freely around the performing area, including getting in among the audience, without loss of sound quality.

It's not just that we can move as we wish with a wireless microphone. Moreover, we can do so without fear of tripping - if there are no wires, the chances of this happening are markedly reduced.

A Clean Machine

Whether we're performing in front of a camera or before hundreds of people inside an auditorium, the less cables that are visible to our audience, the better the experience for them it will be. This is because it gives a 'clean' look to proceedings, meaning that viewers will not be distracted by the presence of wires when watching your visual recording or presentation.

Cable Conundrum

Cabled microphones that are used frequently can very often suffer from frayed wires, especially if they are cheaply made. Therefore, the cord will need to be intermittently replaced or repaired as it becomes damaged, lest it become hazardous. In extreme circumstances, the cable can disconnect from the amplifier itself, causing unnecessary embarrassment and an unwanted break in proceedings.

Handheld Hero

As their name suggests, handheld microphones are clutched in the grasp of the speaker or singer. One of their biggest advantages is the fact that the distance between mouth and microphone can be physically altered at will and with ease, meaning that volume and fidelity can also change. Hence, a number of special audio effects can be achieved, whether it's a higher emphasis on certain key words or for the artistic leanings of a performing vocalist.

Loudspeaker

A loudspeaker, which is also called a speaker, is an item that is used to create the sound in radios, television sets, and electric musical instrument amplifier systems.

Loudspeakers use both electric and mechanical principles to convert an electrical signal from a radio, television set or electric musical instrument into sound. For a loudspeaker to produce sound, the signal from the radio, television set, or electric musical instrument needs to be connected to an electronic amplifier.

Loudspeakers are usually built by using stiff paper cone, a coil of thin copper wire, and a circular magnet. The cone, copper wire, and magnet are usually mounted in a rectangle-shaped wood cabinet. The coil of copper wire moves back and forth when an electrical signal is passed through it. The coil of copper wire and the magnet cause the rigid paper cone to vibrate and reproduce sounds.

Inside loudspeaker can be audio crossover.

Types of Loudspeakers

Some loudspeakers are designed for lower-pitched sounds, such as *woofer* loudspeakers or *sub-woofer* loudspeakers. Other loudspeakers, which are called *tweeters*, are designed to reproduce high-pitched sounds (such as the sound of a whistle or a bird singing).

Loudspeakers for electric musical instruments are usually much stronger and heavier than loudspeakers for radios or television sets. Loudspeakers main function is to convert electrical signals given to it into sound signals.

Johann Philipp Reis installed an electric loudspeaker in his *telephone* in 1861; it was capable of reproducing clear tones, but also could reproduce muffled speech after a few revisions. Alexander Graham Bell patented his first electric loudspeaker (capable of reproducing intelligible speech) as part of his telephone in 1876, which was followed in 1877 by an improved version from Ernst Siemens. During this time, Thomas Edison was issued a British patent for a system using compressed air as an amplifying mechanism for his early cylinder phonographs, but he ultimately settled for the familiar metal horn driven by a membrane attached to the stylus. In 1898, Horace Short patented a design for a loudspeaker driven by compressed air; he then sold the rights to Charles Parsons, who was issued several additional British patents before 1910. A few companies, including the Victor Talking Machine Company and Pathé, produced record players using compressed-air loudspeakers. However, these designs were significantly limited by their poor sound quality and their inability to reproduce sound at low volume. Variants of the system were used for public address applications, and more recently, other variations have been used to test space-equipment resistance to the very loud sound and vibration levels that the launching of rockets produces.

The first experimental moving-coil (also called *dynamic*) loudspeaker was invented by Oliver Lodge in 1898. The first practical moving-coil loudspeakers were manufactured by Danish engineer Peter L. Jensen and Edwin Pridham in 1915, in Napa, California. Like previous loudspeakers these used horns to amplify the sound produced by a small diaphragm. Jensen was denied patents. Being unsuccessful in selling their product to telephone companies, in 1915 they changed their target market to radios and public address systems, and named their product Magnavox. Jensen was, for years after the invention of the loudspeaker, a part owner of The Magnavox Company.

Kellogg and Rice

Prototype moving-coil cone loudspeaker

The first commercial version of the speaker, sold with the RCA Radiola receiver, had only a 6 inch cone.

The moving-coil principle commonly used today in speakers was patented in 1924 by Chester W.

Rice and Edward W. Kellogg. The key difference between previous attempts and the patent by Rice and Kellogg is the adjustment of mechanical parameters so that the fundamental resonance of the moving system is below the frequency where the cone's radiation impedance becomes uniform. About this same period, Walter H. Schottky invented the first ribbon loudspeaker together with Dr. Erwin Gerlach.

These first loudspeakers used electromagnets, because large, powerful permanent magnets were generally not available at a reasonable price. The coil of an electromagnet, called a field coil, was energized by current through a second pair of connections to the driver. This winding usually served a dual role, acting also as a choke coil, filtering the power supply of the amplifier that the loudspeaker was connected to. AC ripple in the current was attenuated by the action of passing through the choke coil. However, AC line frequencies tended to modulate the audio signal going to the voice coil and added to the audible hum. In 1930 Jensen introduced the first commercial fixed-magnet loudspeaker; however, the large, heavy iron magnets of the day were impractical and field-coil speakers remained predominant until the widespread availability of lightweight Alnico magnets after World War II.

In the 1930s, loudspeaker manufacturers began to combine two and three band passes' worth of drivers in order to increase frequency response and sound pressure level. In 1937, the first film industry-standard loudspeaker system, "The Shearer Horn System for Theatres" (a two-way system), was introduced by Metro-Goldwyn-Mayer. It used four 15″ low-frequency drivers, a crossover network set for 375 Hz, and a single multi-cellular horn with two compression drivers providing the high frequencies. John Kenneth Hilliard, James Bullough Lansing, and Douglas Shearer all played roles in creating the system. At the 1939 New York World's Fair, a very large two-way public address system was mounted on a tower at Flushing Meadows. The eight 27″ low-frequency drivers were designed by Rudy Bozak in his role as chief engineer for Cinaudagraph. High-frequency drivers were likely made by Western Electric.

Altec Lansing introduced the *604*, which became their most famous coaxial Duplex driver, in 1943. It incorporated a high-frequency horn that sent sound through the middle of a 15-inch woofer for near-point-source performance. Altec's "Voice of the Theatre" loudspeaker system arrived in the marketplace in 1945, offering better coherence and clarity at the high output levels necessary in movie theaters. The Academy of Motion Picture Arts and Sciences immediately began testing its sonic characteristics; they made it the film house industry standard in 1955.

In 1954, Edgar Villchur developed the acoustic suspension principle of loudspeaker design in Cambridge, Massachusetts. This allowed for better bass response than previously from drivers mounted in smaller cabinets which was important during the transition to stereo recording and reproduction. He and his partner Henry Kloss formed the Acoustic Research company to manufacture and market speaker systems using this principle. Subsequently, continuous developments in enclosure design and materials led to significant audible improvements. The most notable improvements to date in modern dynamic drivers, and the loudspeakers that employ them, are improvements in cone materials, the introduction of higher-temperature adhesives, improved permanent magnet materials, improved measurement techniques, computer-aided design, and finite element analysis. At low frequencies, the application of electrical network theory to the acoustic performance allowed by various enclosure designs (initially by Thiele, and later by Small) has been very important at the design level.

Driver Design: Dynamic Loudspeakers

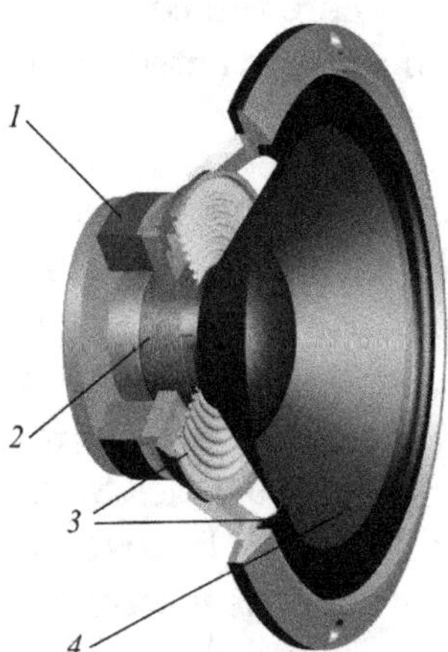

Cutaway view of a dynamic loudspeaker for the bass register

1. Magnet
2. Voice coil
3. Suspension
4. Diaphragm

The most common type of driver, commonly called a dynamic loudspeaker, uses a lightweight diaphragm, or *cone*, connected to a rigid *basket*, or *frame*, via a flexible suspension, commonly called a *spider*, that constrains a voice coil to move axially through a cylindrical magnetic gap. When an electrical signal is applied to the voice coil, a magnetic field is created by the electric current in the voice coil, making it a variable electromagnet. The coil and the driver's magnetic system interact, generating a mechanical force that causes the coil (and thus, the attached cone) to move back and forth, accelerating and reproducing sound under the control of the applied electrical signal coming from the amplifier. The following is a description of the individual components of this type of loudspeaker.

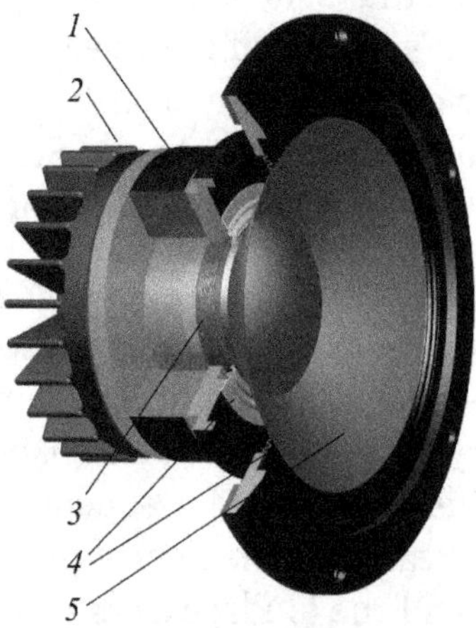

Cutaway view of a dynamic midrange speaker

1. Magnet
2. Cooler (sometimes present)
3. Voice coil
4. Suspension
5. Diaphragm

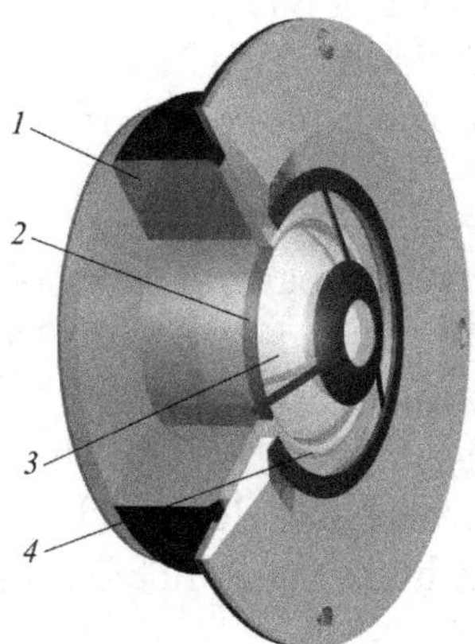

Cutaway view of a dynamic tweeter with acoustic lens and a dome-shaped membrane

1. Magnet
2. Voice coil
3. Diaphragm
4. Suspension

The diaphragm is usually manufactured with a cone- or dome-shaped profile. A variety of different materials may be used, but the most common are paper, plastic, and metal. The ideal material would 1) be rigid, to prevent uncontrolled cone motions; 2) have low mass, to minimize starting force requirements and energy storage issues; 3) be well damped, to reduce vibrations continuing after the signal has stopped with little or no audible ringing due to its resonance frequency as determined by its usage. In practice, all three of these criteria cannot be met simultaneously using existing materials; thus, driver design involves trade-offs. For example, paper is light and typically well damped, but is not stiff; metal may be stiff and light, but it usually has poor damping; plastic can be light, but typically, the stiffer it is made, the poorer the damping. As a result, many cones are made of some sort of composite material. For example, a cone might be made of cellulose paper, into which some carbon fiber, Kevlar, glass, hemp or bamboo fibers have been added; or it might use a honeycomb sandwich construction; or a coating might be applied to it so as to provide additional stiffening or damping.

The chassis, frame, or basket, is designed to be rigid, avoiding deformation that could change critical alignments with the magnet gap, perhaps causing the voice coil to rub against the sides of the gap. Chassis are typically cast from aluminum alloy, or stamped from thin steel sheet, though in some drivers with large magnets cast chassis are preferable as sheet metal can easily be warped in whenever the loudspeaker is subjected to rough handling. Other materials such as molded plastic and damped plastic compound baskets are becoming common, especially for inexpensive, low-mass drivers. Metallic chassis can play an important role in conducting heat away from the voice coil; heating during operation changes resistance, causes physical dimensional changes, and if extreme, may even demagnetize permanent magnets.

The suspension system keeps the coil centered in the gap and provides a restoring (centering) force that returns the cone to a neutral position after moving. A typical suspension system consists of two parts: the *spider*, which connects the diaphragm or voice coil to the frame and provides the majority of the restoring force, and the *surround*, which helps center the coil/cone assembly and allows free pistonic motion aligned with the magnetic gap. The spider is usually made of a corrugated fabric disk, impregnated with a stiffening resin. The name comes from the shape of early suspensions, which were two concentric rings of Bakelite material, joined by six or eight curved "legs." Variations of this topology included the addition of a felt disc to provide a barrier to particles that might otherwise cause the voice coil to rub. The German firm Rulik still offers drivers with uncommon spiders made of wood.

The cone surround can be rubber or polyester foam, or a ring of corrugated, resin coated fabric; it is attached to both the outer diaphragm circumference and to the frame. These diverse surround materials, their shape and treatment can dramatically affect the acoustic output of a driver; each implementation having advantages and disadvantages. Polyester foam, for example, is lightweight and economical, though usually leaking air to some degree, but is degraded by exposure to ozone, UV light, humidity and elevated temperatures, significantly limiting useful life with adequate performance.

The wire in a voice coil is usually made of copper, though aluminum—and, rarely, silver—may be used. The advantage of aluminum is its light weight, which reduces the moving mass compared to copper. This raises the resonant frequency of the speaker and increases its efficiency. A disadvantage of aluminum is that it is not easily soldered, and so connections are instead often crimped together and sealed. These connections must be made well or they may fail in an intense environment of mechanical vibration. Voice-coil wire cross sections can be circular, rectangular, or hexagonal, giving varying amounts of wire volume coverage in the magnetic gap space. The coil is oriented co-axially inside the gap; it moves back and forth within a small circular volume (a hole, slot, or groove) in the magnetic structure. The gap establishes a concentrated magnetic field between the two poles of a permanent magnet; the outside of the gap being one pole, and the center post (called the pole piece) being the other. The pole piece and back plate are often a single piece, called the pole plate or yoke.

Modern driver magnets are almost always permanent and made of ceramic, ferrite, Alnico, or, more recently, rare earth such as neodymium and samarium cobalt. Electro dynamic drivers were often used in musical instrument amplifier/speaker cabinets well into the 1950s; there were economic savings in those using tube amplifiers as the field coil could, and usually did, do double duty as a power supply choke. A trend in design – due to increases in transportation costs and a desire for smaller, lighter devices (as in many home theater multi-speaker installations) – is the use of the last instead of heavier ferrite types. Very few manufacturers still produce electro dynamic loudspeakers with electrically powered field coils, as was common in the earliest designs; one of the last is a French firm. When high field-strength permanent magnets became available after WWII, Alnico, an alloy of aluminum, nickel, and cobalt became popular, since it dispensed with the problems of field-coil drivers. Alnico was used almost exclusively until about 1980, despite the embarrassing problem of Alnico magnets being partially degaussed (i.e., demagnetized) by accidental 'pops' or 'clicks' caused by loose connections, especially if used with a high-power amplifier. The damage can be reversed by "recharging" the magnet, but this requires uncommon specialist equipment and knowledge.

After 1980, most (but not quite all) driver manufacturers switched from Alnico to ferrite magnets, which are made from a mix of ceramic clay and fine particles of barium or strontium ferrite. Although the energy per kilogram of these ceramic magnets is lower than Alnico, it is substantially less expensive, allowing designers to use larger yet more economical magnets to achieve a given performance.

The size and type of magnet and details of the magnetic circuit differ, depending on design goals. For instance, the shape of the pole piece affects the magnetic interaction between the voice coil and the magnetic field, and is sometimes used to modify a driver's behavior. A "shorting ring", or Faraday loop, may be included as a thin copper cap fitted over the pole tip or as a heavy ring situated within the magnet-pole cavity. The benefits of this complication is reduced impedance at high frequencies, providing extended treble output, reduced harmonic distortion, and a reduction in the inductance modulation that typically accompanies large voice coil excursions. On the other hand, the copper cap requires a wider voice-coil gap, with increased magnetic reluctance; this reduces available flux, requiring a larger magnet for equivalent performance.

Driver design—including the particular way two or more drivers are combined in an enclosure to make a speaker system—is both an art, involving subjective perceptions of timbre and sound quality and a science, involving measurements and experiments. Adjusting a design to improve performance is done using a combination of magnetic, acoustic, mechanical, electrical, and material science theory, and tracked with high precision measurements and the observations of experienced listeners. A few of the issues speaker and driver designers must confront are distortion, radiation lobing, phase effects, off-axis response, and crossover artifacts. Designers can use an anechoic chamber to ensure the speaker can be measured independently of room effects, or any of several electronic techniques that, to some extent, substitute for such chambers. Some developers eschew anechoic chambers in favor of specific standardized room setups intended to simulate real-life listening conditions.

Fabrication of finished loudspeaker systems has become segmented, depending largely on price, shipping costs, and weight limitations. High-end speaker systems, which are typically heavier (and often larger) than economic shipping allows outside local regions, are usually made in their target market region and can cost $140,000 or more per pair. Economical mass market speaker systems and drivers available for much lower costs may be manufactured in China or other low-cost manufacturing locations.

Driver Types

A four-way, high fidelity loudspeaker system. Each of the four drivers outputs a different frequency range; the fifth aperture at the bottom is a bass reflex port.

Individual electro dynamic drivers provide their best performance within a limited frequency range. Multiple drivers (e.g., subwoofers, woofers, mid-range drivers, and tweeters) are generally combined into a complete loudspeaker system to provide performance beyond that constraint. The three most commonly used sound radiation systems are the cone, dome and horn type drivers.

Full-range Drivers

A full-range driver is a speaker designed to be used alone to reproduce an audio channel without the help of other drivers, and therefore must cover the entire audio frequency range. These drivers are small, typically 3 to 8 inches (7.6 to 20.3 cm) in diameter to permit reasonable high frequency response, and carefully designed to give low-distortion output at low frequencies, though with reduced maximum output level. Full-range (or more accurately, wide-range) drivers are most commonly heard in public address systems, in televisions (although some models are suitable for hi-fi listening), small radios, intercoms, some computer speakers, etc. In hi-fi speaker systems, the use of wide-range drive units can avoid undesirable interactions between multiple drivers caused by non-coincident driver location or crossover network issues. Fans of wide-range driver hi-fi speaker systems claim a coherence of sound due to the single source and a resulting lack of interference, and likely also to the lack of crossover components. Detractors typically cite wide-range drivers' limited frequency response and modest output abilities (most especially at low frequencies), together with their requirement for large, elaborate, expensive enclosures—such as transmission lines, quarter wave resonators or horns—to approach optimum performance. With the advent of neodymium drivers, low cost quarter wave transmission lines are made possible and are increasingly made availably commercially.

Full-range drivers often employ an additional cone called a *whizzer*: a small, light cone attached to the joint between the voice coil and the primary cone. The whizzer cone extends the high-frequency response of the driver and broadens its high frequency directivity, which would otherwise be greatly narrowed due to the outer diameter cone material failing to keep up with the central voice coil at higher frequencies. The main cone in a whizzer design is manufactured so as to flex more in the outer diameter than in the center. The result is that the main cone delivers low frequencies and the whizzer cone contributes most of the higher frequencies. Since the whizzer cone is smaller than the main diaphragm, output dispersion at high frequencies is improved relative to an equivalent single larger diaphragm.

Limited-range drivers, also used alone, are typically found in computers, toys, and clock radios. These drivers are less elaborate and less expensive than wide-range drivers, and they may be severely compromised to fit into very small mounting locations. In these applications, sound quality is a low priority. The human ear is remarkably tolerant of poor sound quality, and the distortion inherent in limited-range drivers may enhance their output at high frequencies, increasing clarity when listening to spoken word material.

Subwoofer

A subwoofer is a woofer driver used only for the lowest-pitched part of the audio spectrum: typically below 200 Hz for consumer systems,below 100 Hz for professional live sound, and below 80 Hz in THX-approved systems. Because the intended range of frequencies is limited, subwoofer system design is usually simpler in many respects than for conventional loudspeakers, often consisting of a single driver enclosed in a suitable box or enclosure. Since sound in this frequency range can easily bend around corners by diffraction, the speaker aperture does not have to face the audience, and subwoofers can be mounted in the bottom of the enclosure, facing the floor. This is eased by the limitations of human hearing at low frequencies; such sounds cannot be located in space, due to their large wavelengths compared to higher frequencies which produce differential effects in the ears due to shadowing by the head, and diffraction around it, both of which we rely upon for localization clues.

To accurately reproduce very low bass notes without unwanted resonances (typically from cabinet panels), subwoofer systems must be solidly constructed and properly braced to avoid unwanted sounds of cabinet vibrations. As a result, good subwoofers are typically quite heavy. Many subwoofer systems include integrated power amplifiersand electronic subsonic (sub)-filters, with additional controls relevant to low-frequency reproduction (e.g., a crossover knob and a phase switch). These variants are known as "active" or "powered" subwoofers, with the former including a power amplifier. In contrast, "passive" subwoofers require external amplification.

In typical installations, subwoofers are physically separated from the rest of the speaker cabinets. Because of propagation delay, their output may be somewhat out of phase from another subwoofer (on another channel) or slightly out of phase with the rest of the sound. Consequently, a subwoofer's power amp often has a phase-delay adjustment (approximately 1 ms of delay is required for each additional foot of separation from the listener) which may improve performance of the system as a whole at subwoofer frequencies (and perhaps an octave or so above the crossover point). However, the influence of room resonances (sometimes called standing waves) is typically so large that such issues are secondary in practice. Subwoofers are widely used in large concert and mid-sized venue sound reinforcement systems. Subwoofer cabinets are often built with a bass reflex port (i.e., a hole cut into the cabinet with a tube attached to it), a design feature which if properly engineered improves bass performance and increases efficiency.

Woofer

A woofer is a driver that reproduces low frequencies. The driver works with the characteristics of the enclosure to produce suitable low frequencies. Indeed, both are so closely connected that they must be considered together in use. Only at design time do the separate properties of enclosure and woofer matter individually. Some loudspeaker systems use a woofer for the lowest frequencies, sometimes well enough that a subwoofer is not needed. Additionally, some loudspeakers use the woofer to handle middle frequencies, eliminating the mid-range driver. This can be accomplished with the selection of a tweeter that can work low enough that, combined with a woofer that responds high enough, the two drivers add coherently in the middle frequencies.

Mid-range Driver

A mid-range speaker is a loudspeaker driver that reproduces a band of frequencies generally between 1–6 kHz, otherwise known as the 'mid' frequencies (between the woofer and tweeter). Mid-range driver diaphragms can be made of paper or composite materials, and can be direct radiation drivers (rather like smaller woofers) or they can be compression drivers (rather like some tweeter designs). If the mid-range driver is a direct radiator, it can be mounted on the front baffle of a loudspeaker enclosure, or, if a compression driver, mounted at the throat of a horn for added output level and control of radiation pattern.

Tweeter

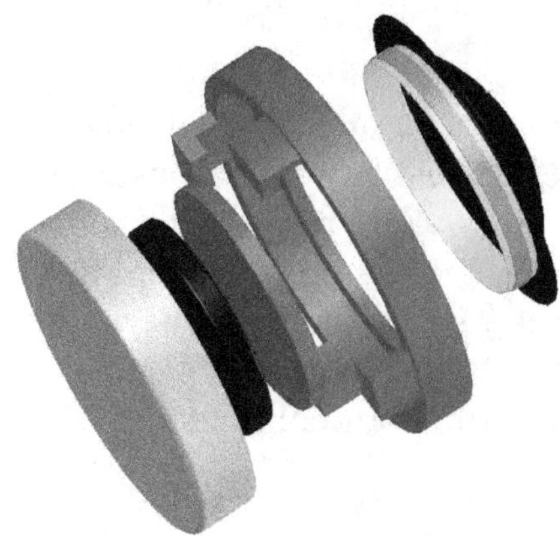

Exploded view of a dome tweeter.

A tweeter is a high-frequency driver that reproduces the highest frequencies in a speaker system. A major problem in tweeter design is achieving wide angular sound coverage (off-axis response), since high frequency sound tends to leave the speaker in narrow beams. Soft-dome tweeters are widely found in home stereo systems, and horn-loaded compression drivers are common in professional sound reinforcement. Ribbon tweeters have gained popularity in recent years, as the output power of some designs has been increased to levels useful for professional sound reinforcement, and their output pattern is wide in the horizontal plane, a pattern that has convenient applications in concert sound.

Coaxial Drivers

A coaxial driver is a loudspeaker driver with two or several combined concentric drivers. Coaxial drivers have been produced by many companies, such as Altec, Tannoy, Pioneer, KEF, SEAS, B&C Speakers, BMS, Cabasse and Genelec.

System Design

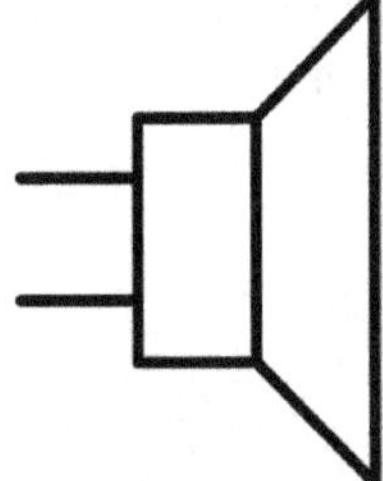

Electronic symbol for a speaker

Crossover

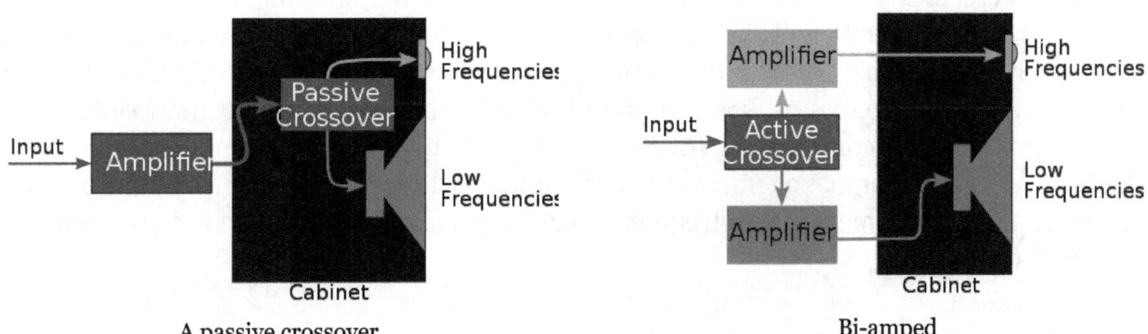

A passive crossover

Bi-amped

Used in multi-driver speaker systems, the crossover is an assembly of filters that separate the input signal into different frequency ranges (i.e. “bands”), according to the requirements of each driver. Hence the drivers receive power only at their operating frequency (the sound frequency range they were designed for), thereby reducing distortion in the drivers and interference between them. The ideal characteristics of a crossover may include perfect out-of-band attenuation at the output of each filter, no amplitude variation (“ripple”) within each pass band, no phase delay between overlapping frequency bands, to name just a few.

Crossovers can be *passive* or *active*. A passive crossover is an electronic circuit that uses a combination of one or more resistors, inductors, or non-polar capacitors. These components are combined to form a filter network and are most often placed between the full frequency-range power amplifier and the loudspeaker drivers to divide the amplifier’s signal into the necessary frequency bands before being delivered to the individual drivers. Passive crossover circuits need no external power beyond the audio signal itself, but have some disadvantages: they may require larger inductors and capacitors due to power handling requirements (being driven by the amplifier), limited component availability to optimize the crossover’s characteristics at such power levels, etc. Unlike active crossovers which include a built-in amplifier, passive crossovers have an inherent attenuation within the pass band, typically leading to a reduction in damping factor before the voice coil An active crossover is an electronic filter circuit that divides the signal into individual frequency bands *before* power amplification, thus requiring at least one power amplifier for each bandpass. Passive filtering may also be used in this way before power amplification, but it is an uncommon solution, being less flexible than active filtering. Any technique that uses crossover filtering followed by amplification is commonly known as bi-amping, tri-amping, quad-amping, and so on, depending on the minimum number of amplifier channels.

Some loudspeaker designs use a combination of passive and active crossover filtering, such as a passive crossover between the mid- and high-frequency drivers and an active crossover between the low-frequency driver and the combined mid- and high frequencies.

Passive crossovers are commonly installed inside speaker boxes and are by far the most usual type of crossover for home and low-power use. In car audio systems, passive crossovers may be in a separate box, necessary to accommodate the size of the components used. Passive crossovers may be simple for low-order filtering, or complex to allow steep slopes such as 18 or 24 dB per octave.

Passive crossovers can also be designed to compensate for undesired characteristics of driver, horn, or enclosure resonances, and can be tricky to implement, due to component interaction. Passive crossovers, like the driver units that they feed, have power handling limits, have insertion losses (10% is often claimed), and change the load seen by the amplifier. The changes are matters of concern for many in the hi-fi world. When high output levels are required, active crossovers may be preferable. Active crossovers may be simple circuits that emulate the response of a passive network, or may be more complex, allowing extensive audio adjustments. Some active crossovers, usually digital loudspeaker management systems, may include electronics and controls for precise alignment of phase and time between frequency bands, equalization, dynamic range compression and limiting) control.

Enclosures

An unusual three-way speaker system. The cabinet is narrow to raise the frequency where a diffraction effect called the "baffle step" occurs

Most loudspeaker systems consist of drivers mounted in an enclosure, or cabinet. The role of the enclosure is to prevent sound waves emanating from the back of a driver from interfering destructively with those from the front. The sound waves emitted from the back are 180° out of phase with those emitted forward, so without an enclosure they typically cause cancellations which significantly degrade the level and quality of sound at low frequencies.

The simplest driver mount is a flat panel (i.e., baffle) with the drivers mounted in holes in it. However, in this approach, sound frequencies with a wavelength longer than the baffle dimensions are canceled out, because the antiphase radiation from the rear of the cone interferes with the radiation from the front. With an infinitely large panel, this interference could be entirely prevented. A sufficiently large sealed box can approach this behavior.

Since panels of infinite dimensions are impossible, most enclosures function by containing the rear radiation from the moving diaphragm. A sealed enclosure prevents transmission of the sound emitted from the rear of the loudspeaker by confining the sound in a rigid and airtight box. Techniques used to reduce transmission of sound through the walls of the cabinet include thicker cabinet walls, lossy wall material, internal bracing, curved cabinet walls—or more rarely, visco-elastic materials (e.g., mineral-loaded bitumen) or thin lead sheeting applied to the interior enclosure walls.

However, a rigid enclosure reflects sound internally, which can then be transmitted back through the loudspeaker diaphragm—again resulting in degradation of sound quality. This can be reduced by internal absorption using absorptive materials (often called "damping"), such as glass wool, wool, or synthetic fiber batting, within the enclosure. The internal shape of the enclosure can also be designed to reduce this by reflecting sounds away from the loudspeaker diaphragm, where they may then be absorbed.

Other enclosure types alter the rear sound radiation so it can add constructively to the output from the front of the cone. Designs that do this (including *bass reflex*, *passive radiator*, *transmission line*, etc.) are often used to extend the effective low-frequency response and increase low-frequency output of the driver.

To make the transition between drivers as seamless as possible, system designers have attempted to time-align (or phase adjust) the drivers by moving one or more driver mounting locations forward or back so that the acoustic center of each driver is in the same vertical plane. This may also involve tilting the face speaker back, providing a separate enclosure mounting for each driver, or (less commonly) using electronic techniques to achieve the same effect. These attempts have resulted in some unusual cabinet designs.

The speaker mounting scheme (including cabinets) can also cause diffraction, resulting in peaks and dips in the frequency response. The problem is usually greatest at higher frequencies, where wavelengths are similar to, or smaller than, cabinet dimensions. The effect can be minimized by rounding the front edges of the cabinet, curving the cabinet itself, using a smaller or narrower enclosure, choosing a strategic driver arrangement, using absorptive material around a driver, or some combination of these and other schemes.

Horn Loudspeakers

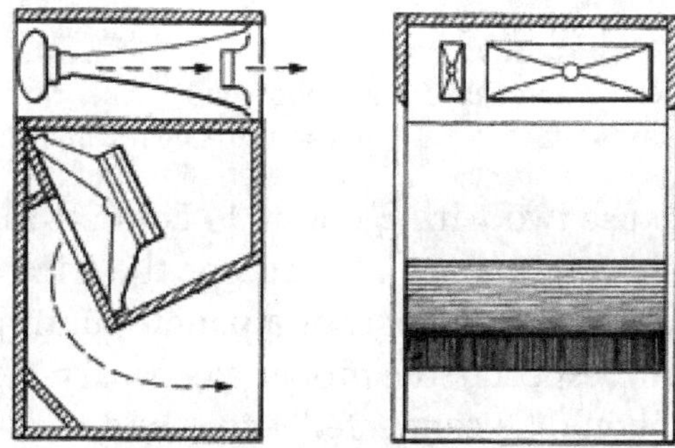

A three-way loudspeaker that uses horns in front of each of the three drivers: a shallow horn for the tweeter, a long, straight horn for mid frequencies and a folded horn for the woofer

Horn loudspeakers are the oldest form of loudspeaker system. The use of horns as voice-amplifying megaphones dates at least to the 17th century, and horns were used in mechanical gramophones as early as 1857. Horn loudspeakers use a shaped waveguide in front of or behind the driver to increase the directivity of the loudspeaker and to transform a small diameter, high pressure condition at the driver cone surface to a large diameter, low pressure condition at the mouth of the horn. This improves the acoustic—electro/mechanical impedance match between the driver and ambient air, increasing efficiency, and focusing the sound over a narrower area.

The size of the throat, mouth, the length of the horn, as well as the area expansion rate along it must be carefully chosen to match the drive to properly provide this transforming function over a range of frequencies (every horn performs poorly outside its acoustic limits, at both high and low frequencies). The length and cross-sectional mouth area required to create a bass or sub-bass horn require a horn many feet long. 'Folded' horns can reduce the total size, but compel designers to make compromises and accept increased complication such as cost and construction. Some horn designs not only fold the low frequency horn, but use the walls in a room corner as an extension of the horn mouth. In the late 1940s, horns whose mouths took up much of a room wall were not unknown amongst hi-fi fans. Room sized installations became much less acceptable when two or more were required.

A horn loaded speaker can have a sensitivity as high as 110 dB at 2.83 volts (1 watt at 8 ohms) at 1 meter. This is a hundredfold increase in output compared to a speaker rated at 90 dB sensitivity, and is invaluable in applications where high sound levels are required or amplifier power is limited.

Wiring Connections

Two-way binding posts on a loudspeaker, connected using banana plugs.

A 4-ohm loudspeaker with two pairs of binding posts capable of accepting bi-wiring after the removal of two metal straps.

Most home hi-fi loudspeakers use two wiring points to connect to the source of the signal (for example, to the audio amplifier or receiver). To accept the wire connection, the loudspeaker enclosure may have binding posts, spring clips, or a panel-mount jack. If the wires for a pair of speakers are not connected with respect to the proper electrical polarity (the + and – connections on the speaker and amplifier should be connected + to + and – to –; speaker cable is almost always marked so that one conductor of a pair can be distinguished from the other, even if it has run under or behind things in its run from amplifier to speaker location), the loudspeakers are said to be "out of phase" or more properly "out of polarity". Given identical signals, motion in one cone is in the opposite direction of the other. This typically causes monophonic material in a stereo recording to be canceled out, reduced in level, and made more difficult to localize, all due to destructive interference of the sound waves. The cancellation effect is most noticeable at frequencies where the loudspeakers are separated by a quarter wavelength or less; low frequencies are affected the most. This type of miswiring error does not damage speakers, but is not optimal for listening.

With sound reinforcement system, PA system and instrument amplifier speaker enclosures, cables and some type of jack or connector are typically used. Lower- and mid-priced sound system and instrument speaker cabinets often use 1/4" speaker cable jacks. Higher-priced and higher powered sound system cabinets and instrument speaker cabinets often use Speakon connectors. Speakon connectors are considered to be safer for high wattage amplifiers, because the connector is designed so that human users cannot touch the connectors.

Wireless Speakers

HP Roar Wireless Speaker

Wireless speakers are very similar to traditional (wired) loudspeakers, but they receive audio signals using radio frequency (RF) waves rather than over audio cables. There is normally an amplifier integrated in the speaker's cabinet because the RF waves alone are not enough to drive the speaker. This integration of amplifier and loudspeaker is known as an active loudspeaker. Manufacturers of these loudspeakers design them to be as lightweight as possible while producing the maximum amount of audio output efficiency.

Wireless speakers still need power, so require a nearby AC power outlet, or possibly batteries. Only the wire to the amplifier is eliminated.

Specifications

Specifications label on a loudspeaker.

Speaker specifications generally include:

- Speaker or driver type (individual units only): Full-range, woofer, tweeter, or mid-range.
- Size of individual drivers. For cone drivers, the quoted size is generally the outside diameter of the basket. However, it may less commonly also be the diameter of the cone surround, measured apex to apex, or the distance from the center of one mounting hole to its opposite.

Voice-coil diameter may also be specified. If the loudspeaker has a compression horn driver, the diameter of the horn throat may be given.

- Rated Power: Nominal (or even continuous) power, and peak (or maximum short-term) power a loudspeaker can handle (i.e., maximum input power before destroying the loudspeaker; it is never the sound output the loudspeaker produces). A driver may be damaged at much less than its rated power if driven past its mechanical limits at lower frequencies. Tweeters can also be damaged by amplifier clipping (amplifier circuits produce large amounts of energy at high frequencies in such cases) or by music or sine wave input at high frequencies. Each of these situations might pass more energy to a tweeter than it can survive without damage. In some jurisdictions, power handling has a legal meaning allowing comparisons between loudspeakers under consideration. Elsewhere, the variety of meanings for power handling capacity can be quite confusing.
- Impedance: Typically 4 Ω (ohms), 8 Ω, etc.
- Baffle or enclosure type (enclosed systems only): Sealed, bass reflex, etc.
- Number of drivers (complete speaker systems only): Two-way, three-way, etc.
- Class of loudspeaker:
  - Class 1: maximum SPL 110-119 dB, the type of loudspeaker used for reproducing a person speaking in a small space or for background music; mainly used as fill speakers for Class 2 or Class 3 speakers; typically small 4" or 5" woofers and dome tweeters.
  - Class 2: maximum SPL 120-129 dB, the type of medium power-capable loudspeaker used for reinforcement in small to medium spaces or as fill speakers for Class 3 or Class 4 speakers; typically 5" to 8" woofers and dome tweeters.
  - Class 3: maximum SPL 130-139 dB, high power-capable loudspeakers used in main systems in small to medium spaces; also used as fill speakers for class 4 speakers; typically 6.5" to 12" woofers and 2" or 3" compression drivers for high frequencies.
  - Class 4: maximum SPL 140 dB and higher, very high power-capable loudspeakers used as mains in medium to large spaces (or for fill speakers for these medium to large spaces); 10" to 15" woofers and 3" compression drivers.
- Crossover frequency(ies) (multi-driver systems only): The nominal frequency boundaries of the division between drivers.
- Frequency response: The measured, or specified, output over a specified range of frequencies for a constant input level varied across those frequencies. It sometimes includes a variance limit, such as within "± 2.5 dB."
- Thiele/Small parameters (individual drivers only): these include the driver's F_s (resonance frequency), Q_{ts} (a driver's Q; more or less, its damping factor at resonant frequency), V_{as} (the equivalent air compliance volume of the driver), etc.
- Sensitivity: The sound pressure level produced by a loudspeaker in a non-reverberant environment, often specified in dB and measured at 1 meter with an input of 1 watt (2.83 rms

volts into 8 Ω), typically at one or more specified frequencies. Manufacturers often use this rating in marketing material.

- Maximum sound pressure level: The highest output the loudspeaker can manage, short of damage or not exceeding a particular distortion level. Manufacturers often use this rating in marketing material—commonly without reference to frequency range or distortion level.

Electrical Characteristics of Dynamic Loudspeakers

The load that a driver presents to an amplifier consists of a complex electrical impedance—a combination of resistance and both capacitive and inductive reactance, which combines properties of the driver, its mechanical motion, the effects of crossover components (if any are in the signal path between amplifier and driver), and the effects of air loading on the driver as modified by the enclosure and its environment. Most amplifiers' output specifications are given at a specific power into an ideal resistive load; however, a loudspeaker does not have a constant impedance across its frequency range. Instead, the voice coil is inductive, the driver has mechanical resonances, the enclosure changes the driver's electrical and mechanical characteristics, and a passive crossover between the drivers and the amplifier contributes its own variations. The result is a load impedance that varies widely with frequency, and usually a varying phase relationship between voltage and current as well, also changing with frequency. Some amplifiers can cope with the variation better than others can.

To make sound, a loudspeaker is driven by modulated electric current (produced by an amplifier) that pass through a "speaker coil" which then (through inductance) creates a magnetic field around the coil, creating a magnetic field. The electric current variations that pass through the speaker are thus converted to a varying magnetic field, whose interaction with the driver's magnetic field moves the speaker diaphragm, which thus forces the driver to produce air motion that is similar to the original signal from the amplifier.

Electromechanical Measurements

Examples of typical measurements are: amplitude and phase characteristics vs. frequency; impulse response under one or more conditions (e.g., square waves, sine wave bursts, etc.); directivity vs. frequency (e.g., horizontally, vertically, spherically, etc.); harmonic and intermodulation distortion vs. sound pressure level (SPL) output, using any of several test signals; stored energy (i.e., ringing) at various frequencies; impedance vs. frequency; and small-signal vs. large-signal performance. Most of these measurements require sophisticated and often expensive equipment to perform, and also good judgment by the operator, but the raw sound pressure level output is rather easier to report and so is often the only specified value—sometimes in misleadingly exact terms. The sound pressure level (SPL) a loudspeaker produces is measured in decibels.

Efficiency vs. Sensitivity

Loudspeaker efficiency is defined as the sound power output divided by the electrical power input. Most loudspeakers are inefficient transducers; only about 1% of the electrical energy sent by an amplifier to a typical home loudspeaker is converted to acoustic energy. The remainder is converted to heat, mostly in the voice coil and magnet assembly. The main reason for this is the difficulty of achieving proper impedance matching between the acoustic impedance of the drive unit and the air it radiates into. (At low frequencies, improving this match is the main purpose of speaker enclosure designs). The efficiency of loudspeaker drivers varies with frequency as well. For instance, the output of a woofer driver decreases as the input frequency decreases because of the increasingly poor match between air and the driver.

Driver ratings based on the SPL for a given input are called sensitivity ratings and are notionally similar to efficiency. Sensitivity is usually defined as so many decibels at 1 W electrical input, measured at 1 meter (except for headphones), often at a single frequency. The voltage used is often 2.83 V_{RMS}, which is 1 watt into an 8 Ω (nominal) speaker impedance (approximately true for many speaker systems). Measurements taken with this reference are quoted as dB with 2.83 V @ 1 m.

The sound pressure output is measured at (or mathematically scaled to be equivalent to a measurement taken at) one meter from the loudspeaker and on-axis (directly in front of it), under the condition that the loudspeaker is radiating into an infinitely large space and mounted on an infinite baffle. Clearly then, sensitivity does not correlate precisely with efficiency, as it also depends on the directivity of the driver being tested and the acoustic environment in front of the actual loudspeaker. For example, a cheerleader's horn produces more sound output in the direction it is pointed by concentrating sound waves from the cheerleader in one direction, thus "focusing" them. The horn also improves impedance matching between the voice and the air, which produces more acoustic power for a given speaker power. In some cases, improved impedance matching (via careful enclosure design) lets the speaker produce more acoustic power:

- Typical home loudspeakers have sensitivities of about 85 to 95 dB for 1 W @ 1 m—an efficiency of 0.5–4%.
- Sound reinforcement and public address loudspeakers have sensitivities of perhaps 95 to 102 dB for 1 W @ 1 m—an efficiency of 4–10%.
- Rock concert, stadium PA, marine hailing, etc. speakers generally have higher sensitivities of 103 to 110 dB for 1 W @ 1 m—an efficiency of 10–20%.

A driver with a higher maximum power rating cannot necessarily be driven to louder levels than a lower-rated one, since sensitivity and power handling are largely independent properties. In the examples that follow, assume (for simplicity) that the drivers being compared have the same electrical impedance, are operated at the same frequency within both driver's respective pass bands, and that power compression and distortion are low. For the first example, a speaker 3 dB more sensitive than another produces double the sound power (is 3 dB louder) for the same power input. Thus, a 100 W driver ("A") rated at 92 dB for 1 W @ 1 m sensitivity puts out twice as much acoustic power as a 200 W driver ("B") rated at 89 dB for 1 W @ 1 m when both are driven with 100 W of input power. In this particular example, when driven at 100 W, speaker A produces the same SPL, or loudness as speaker B would produce with 200 W input. Thus, a 3 dB increase in sensitivity of the speaker means that it needs half the amplifier power to achieve a given SPL. This translates into a smaller, less complex power amplifier—and often, to reduced overall system cost.

It is typically not possible to combine high efficiency (especially at low frequencies) with compact enclosure size and adequate low frequency response. One can, for the most part, choose only two of the three parameters when designing a speaker system. So, for example, if extended low-frequency performance and small box size are important, one must accept low efficiency. This rule of thumb is sometimes called Hofmann's Iron Law (after J.A. Hofmann, the "H" in KLH).

Listening Environment

At Jay Pritzker Pavilion, a LARES system is combined with a zoned sound reinforcement system, both suspended on an overhead steel trellis, to synthesize an indoor acoustic environment outdoors.

The interaction of a loudspeaker system with its environment is complex and is largely out of the loudspeaker designer's control. Most listening rooms present a more or less reflective environment, depending on size, shape, volume, and furnishings. This means the sound reaching a listener's ears consists not only of sound directly from the speaker system, but also the same sound delayed by traveling to and from (and being modified by) one or more surfaces. These reflected sound waves, when added to the direct sound, cause cancellation and addition at assorted frequencies (e.g., from resonant room modes), thus changing the timbre and character of the sound at the listener's ears. The human brain is very sensitive to small variations, including some of these, and this is part of the reason why a loudspeaker system sounds different at different listening positions or in different rooms.

A significant factor in the sound of a loudspeaker system is the amount of absorption and diffusion present in the environment. Clapping one's hands in a typical empty room, without draperies or carpet, produces a zippy, fluttery echo due both to a lack of absorption and to reverberation (that is, repeated echoes) from flat reflective walls, floor, and ceiling. The addition of hard surfaced furniture, wall hangings, shelving and even baroque plaster ceiling decoration changes the echoes, primarily because of diffusion caused by reflective objects with shapes and surfaces having sizes on the order of the sound wavelengths. This somewhat breaks up the simple reflections otherwise caused by bare flat surfaces, and spreads the reflected energy of an incident wave over a larger angle on reflection.

Placement

In a typical rectangular listening room, the hard, parallel surfaces of the walls, floor and ceiling cause primary acoustic resonance nodes in each of the three dimensions: left-right, up-down and forward-backward. Furthermore, there are more complex resonance modes involving three, four, five and even all six boundary surfaces combining to create standing waves. Low frequencies excite these modes the most, since long wavelengths are not much affected by furniture compositions or placement. The mode spacing is critical, especially in small and medium size rooms like recording studios, home theaters and broadcast studios. The proximity of the loudspeakers to room boundaries affects how strongly the resonances are excited as well as affecting the relative strength at each frequency. The location of the listener is critical, too, as a position near a boundary can have a great effect on the perceived balance of frequencies. This is because standing wave patterns are most easily heard in these locations and at lower frequencies, below the Schroeder frequency – typically around 200–300 Hz, depending on room size.

Directivity

Acousticians, in studying the radiation of sound sources have developed some concepts important to understanding how loudspeakers are perceived. The simplest possible radiating source is a point source, sometimes called a simple source. An ideal point source is an infinitesimally small point radiating sound. It may be easier to imagine a tiny pulsating sphere, uniformly increasing and decreasing in diameter, sending out sound waves in all directions equally, independent of frequency.

Any object radiating sound, including a loudspeaker system, can be thought of as being composed of combinations of such simple point sources. The radiation pattern of a combination of point sources is not the same as for a single source, but depends on the distance and orientation between the sources, the position relative to them from which the listener hears the combination, and the frequency of the sound involved. Using geometry and calculus, some simple combinations of sources are easily solved; others are not.

One simple combination is two simple sources separated by a distance and vibrating out of phase, one miniature sphere expanding while the other is contracting. The pair is known as a doublet, or dipole, and the radiation of this combination is similar to that of a very small dynamic loudspeaker operating without a baffle. The directivity of a dipole is a figure 8 shape with maximum output along a vector that connects the two sources and minimums to the sides when the observing point is equidistant from the two sources, where the sum of the positive and negative waves cancel each other. While most drivers are dipoles, depending on the enclosure to which they are attached, they may radiate as monopoles, dipoles (or bipoles). If mounted on a finite baffle, and these out of phase waves are allowed to interact, dipole peaks and nulls in the frequency response result. When the rear radiation is absorbed or trapped in a box, the diaphragm becomes a monopole radiator. Bipolar speakers, made by mounting in-phase monopoles (both moving out of or into the box in unison) on opposite sides of a box, are a method of approaching omnidirectional radiation patterns.

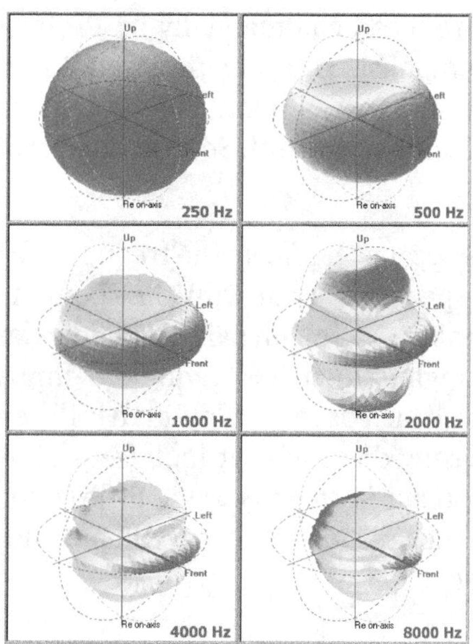

Polar plots of a four-driver industrial columnar public address loudspeaker taken at six frequencies.

In real life, individual drivers are complex 3D shapes such as cones and domes, and they are placed on a baffle for various reasons. A mathematical expression for the directivity of a complex shape, based on modeling combinations of point sources, is usually not possible, but in the far field, the directivity of a loudspeaker with a circular diaphragm is close to that of a flat circular piston, so it can be used as an illustrative simplification for discussion. As a simple example of the mathematical physics involved, consider the following: the formula for far field directivity of a flat circular piston in an infinite baffle is $p(\theta)=\dfrac{p_0 J_1(k_a \sin\theta)}{k_a \sin\theta}$

where $k_a=\dfrac{2\pi a}{\lambda}$, p_o is the pressure on axis, a is the piston radius, λ is the wavelength $\left(i.e\,\lambda=\dfrac{c}{f}=\dfrac{\text{speed of sound}}{\text{frequency}}\right)$ θ is the angle off axis and j_1 is the Bessel function of the first kind.

A planar source radiates sound uniformly for low frequencies' wavelengths longer than the dimensions of the planar source, and as frequency increases, the sound from such a source focuses into an increasingly narrower angle. The smaller the driver, the higher the frequency where this narrowing of directivity occurs. Even if the diaphragm is not perfectly circular, this effect occurs such that larger sources are more directive. Several loudspeaker designs approximate this behavior. Most are electrostatic or planar magnetic designs.

Various manufacturers use different driver mounting arrangements to create a specific type of sound field in the space for which they are designed. The resulting radiation patterns may be intended to more closely simulate the way sound is produced by real instruments, or simply create a controlled energy distribution from the input signal (some using this approach are called monitors, as they are useful in checking the signal just recorded in a studio). An example of the first is a room corner system with many small drivers on the surface of a 1/8 sphere. A system design of this type was patented and produced commercially by Professor Amar Bose—the 2201. Later Bose models have deliberately emphasized production of both direct and reflected sound by the loudspeaker itself, regardless of its environment. The designs are controversial in high fidelity circles, but have proven commercially successful. Several other manufacturers' designs follow similar principles.

Directivity is an important issue because it affects the frequency balance of sound a listener hears, and also the interaction of the speaker system with the room and its contents. A very directive (sometimes termed 'beamy') speaker (i.e., on an axis perpendicular to the speaker face) may result in a reverberant field lacking in high frequencies, giving the impression the speaker is deficient in treble even though it measures well on axis (e.g., "flat" across the entire frequency range). Speakers with very wide, or rapidly increasing directivity at high frequencies, can give the impression that there is too much treble (if the listener is on axis) or too little (if the listener is off axis). This is part of the reason why on-axis frequency response measurement is not a complete characterization of the sound of a given loudspeaker.

Other Speaker Designs

While dynamic cone speakers remain the most popular choice, many other speaker technologies exist.

With a Diaphragm

Moving-iron Loudspeakers

The moving iron speaker was the first type of speaker that was invented. Unlike the newer dynamic (moving coil) design, a moving-iron speaker uses a stationary coil to vibrate a magnetized piece of metal (called the iron, reed, or armature). The metal is either attached to the diaphragm or is the diaphragm itself. This design was the original loudspeaker design, dating back to the early telephone. Moving iron drivers are inefficient and can only produce a small band of sound. They require large magnets and coils to increase force.

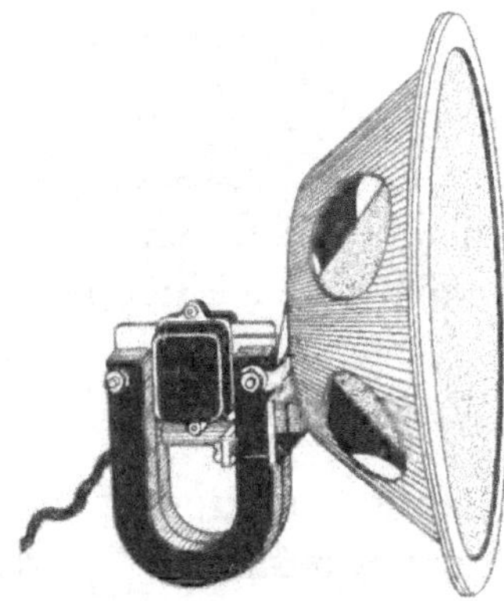

Moving iron speaker

Balanced armature drivers (a type of moving iron driver) use an armature that moves like a seesaw or diving board. Since they are not damped, they are highly efficient, but they also produce strong resonances. They are still used today for high end earphones and hearing aids, where small size and high efficiency are important.

Piezoelectric Speakers

A piezoelectric buzzer.

Piezoelectric speakers are frequently used as beepers in watches and other electronic devices, and are sometimes used as tweeters in less-expensive speaker systems, such as computer speakers and portable radios. Piezoelectric speakers have several advantages over conventional loudspeakers: they are resistant to overloads that would normally destroy most high frequency drivers, and they can be used without a crossover due to their electrical properties. There are also disadvantages: some amplifiers can oscillate when driving capacitive loads like most piezoelectrics, which results in distortion or damage to the amplifier. Additionally, their frequency response, in most cases, is inferior to that of other technologies. This is why they are generally used in single frequency (beeper) or non-critical applications.

Piezoelectric speakers can have extended high frequency output, and this is useful in some specialized circumstances; for instance, sonar applications in which piezoelectric variants are used as both output devices (generating underwater sound) and as input devices (acting as the sensing components of underwater microphones). They have advantages in these applications, not the least of which is simple and solid state construction that resists seawater better than a ribbon or cone based device would.

In 2013, Kyocera introduced piezoelectric ultra-thin medium-size film speakers with only 1 millimeter of thickness and 7 grams of weight for their 55" OLED televisions and they hope the speakers will also be used in PCs and tablets. Besides medium-size, there are also large and small sizes which can all produce relatively the same quality of sound and volume within 180 degrees. The highly responsive speaker material provides better clarity than traditional TV speakers.

Magnetostatic Loudspeakers

Instead of a voice coil driving a speaker cone, a magnetostatic speaker uses an array of metal strips bonded to a large film membrane. The magnetic field produced by signal current flowing through the strips interacts with the field of permanent bar magnets mounted behind them. The force produced moves the membrane and so the air in front of it. Typically, these designs are less efficient than conventional moving-coil speakers.

Magnetostatic loudspeaker

Magnetostrictive Speakers

Magnetostrictive transducers, based on magnetostriction, have been predominantly used as sonar ultrasonic sound wave radiators, but their use has spread also to audio speaker systems. Magnetostrictive speaker drivers have some special advantages: they can provide greater force (with smaller excursions) than other technologies; low excursion can avoid distortions from large excursion as in other designs; the magnetizing coil is stationary and therefore more easily cooled; they are robust because delicate suspensions and voice coils are not required. Magnetostrictive speaker modules have been produced by Fostex and FeONIC and subwoofer drivers have also been produced.

Electrostatic Loudspeakers

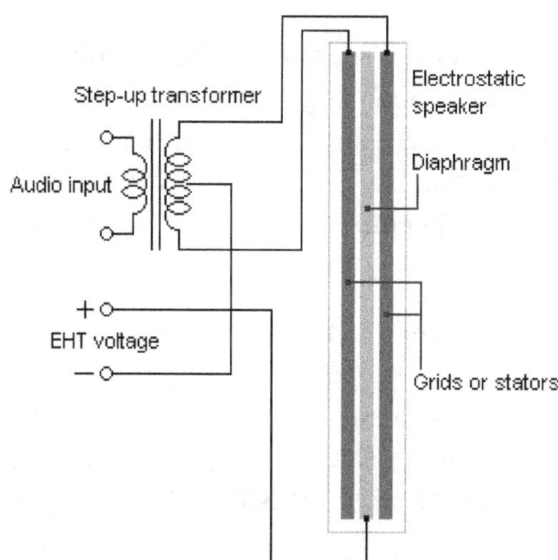

Schematic showing an electrostatic speaker's construction and its connections. The thickness of the diaphragm and grids has been exaggerated for the purpose of illustration.

Electrostatic loudspeakers use a high voltage electric field (rather than a magnetic field) to drive a thin statically charged membrane. Because they are driven over the entire membrane surface rather than from a small voice coil, they ordinarily provide a more linear and lower-distortion motion than dynamic drivers. They also have a relatively narrow dispersion pattern that can make for precise sound-field positioning. However, their optimum listening area is small and they are not very efficient speakers. They have the disadvantage that the diaphragm excursion is severely limited because of practical construction limitations—the further apart the stators are positioned, the higher the voltage must be to achieve acceptable efficiency. This increases the tendency for electrical arcs as well as increasing the speaker's attraction of dust particles. Arcing remains a potential problem with current technologies, especially when the panels are allowed to collect dust or dirt and are driven with high signal levels.

Electrostatics are inherently dipole radiators and due to the thin flexible membrane are less suited for use in enclosures to reduce low frequency cancellation as with common cone drivers. Due to this and the low excursion capability, full range electrostatic loudspeakers are large by nature, and the bass rolls off at a frequency corresponding to a quarter wavelength of the narrowest panel dimension. To reduce the size of commercial products, they are sometimes used as a high frequency driver in combination with a conventional dynamic driver that handles the bass frequencies effectively.

Electrostatics are usually driven through a step-up transformer that multiplies the voltage swings produced by the power amplifier. This transformer also multiplies the capacitive load that is inherent in electrostatic transducers, which means the effective impedance presented to the power amplifiers varies widely by frequency. A speaker that is nominally 8 ohms may actually present a load of 1 ohm at higher frequencies, which is challenging to some amplifier designs.

Ribbon and Planar Magnetic Loudspeakers

A ribbon speaker consists of a thin metal-film ribbon suspended in a magnetic field. The electrical signal is applied to the ribbon, which moves with it to create the sound. The advantage of a ribbon driver is that the ribbon has very little mass; thus, it can accelerate very quickly, yielding very good high-frequency response. Ribbon loudspeakers are often very fragile—some can be torn by a strong gust of air. Most ribbon tweeters emit sound in a dipole pattern. A few have backings that limit the dipole radiation pattern. Above and below the ends of the more or less rectangular ribbon, there is less audible output due to phase cancellation, but the precise amount of directivity depends on ribbon length. Ribbon designs generally require exceptionally powerful magnets, which makes them costly to manufacture. Ribbons have a very low resistance that most amplifiers cannot drive directly. As a result, a step down transformer is typically used to increase the current through the ribbon. The amplifier "sees" a load that is the ribbon's resistance times the transformer turns ratio squared. The transformer must be carefully designed so that its frequency response and parasitic losses do not degrade the sound, further increasing cost and complication relative to conventional designs.

Planar magnetic speakers (having printed or embedded conductors on a flat diaphragm) are sometimes described as ribbons, but are not truly ribbon speakers. The term planar is generally reserved for speakers with roughly rectangular flat surfaces that radiate in a bipolar (i.e., front and back) manner. Planar magnetic speakers consist of a flexible membrane with a voice coil printed or mounted on it. The current flowing through the coil interacts with the magnetic field of carefully placed magnets on either side of the diaphragm, causing the membrane to vibrate more or less uniformly and without much bending or wrinkling. The driving force covers a large percentage of the membrane surface and reduces resonance problems inherent in coil-driven flat diaphragms.

Bending Wave Loudspeakers

Bending wave transducers use a diaphragm that is intentionally flexible. The rigidity of the material increases from the center to the outside. Short wavelengths radiate primarily from the inner area, while longer waves reach the edge of the speaker. To prevent reflections from the outside back into the center, long waves are absorbed by a surrounding damper. Such transducers can cover a wide frequency range (80 Hz to 35,000 Hz) and have been promoted as being close to an ideal point sound source. This uncommon approach is being taken by only a very few manufacturers, in very different arrangements.

The Ohm Walsh loudspeakers use a unique driver designed by Lincoln Walsh, who had been a radar development engineer in WWII. He became interested in audio equipment design and his last project was a unique, one-way speaker using a single driver. The cone faced down into a sealed, airtight enclosure. Rather than move back-and-forth as conventional speakers do, the cone rippled and created sound in a manner known in RF electronics as a "transmission line". The new speaker created a cylindrical sound field. Lincoln Walsh died before his speaker was released to the public. The Ohm Acoustics firm has produced several loudspeaker models using the Walsh driver design since then. German Physiks, an audio equipment firm in Germany, also produces speakers using this approach.

The German firm, Manger, has designed and produced a bending wave driver that at first glance appears conventional. In fact, the round panel attached to the voice coil bends in a carefully controlled way to produce full range sound. Josef W. Manger was awarded with the "Diesel Medal" for extraordinary developments and inventions by the German institute of inventions.

Flat Panel Loudspeakers

There have been many attempts to reduce the size of speaker systems, or alternatively to make them less obvious. One such attempt was the development of "exciter" transducer coils mounted to flat panels to act as sound sources, most accurately called exciter/panel drivers. These can then be made in a neutral color and hung on walls where they are less noticeable than many speakers, or can be deliberately painted with patterns, in which case they can function decoratively. There are two related problems with flat panel techniques: first, a flat panel is necessarily more flexible than a cone shape in the same material, and therefore moves as a single unit even less, and second, resonances in the panel are difficult to control, leading to considerable distortions. Some progress has been made using such lightweight, rigid, materials such as Styrofoam, and there have been several flat panel systems commercially produced in recent years.

Heil Air Motion Transducers

Oskar Heil invented the air motion transducer in the 1960s. In this approach, a pleated diaphragm is mounted in a magnetic field and forced to close and open under control of a music signal. Air is forced from between the pleats in accordance with the imposed signal, generating sound. The drivers are less fragile than ribbons and considerably more efficient (and able to produce higher absolute output levels) than ribbon, electrostatic, or planar magnetic tweeter designs. ESS, a California manufacturer, licensed the design, employed Heil, and produced a range of speaker systems using his tweeters during the 1970s and 1980s. Lafayette Radio, a large US retail store chain, also sold speaker systems using such tweeters for a time. There are several manufacturers of these drivers (at least two in Germany—one of which produces a range of high-end professional speakers using tweeters and mid-range drivers based on the technology) and the drivers are increasingly used in professional audio. Martin Logan produces several AMT speakers in the US and Golden Ear. Technologies incorporates them in its entire speaker line.

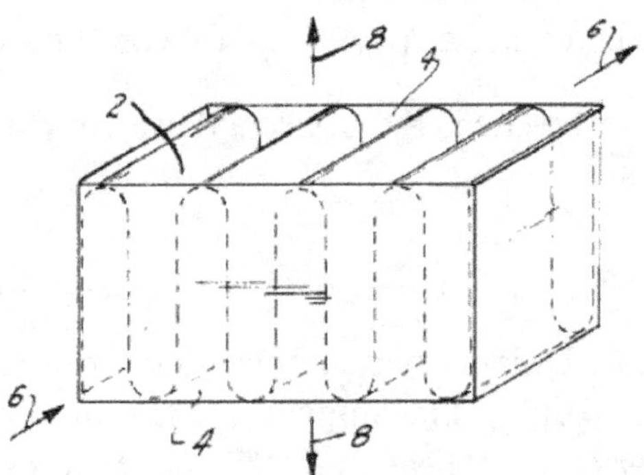

In Heil's air motion transducer, current through the membrane 2 causes it to move left and right in magnetic field 6, moving air in and out along directions 8; barriers 4 prevent air from moving in unintended directions.

Transparent Ionic Conduction Speaker

In 2013, a research team introduced Transparent ionic conduction speaker which a 2 layers transparent conductive gel and a layer of transparent rubber in between to make high voltage and high actuation work to reproduce good sound quality. The speaker is suitable for robotics, mobile computing and adaptive optics fields.

Without a Diaphragm

Plasma arc Speakers

Plasma speaker

Plasma arc loudspeakers use electrical plasma as a radiating element. Since plasma has minimal mass, but is charged and therefore can be manipulated by an electric field, the result is a very linear output at frequencies far higher than the audible range. Problems of maintenance and reliability for this approach tend to make it unsuitable for mass market use. In 1978 Alan E. Hill of the Air Force Weapons Laboratory in Albuquerque, NM, designed the PlasmatronicsHill Type I, a tweeter whose plasma was generated from helium gas.This avoided the ozone and nitrous oxide produced by RF decomposition of air in an earlier generation of plasma tweeters made by the pioneering DuKane Corporation, who produced the Ionovac (marketed as the Ionofane in the UK) during the 1950s. Currently, there remain a few manufacturers in Germany who use this design, and a do-it-yourself design has been published and has been available on the Internet.

A less expensive variation on this theme is the use of a flame for the driver, as flames contain ionized (electrically charged) gases.

Thermoacoustic Speakers

In 2008, researchers of Tsinghua University demonstrated a thermoacoustic loudspeaker of carbon nanotube thin film, whose working mechanism is a thermoacoustic effect. Sound frequency electric currents are used to periodically heat the CNT and thus result in sound generation in the surrounding air. The CNT thin film loudspeaker is transparent, stretchable and flexible. In 2013, researchers of Tsinghua University further present a thermoacoustic earphone of carbon nanotube thin yarn and a thermoacoustic surface-mounted device. They are both fully integrated devices and compatible with Si-based semiconducting technology.

Rotary Woofers

A rotary woofer is essentially a fan with blades that constantly change their pitch, allowing them to easily push the air back and forth. Rotary woofers are able to efficiently reproduce infrasound frequencies, which are difficult to impossible to achieve on a traditional speaker with a diaphragm. They are often employed in movie theaters to recreate rumbling bass effects, such as explosions.

New Technologies

Digital Speakers

Digital speakers have been the subject of experiments performed by Bell Labs as far back as the 1920s. The design is simple; each bit controls a driver, which is either fully ‹on' or ‹off'. Problems with this design have led manufacturers to abandon it as impractical for the present. First, for a reasonable number of bits (required for adequate sound reproduction quality), the physical size of a speaker system becomes very large. Secondly, due to inherent analog digital conversion problems, the effect of aliasing is unavoidable, so that the audio output is "reflected" at equal amplitude in the frequency domain, on the other side of the sampling frequency, causing an unacceptably high level of ultrasonics to accompany the desired output. No workable scheme has been found to adequately deal with this.

The term "digital" or "digital-ready" is often used for marketing purposes on speakers or headphones, but these systems are not digital in the sense described above. Rather, they are conventional speakers that can be used with digital sound sources (e.g., optical media, MP3 players, etc.), as can any conventional speaker.

Videoconferencing

Videoconferencing (or video conference) means to conduct a conference between two or more participants at different sites by using computer networks to transmit audio and video data. For example, a *point-to-point* (two-person) video conferencing system works much like a video telephone. Each participant has a video camera, microphone, and speakers mounted on his or her computer. As the two participants speak to one another, their voices are carried over the network and delivered to the other's speakers, and whatever images appear in front of the video camera appear in a window on the other participant's monitor.

Multipoint videoconferencing allows three or more participants to sit in a virtual conference room and communicate as if they were sitting right next to each other. Until the mid-90s, the hardware costs made videoconferencing prohibitively expensive for most organizations, but that situation is changing rapidly. Many analysts believe that videoconferencing will be one of the fastest-growing segments of the computer industry in the latter half of the decade.

Point-to-point Video Conferencing

Video-enabled meetings happen in two distinct ways: either point-to-point or with multi-point. In point-to-point, the simplest scenario is where one person or group is connected to another. The physical components (i.e. microphone and camera) that enable the meeting to take place are often integrated in to desktop computing solutions like a laptop or tablet, or can be combined into dedicated, room-based hardware solutions.

Point-to-point video conferencing

Where desktop solutions tend to be used by individuals, room-based solutions utilize dedicated video conferencing technology where groups of people can be seen, heard and can naturally participate in the meeting.

Multi-point Video Conferencing

In multi-point video calls, three or more locations are connected together, where all participants can see and hear each other, as well as see any content being shared during the meeting.

A use case scenario of multi-point Video Conferencing

In this scenario, digital information streams of voice, video and content are processed by a central, independent software program. Combining the individual participant's video and voice traffic, the program re-sends a collective data stream back to meeting participants in the form of real-time audio and video imagery.

Individuals can participate in a meeting in an "audio only" mode, or combine audio with video images of the meeting on screen. Depending upon the technical capability of the video conferencing system being used, images seen by participants are either classified as "active speaker" or "continuous presence."

In "active speaker" mode, the screen only provides an image of the person that is speaking at any point in time. In more advanced solutions with "continuous presence" mode, the bridge divides the image on the screen into a number of different areas. The person speaking at any point in time is presented in a large central area, and other meeting participants are shown displayed around the central image.

The "continuous presence" mode thus allows meeting participants to view and interact with all meeting participants in a 'virtual meeting room.'

The software program which creates the "virtual meeting room" and the digital processing hardware on which it resides, is often called a video bridge, or "bridge", for short. Another term for a bridge which is often used is a video conferencing "multi-point control unit" or "MCU."

Whereas point-to-point video conferencing is relatively simple, the creation and management of multipoint video conferences can be complex. An MCU must be able to create, control and facilitate multiple simultaneous live video conferencing meetings. A further complexity is added when different locations may connect to the meeting over digital or analogue streams at different speeds, with different data transport and signalling protocols employed to facilitate the communication. To link these users into a common, virtual meeting, the MCU must therefore be able to understand and translate between several different protocols (i.e. H.264 for communication over IP, and H.263 for ISDN).

The MCU will also allow those joining the video bridge to do so at the highest speed and the best possible quality that their individual system can support. Although there are two separate processes taking place here, this is often jointly referred to as "transcoding." It is important to note that not all bridges provide such transcoding capability, and failure to do this can seriously impact the quality and experience of video calls. When transcoding is not provided and users dial into a bridge over a range of different connection speeds, it is possible that the bridge may only be able to support the video meeting by establishing the connections at the lowest common denominator.

To illustrate the negative effect of this, consider a meeting that takes place with most users joining the bridge from the high-speed corporate network, but where one or two individuals dial into the meeting from home on low-bandwidth DSL or ISDN. In this case the experience of the many corporate users is downgraded to the lowest common denominator of the home-users, potentially making the video call ineffective. Where effective transcoding is supported by the MCU, those on the corporate network will continue to enjoy HD video quality, while remote users receive quality commensurate with their connection speeds.

In summary, when an MCU is designed well, integrating easily with multiple vendors and allowing users to call in at the data rate and resolution they want or need to—the result is an easy, seamless experience for all users, allowing people to focus on the meeting, not the technology.

Language of Video Conferencing

As video conferencing technology has evolved, two main protocols have emerged to provide the signalling control for the establishment, control and termination of video conferencing calls: SIP (Session Initiation Protocol) and H.323.

For the encoding and decoding of visual information, the industry is moving towards the industry standard known as H.264, which was developed to provide high-quality video at lower bandwidth over a wide range of networks and systems. An extension to the H.264 protocol is Scalable Video Coding (SVC), which is established to facilitate the enablement of video conferencing on a wider range of devices, such as tablets and mobile phones.

Bridging Architecture and Functionality

The combination of software and the hardware that creates the virtual meeting rooms is called a "video bridge." Virtual meeting rooms are identified by their "bridge numbers." With multiple calls taking place simultaneously, software analyses all the different data streams coming into the bridge processors, and assigns data streams accordingly. At the simplest level, the processing workload for bridges is dependent upon four factors:

- The number of locations that dial into each bridge.
- The number of conferencing calls that each bridge must handle simultaneously.
- The amount of data that is being received on each digital stream: higher resolutions of images and sound (i.e. High Definition) generate more data that needs to be processed.
- The degree of transcoding that the bridge must perform while handling calls being received at different connection speeds and utilizing different protocols.

As the workload increases, each bridge must process more data. Performance can therefore be improved by increasing the number of Digital Signalling Processors (DSPs) utilized to decode and encode the digital streams entering and leaving MCUs. If the bridging function becomes overloaded, video and voice information may be lost, causing latency to be introduced into calls, both of which can degrade the video meeting experience.

Extra processing resource can be provided for the bridging function by either utilizing a more powerful bridge (with a greater number of DSPs) or through a virtual software approach, where the software that controls the signalling function can operate independently of the physical hardware. A conference call with an assigned conference number does not have to take place, or be processed by a dedicated piece of hardware. The call can be "virtualized", and assigned to whatever physical bridge has the correct resource or capacity to handle the call. A virtualization manager oversees which physical bridge has the capacity, and assigns incoming calls accordingly. In extreme, but rare circumstances, the virtualization manager may assign resources for a call across several different physical bridges that work in tandem together. Known as "auto-cascading", the resources within the physical bridge can be instructed by the software to operate in a "parent-child" arrangement, with one bridge "owning" the conference call, and the others sharing the workload. In the continuous presence mode of presentation, the bridge will automatically provide the screen templates in which the viewers will see the other meeting participants.

The bridge can also provide some administrative functionality for the call, such as assigning passwords to enter each meeting, and providing Interactive Voice Response (IVR) functionality, where call participants can be greeted and instructed by customized voice greetings. Although most participants will actively dial into a video conferencing meeting, the bridge can be programmed to automatically dial out to participating locations and automatically connect them in to a meeting. For example, the bridge could automatically wake up the cameras in remote meeting rooms, and link those meeting rooms into a prescheduled call. Participants of such a meeting would simply have to walk into the video room at the correct time, and join the meeting.

Video Call Management and Protocol Conversion

In order to build an architecture that scales, the software platform must be able to provide call signalling functionality, and dynamically manage the set-up and maintenance of a large number of video calls. The software architecture has to be capable of reconfiguring itself and its resources in real-time, so that these resources are used to their best ability. In addition, the software architecture has to understand the bandwidth requirements of each call being placed, the policy that is associated with each call (the prioritization and importance of a call), and where the participants of a call are geographically located. By understanding this, the software platform can utilize local resources instead of redirecting data streams and call signalling to resources that are far away, an approach which would eat up large amounts of bandwidth on WAN links that are costly.

Let us consider three examples of this approach and see how it simplifies the process:

Example A	Customer A in California wants to meet with Customer B in New York, Customer C in London and Customer D in Paris. The Customer has a video bridge in Denver and a video bridge in Paris and a virtualization manager on a server in London. In this situation, the virtualization management software would identify that two participants wanted to join the call from the U.S., and may, for example purposes, direct them to the resources on the Denver bridge. Likewise, the European participants may be directed to the Paris bridge, with overall control of the call being given to the Master Denver bridge. Under this scheme, large amounts of video data are not shipped across a transatlantic WAN, thereby potentially providing cost savings.

Example B	In the above example, the U.S. customers are using an H.264 based system, and in Europe they are using Microsoft® Lync® enabled video conferencing based upon RTV. In this scenario, the virtualization management software on the London server acts as a gateway between Microsoft® and the U.S. video resources, converts the Microsoft signalling, and establishes the whole call using the bridges in the U.S. and Paris.
Example C	Example C In this example, the call is proceeding but the bridge in Denver suddenly stops functioning due to a fire in the data centre. The Virtualization Manager in London detects this, and redirects the video traffic across the WAN link to the Paris bridge. Users connecting via H.323 simply redial to re-join the call, with the administration and management being performed seamlessly in the background. However, for SIP based calls there is an added advantage: the platform will detect the problem and reconnect the participants back into the call automatically, hopefully before the user has even noticed that there was a problem.

The software platform should also be able to instantly detect any failure of hardware resources or loss of communication across infrastructure links, so that it can re-direct traffic and re-establish calls utilizing alternative resources, without overly impacting video calls or their quality. When systems on different customer premises try to join the same video call using devices which run different protocols (i.e. H.323, RTV or SIP), the video conferencing platform must first perform protocol conversion to a common language so the infrastructure can understand and process information correctly. In other words, the software platform should provide intrinsic gateway functionality between devices that talk different languages.

The Polycom Real Presence DMA sits in front of the bridges, and interfaces between the outside world and the bridging resources. This optimizes how incoming video calls are handled by virtual resources at its disposal. The Polycom Real Presence DMA can apply business rules that help it place incoming meetings on bridges that make the most sense, either for capacity, geography, or other priority rules.

Device Management

To enable large-scale deployment and management of video conferencing solutions, the software platform provides for the management and maintenance of hardware infrastructure components through a separate functional area: The Device Manager. The Device Manager can help dynamically provision devices and components of the video conferencing infrastructure. Once component hardware is deployed within the network and its infrastructure, the Device Manager will monitor and help troubleshoot problems with these devices. When software updates are required, the Device Manager will help deploy them.

A significant contributing factor to the rise in demand for video conferencing is because of the ease of use by which calls can be established by users. The scheduling and management of calls has become easy, through the creation of user-friendly scheduling portals, or via integration into Microsoft Outlook. The Device Manager will also provide reporting, and comprehensive details of video calls, processing the information to evaluate current system usage, and expansion plans for the video network.

Security

Many organizations who have invested in video conferencing will inevitably need to be able to assist mobile or home workers wanting to dial into their company network, and participate in video calls with colleagues. The software platform must therefore provide the capability to enable, and manage this. Likewise, video conferencing-enabled organizations will also want to use the technology to communicate with their partners and customers. This will only be possible if video traffic is able to securely traverse the firewalls from one customer to another. Firewall traversal is a particular challenge to video, as the data firewalls try to re-organize data packets. The implementation of a video firewall such as the Polycom VBP (H323) can eliminate this issue.

Content Management

Historically, the primary motivating factor for most companies has been to use video conferencing as a way of saving business travel costs. Recently, organizations are beginning to understand that the benefits of video conferencing can impact many different parts of an organization including; training, marketing, education, compliance, internal communications, advertising, PR, to name just a few.

As the usage of video conferencing in these fields has begun to grow, customers have discovered the potential to not only use video conferencing to communicate in real-time, but also to uncover the possibilities that exist for re-using digital recordings of past events and communications. Moving beyond "meetings," the same technology is being used to create digitally encapsulated rich media, which can then be edited, enhanced, archived, and broadcast across multiple media. These assets can be made available to target audiences on-demand.

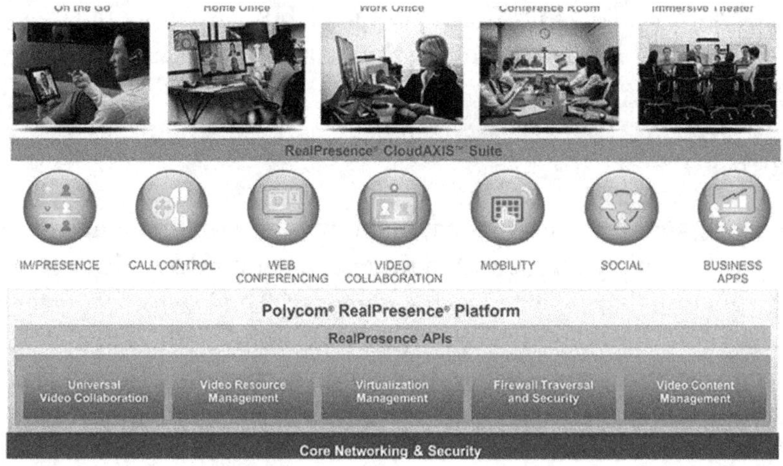

For example:

- Live event multicasting: The software platform enables the streaming of recorded webcasts, and supports both the push and pull of video to the streaming servers.
- Video-on-demand: The software platform automates the creation of archived versions of any live event webcast so that customers can replay them on demand, as desired.

- Media management: The software platform can be used to control how video content will be aggregated, approved, categorised, edited and published.
- Storage and archiving—The software platform establishes rules for the lifecycle of storage for bandwidth-intensive video content: customers can determine how the content will be retained, transcoded and stored in the Cloud, or across corporate resources without daily, hands-on maintenance.

Polycom Real Presence

The five basic functional areas that constitute the software platform Polycom has developed to enable scalable, reliable, and cost-efficient video conferencing solutions. The Polycom Real Presence platform breaks down the core infrastructure for enabling video conferencing into universal video collaboration, virtualization management, video resource management, universal access and security and video content management.

Universal Video Collaboration

Providing the bridging capability at the core of video conferencing, this provides the software for multipoint video, voice and content collaboration that connects the most people at highest quality and lowest cost. Virtualization management Providing the call management and protocol conversion that allows the bridging resources to be virtualized, this provides the software that enables multi-tenancy and massive scale, redundancy and resiliency.

Video Resource Management

Providing the device and software management of endpoints and infrastructure, enabling central management, monitoring and the delivery of video collaboration across organizations.

Universal Access and Security

The software that easily and securely connects video participants in and outside a customer firewall and optimizes for a best collaboration experience.

Video Content Management

Software that enables organizations to support their business customers for secure video capture, content management, administration and delivery.

Benefits of Online Video Conferencing

- Reduced Travel Time and Costs

  The oldest recognised benefit of video conferencing is reduced travel time and expenses. The ability for managers, internal teams, and IT personnel to be in client meetings or solve issues without leaving their offices can help drive business productivity. Providing video capacity for your customers can create a competitive offering. Even hiring can be less of a hassle if persons unable to be part of the live interview process can evaluate the candidate from the recorded video call.

- Optimised Attendance

  Increased attendance from dispersed internal teams and clients is possible for participants who otherwise would have been debilitated by location. Further, video recording capabilities mean that, if needed, all individuals who need the data (such as staff training or presentations) can get the information when it is easiest for them, rather than delaying or not attending the meetings.

- Structured Meetings with Improved Communications

  Because people are calling from different locations, defined start and end-times are often agreed upon prior to the video call. This allows for a more intensive discussion with less chit-chat, and participants are more likely to stay alert and focused on what is discussed. Instead of frustrating email trains where meaning or intent behind messages can be obscured, participants can see important visual cues in body-language from customers, partners, and colleagues. Expressions of satisfaction, concern, or understanding can be addressed more easily than through a myriad of emails, IMs and voicemails, making video conferencing the closest thing to being there.

- Increased Productivity

  As a result of improved communications, participants are more in sync, decisions are able to be made faster, and productivity increases. Indeed, a 2013 survey found 94% of video conferencing software users thought the biggest benefit was increased efficiency and productivity. Problems can be resolved faster and services for clients can be developed more quickly, providing a serious competitive edge for your company.

- Employee Retention

  The mobility offered by cloud-based video conferencing positively contributes to employee retention. Less travel requirements allow a better work/life balance and employees can choose to work from home to alleviate cost of commuting. Remote employees can still have close relationships with team members, as video's real-time face-to-face interactions are richer than any alternative to in-person meetings.

- Sustained Competitive Advantage

  All of these aspects mean video conferencing provides a strong competitive advantage for your business. There's no benefit to being second, but with the right unified communication system, you can maintain a strong business position through effective collaboration and productivity improvement.

Disadvantages of Video Conferencing

- Lack of personal interaction: Some meetings require a personal touch to be successful. Video conferencing can be less personal than meeting face to face, and it can be possible to miss out on vital body language when you're struggling with a pixelated image or stuttering video.

- Technical problems: The major disadvantages are the technical difficulties associated with smooth transmissions that could result from software, hardware or network failure. Remote connections are sometimes known to be hampered by environmental changes. On some occasions, the absence of technical support personnel creates difficulty for participants who are unfamiliar with the videoconferencing technological concepts.
- International time zones: One of the very real disadvantages of using video conferencing is that if you communicate regularly with people in other countries you will be available at different times to them. Unfortunately without the skills of a time lord there's not really a practical way to overcome this.
- High cost of setup: Setting up video conferencing in an office can be a bit expensive for small-sized companies. Simple features can fit into the budget, but if advanced features are required, then a substantial amount of expenditure must be done.

References

- Crow, Michael M (1998). Limited by design: R&D laboratories in the U.S. national innovation system. New York City, NY: Columbia University Press. p. 145. ISBN 0231109822
- Advantages-public-address-system: cescomplete.com, Retrieved 12 March 2018
- Paritsky, Alexander; Kots, A. (1997). "Fiber optic microphone as a realization of fiber optic positioning sensors". Proc. of International Society for Optical Engineering (SPIE). 10th Meeting on Optical Engineering in Israel. 3110: 408–409. doi:10.1117/12.281371
- Public-speaking-microphones: speechmastery.com, Retrieved 10 June 2018
- "Multimedia systems - Guide to the recommended characteristics of analogue interfaces to achieve interoperability". Webstore.iec.ch. IEC 61938:2013. Retrieved 3 March 2017
- 6-benefits-online-video-conferencing: vitaenterprisesolutions.com.au, Retrieved 11 July 2018
- J. Eargle and M. Gander (2004). "Historical Perspectives and Technology Overview of Loudspeakers for Sound Reinforcemen" (PDF). Journal of the Audio Engineering Society. 52 (4): 412–432 (p. 416)
- Advantages-and-disadvantages-of-video-conferencing, video-conference: eztalks.com, Retrieved 31 May 2018
- Hogan, Michael (2006). Woodrow Wilson's Western Tour: Rhetoric, Public Opinion, And the League of Nations. Texas A&M University Press. p. 10. ISBN 9781585445332. Retrieved 16 November 2015

5

Effective Communication Practices

Effective communication involves a number of skills related to listening, observing, questioning, interpersonal processing, gestures, evaluating and speaking. The diverse communications skills, communication types, theories of communication, etc. have been elucidated in this chapter.

Communication

Communication is the process of sending and receiving messages through verbal or nonverbal means, including speech, or oral communication; writing and graphical representations (such as info graphics, maps, and charts); and signs, signals, and behavior. More simply, communication is said to be "the creation and exchange of meaning."

Media critic and theorist James Carey defined communication as "a symbolic process whereby reality is produced, maintained, repaired and transformed" in his 1992 book "Communication as Culture," positing that we define our reality via sharing our experience with others.

All creatures on earth have developed means in which to convey their emotions and thoughts to one another. However, it's the ability of humans to use words and language to transfer specific meanings that sets them apart from the animal kingdom.

Eight Essential Components of Communication

In order to better understand the communication process, we can break it down into a series of eight essential components:

1. Source
2. Message
3. Channel
4. Receiver
5. Feedback
6. Environment
7. Context
8. Interference

Each of these eight components serves an integral function in the overall process.

Source

The source imagines, creates, and sends the message. In a public speaking situation, the source is the person giving the speech. He or she conveys the message by sharing new information with the audience. The speaker also conveys a message through his or her tone of voice, body language, and choice of clothing. The speaker begins by first determining the message—what to say and how to say it. The second step involves encoding the message by choosing just the right order or the perfect words to convey the intended meaning. The third step is to present or send the information to the receiver or audience. Finally, by watching for the audience's reaction, the source perceives how well they received the message and responds with clarification or supporting information.

Message

The message is the stimulus or meaning produced by the source for the receiver or audience. When you plan to give a speech or write a report, your message may seem to be only the words you choose that will convey your meaning. But that is just the beginning. The words are brought together with grammar and organization. You may choose to save your most important point for last. The message also consists of the way you say it—in a speech, with your tone of voice, your body language, and your appearance—and in a report, with your writing style, punctuation, and the headings and formatting you choose. In addition, part of the message may be the environment or context you present it in and the noise that might make your message hard to hear or see.

Imagine, for example, that you are addressing a large audience of sales reps and are aware there is a World Series game tonight. Your audience might have a hard time settling down, but you may choose to open with, "I understand there is an important game tonight." In this way, by expressing verbally something that most people in your audience are aware of and interested in, you might grasp and focus their attention.

Channel

The channel is the way in which a message or messages travel between source and receiver. For example, think of your television. How many channels do you have on your television? Each channel takes up some space, even in a digital world, in the cable or in the signal that brings the message of each channel to your home. Television combines an audio signal you hear with a visual signal you see. Together they convey the message to the receiver or audience. Turn off the volume on your television. Can you still understand what is happening? Many times you can, because the body language conveys part of the message of the show. Now turn up the volume but turn around so that you cannot see the television. You can still hear the dialogue and follow the story line.

Similarly, when you speak or write, you are using a channel to convey your message. Spoken channels include face-to-face conversations, speeches, telephone conversations and voice mail messages, radio, public address systems, and voice over Internet protocol (VoIP). Written channels include letters, memorandums, purchase orders, invoices, newspaper and magazine articles, blogs, e-mail, text messages, tweets, and so forth.

Receiver

The receiver receives the message from the source, analyzing and interpreting the message in ways both intended and unintended by the source. To better understand this component, think of a receiver on a football team. The quarterback throws the football (message) to a receiver, who must see and interpret where to catch the ball. The quarterback may intend for the receiver to "catch" his message in one way, but the receiver may see things differently and miss the football (the intended meaning) altogether.

As a receiver you listen, see, touch, smell, and taste to receive a message. Your audience "sizes you up," much as you might check them out long before you take the stage or open your mouth. The nonverbal responses of your listeners can serve as clues on how to adjust your opening. By imagining yourself in their place, you anticipate what you would look for if you were them. Just as a quarterback plans where the receiver will be in order to place the ball correctly, you too can recognize the interaction between source and receiver in a business communication context. All of this happens at the same time, illustrating why and how communication is always changing.

Feedback

When you respond to the source, intentionally or unintentionally, you are giving feedback. Feedback is composed of messages the receiver sends back to the source. Verbal or nonverbal, all these feedback signals allow the source to see how well, how accurately (or how poorly and inaccurately) the message was received. Feedback also provides an opportunity for the receiver or audience to ask for clarification, to agree or disagree, or to indicate that the source could make the message more interesting. As the amount of feedback increases, the accuracy of communication also increases.

For example, suppose you are a sales manager participating in a conference call with four sales reps. As the source, you want to tell the reps to take advantage of the fact that it is World Series season to close sales on baseball-related sports gear. You state your message, but you hear no replies from your listeners. You might assume that this means they understood and agreed with you, but later in the month you might be disappointed to find that very few sales were made. If you followed up your message with a request for feedback ("Does this make sense? Do any of you have any questions?"). You might have an opportunity to clarify your message, and to find out whether any of the sales reps believed your suggestion would not work with their customers.

Environment

The environment is the atmosphere, physical and psychological, where you send and receive messages. The environment can include the tables, chairs, lighting, and sound equipment that are in the room. The room itself is an example of the environment. The environment can also include factors like formal dress, that may indicate whether a discussion is open and caring or more professional and formal. People may be more likely to have an intimate conversation when they are physically close to each other, and less likely when they can only see each other from across the room. In that case, they may text each other, itself an intimate form of communication. The choice to text is influenced by the environment. As a speaker, your environment will impact and play a role in your speech. It's always a good idea to go check out where you'll be speaking before the day of the actual presentation.

Context

The context of the communication interaction involves the setting, scene, and expectations of the individuals involved. A professional communication context may involve business suits (environmental cues) that directly or indirectly influence expectations of language and behavior among the participants.

A presentation or discussion does not take place as an isolated event. When you came to class, you came from somewhere. So did the person seated next to you, as did the instructor. The degree to which the environment is formal or informal depends on the contextual expectations for communication held by the participants. The person sitting next to you may be used to informal communication with instructors, but this particular instructor may be used to verbal and nonverbal displays of respect in the academic environment. You may be used to formal interactions with instructors as well, and find your classmate's question of "Hey Teacher, do we have homework today?" as rude and inconsiderate when they see it as normal. The nonverbal response from the instructor will certainly give you a clue about how they perceive the interaction, both the word choices and how they were said.

Context is all about what people expect from each other, and we often create those expectations out of environmental cues. Traditional gatherings like weddings are often formal events. There is a time for quiet social greetings, a time for silence as the bride walks down the aisle, or the father may have the first dance with his daughter as she is transformed from a girl to womanhood in the eyes of her community. In either celebration there may come a time for rambunctious celebration and dancing. You may be called upon to give a toast, and the wedding context will influence your presentation, timing, and effectiveness.

Context is all about what people expect from each other.

In a business meeting, who speaks first? That probably has some relation to the position and role of each person has outside the meeting. Context plays a very important role in communication, particularly across cultures.

Interference

Interference, also called noise, can come from any source. "Interference is anything that blocks or changes the source's intended meaning of the message." For example, if you drove a car to work or school, chances are you were surrounded by noise. Car horns, billboards, or perhaps the radio in your car interrupted your thoughts, or your conversation with a passenger.

Psychological noise is what happens when your thoughts occupy your attention while you are hearing, or reading, a message. Imagine that it is 4:45 p.m. and your boss, who is at a meeting in another city, e-mails you asking for last month's sales figures, an analysis of current sales projections, and the sales figures from the same month for the past five years. You may open the e-mail, start to read, and think, "Great—no problem—I have those figures and that analysis right here in my computer." You fire off a reply with last month's sales figures and the current projections attached. Then, at five o'clock, you turn off your computer and go home. The next morning, your boss calls on the phone to tell you he was inconvenienced because you neglected to include the sales figures from the previous years. What was the problem? Interference: by thinking about how you wanted to respond to your boss's message, you prevented yourself from reading attentively enough to understand the whole message.

Interference can come from other sources, too. Perhaps you are hungry, and your attention to your current situation interferes with your ability to listen. Maybe the office is hot and stuffy. If you were a member of an audience listening to an executive speech, how could this impact your ability to listen and participate?

Noise interferes with normal encoding and decoding of the message carried by the channel between source and receiver. Not all noise is bad, but noise interferes with the communication process. For example, your cell phone ringtone may be a welcome noise to you, but it may interrupt the communication process in class and bother your classmates.

Two Models of Communication

Researchers have observed that when communication takes place, the source and the receiver may send messages at the same time, often overlapping. You, as the speaker, will often play both roles, as source and receiver. You'll focus on the communication and the reception of your messages to the audience. The audience will respond in the form of feedback that will give you important clues. While there are many models of communication, here we will focus on two that offer perspectives and lessons for business communicators.

Rather than looking at the source sending a message and someone receiving it as two distinct acts, researchers often view communication as a transactional process "Transactional Model of Communication"), with actions often happening at the same time. The distinction between source and receiver is blurred in conversational turn-taking, for example, where both participants play both roles simultaneously.

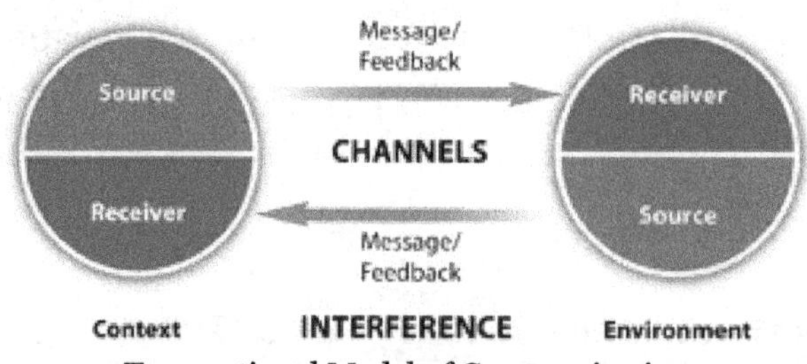

Transactional Model of Communication

Researchers have also examined the idea that we all construct our own interpretations of the message. In the constructivist model, we focus on the negotiated meaning, or common ground, when trying to describe communication.

Imagine that you are visiting Atlanta, Georgia, and go to a restaurant for dinner. When asked if you want a "Coke," you may reply, "sure." The waiter may then ask you again, "what kind?" and you may reply, "Coke is fine." The waiter then may ask a third time, "what kind of soft drink would you like?" The misunderstanding in this example is that in Atlanta, the home of the Coca-Cola Company, most soft drinks are generically referred to as "Coke." When you order a soft drink, you need to specify what type, even if you wish to order a beverage that is not a cola or not even made by the Coca-Cola Company. To someone from other regions of the United States, the words "pop," "soda pop," or "soda" may be the familiar way to refer to a soft drink; not necessarily the brand "Coke." In this example, both you and the waiter understand the word "Coke," but you each understand it to mean something different. In order to communicate, you must each realize what the term means to the other person, and establish common ground, in order to fully understand the request and provide an answer.

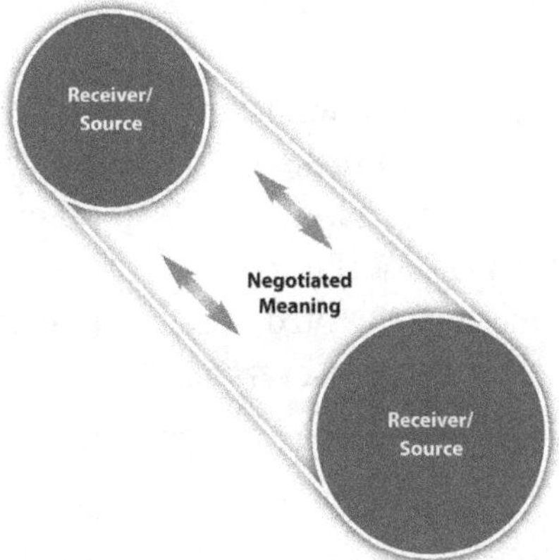

Constructivist Model of Communication

Because we carry the multiple meanings of words, gestures, and ideas within us, we can use a dictionary to guide us, but we will still need to negotiate meaning.

Development of Different Languages

Simple verbal communication has existed since the evolution of languages. History of communication dates back to 3,300 BC when writing was invented and used for the first time, in Iraq. After that, there was an evolution of different kinds of writing styles.

First Postal System

In 900 BC, the first ever postal system was established by the Government of China. Later on, other civil including Rome, Persia, Syria and Egypt too contributed towards the progress of the postal system. Horses were used as the main carriers in this very early postal system. There were relay stations established where the horses were required to deliver the information.

Development of Writing Materials

Previously there was no concept of paper. People used to communicate by writing messages on stones, leaves, bones or horsebacks. Moreover, there were no proper means for wiring. The messages were penned down with coal or other useful tools. This kind of information exchange was most common in China and Egypt. In 1700 BC, there was some development done to improve the writing surfaces. People made use of the Papyrus rolls and light weight parchments derived from dried reeds. These surfaces were much better as they were easily portable and could retain the colour of writing for a longer period. Otherwise writing on stones, bones and horsebacks was prone to fading in a very less time. Hence, creating difficulty for the people to understand what was exactly written by the sender.

In 776 BC, a new idea was introduced to utilise homing pigeons as carriers of messages, and the technique really worked out well. A written message was tied with the wings of a pigeon, and the pigeon used to deliver it to the intended recipient. It was good as it saved time and pigeons' travelling time was relatively less. But it was not a reliable way of communication. The message transfer was solely dependent on the well-being of the bird, and if a pigeon was caught up in danger, which was a common occurrence, then the message was wasted.

Invention of Printing

The next advancement towards better communication was the invention of print technology. Printing was first invented by the Chinese in 1500 BC. Also the first ever writing device, the pencil, was invented in 1565.

Printing was first developed to be done by blocks in the 6th century. The first known book published at that time using block printing was the Diamond Sutra of 686. Later in the mid of 15th century, a person named Johannes Gutenberg in Europe invented the press. This revolutionised the communication process, as the printing of books became easier and cheaper. It also laid down the foundation for newspaper printing. Later the idea for printing press started gaining popularity in the other nations as well.

The introduction of newspapers led to increased interest of people in printing and served to advance communication mechanisms.

Invention of the Newspaper

The printing press established by Gutenberg in the 15th century introduced the idea of newspapers, thus newspaper printing was invented. The first ever newspaper that was published was in England in 1641. However, the name 'newspaper' was not coined until 1670.

Communication in the 19th Century

The developments in communication gradually continued to expose people to new and effective ideas and concepts. The beginning of 19th century saw the introduction of several new concepts in the world of communication. It accounts for remarkable inventions including carbon paper and the telegraph. Instead of relay stations, there were developments for laying down the foundation for proper channels that made it possible to communicate across the Atlantic.

By the mid of 19th century, the fax machine was invented. The year 1876 accounts for the incredible invention of the telephone by Alexander Graham Bell. This device was different from the previous inventions as it significantly reduced the time required for conveying information over long distances.

Communication in the 20th Century

In the 20th century, there was an evolution which led to the discovery of radio and television broadcasting. Communication was transformed to be conducted through electronic means.

In 1960, communication satellites were introduced. Scientists introduced different techniques to create wonders in communication. Echoes and laser technology were invented to revolutionise communication. Bulky telephones transformed into precisely structured mobile phones. Also, the internet and web services became eminent in the late 19th century.

Communication Purposes

Communication serves as a mean for connecting people and places. Communication has expanded to relate to diverse perspectives. It can be used to share different kinds of information in different ways.

Social Communication

It is not necessary to hold a solid reason to communicate with others. With the evolution of the internet, communication has been adopted as a mean to expand one's social circle. Social communication is purely conducted for one's entertainment or to develop relationships with others, either in a verbal, written or a non-verbal way. Social communication includes web surfing, internet chatting and mobile texting.

Formal Communication

Formal communication is meant to establish strong business or work relationships. Businesses and organisation use formal communication to communicate more effectively with their intended clients and employees. This includes meetings and interviews. Communication conducted employing coded words is also referred to as formal communication. This includes the coded information conducted between the defence personnel or engineers.

Notifications

Communication is also used to notify or warn someone. It usually comprises of written circulars and pamphlets that are rotated over the internet or door to door for certain reasons.

Modern Perspectives of Communication

The phenomenon of communication has travelled far from the concept of paper and pen. Now, with the evolution of the internet, almost every electronic and digital device has become a means of communication. Besides computers and mobile phones, from fuelling devices on the petrol pump to the radars, all devices have been transformed to share information. These devices amazingly carry and deliver information over considerable distances and time lapses. The delivery time for sharing information has almost diminished. One can send and receive the information in a blink of an eye.

Challenges and Criticisms of Communication

However, the challenges for sharing information over time have majorly been resolved, but still, there are some barriers that hinder the communication process.

Personal Barriers

Communication carried between individuals is greatly influenced by one's capability of speaking and writing. If the message is not written or spoken well, it may make the message and its meaning ambiguous for the receiver. The translation of written message can be misconceived as different recipients will interpret a certain message on the basis of their individual perceptions and knowledge. The receiver may face difficulty in understanding the information, and there are high possibilities that he may conceive wrong information. So a message must be written in such a way and with words that the intended recipient can easily understand.

Systemic Barriers

When communication involves electronic and digital means, the machine and network errors can affect the effectiveness of communication. Usually, if there is a problem encountered, there will be an unwanted delay in information.

Constitutes of Good Communication

While listening and speaking are important in communication, there are other facts that are very vital to efficient communication in the workplace:

1. Being able to listen to others is imperative in the communication process. This means not only listening with your ears, but also being able to comprehend what the person is saying. Giving co-workers your full attention when they are conveying an idea can go a long way in building relationships and furthering progress.

2. Having empathy is very useful in communication. Empathy involves seeing things from the point of view of others. Put yourself in the other person's position instead of being judgmental or biased by your own beliefs. While this may be difficult for some, empathizing with others can be very helpful to keep in tune with your own emotions and ideas.

3. Encouraging others will heighten morale and appreciation in the workplace. By praising and offering words of encouragement, you help others feel they are wanted, welcomed and

respected by co-workers. People are much more likely to put forth their best effort if they know they are valued.

4. Being aware of others and their emotions means being sympathetic to misfortunes and praising positive milestones. To achieve this successfully, you need to know what is going on in other people's lives. Getting to know co-workers on a first-name basis and holding meaningful conversations through the work week creates a better and more productive work environment.
5. Body language can greatly impact how others perceive you in the workplace. Maintaining an extroverted, friendly persona lets co-workers know you are open to hearing their opinions about projects or new designs. Body language is a large part of being empathetic and encouraging. Be sure to maintain eye contact the majority of the time you are speaking with someone, and use hand gestures to help you form clearer thoughts. Smiling is incredibly dynamic and creates a noticeable difference in how you are perceived. People who smile more are seen as more approachable and trustworthy.

Features of Good Communicators

When it comes to communication, we all tend to think we're pretty good at it. Truth is, even those of us who are good communicators aren't nearly as good as we think we are. This overestimation of our ability to communicate is magnified when interacting with people we know well.

Researchers put this theory to the test and what they discovered is startling. In the study, the researchers paired subjects with people they knew well and then again with people they'd never met. The researchers discovered that people who knew each other well understood each other no better than people who'd just met. Even worse, participants frequently overestimated their ability to communicate, and this was more pronounced with people they knew well.

When communicating with people we know well, we make presumptions about what they understand—presumptions that we don't dare make with strangers. This tendency to overestimate how well we communicate (and how well we're understood) is so prevalent that psychologists even have a name for it: closeness-communication bias.

"The understanding, 'What I know is different from what you know' is essential for effective communication," said study lead Kenneth Savitsky, "but that insight can be elusive. Some people may indeed be on the same wavelength, but maybe not as much as they think. You get rushed and preoccupied, and you stop taking the perspective of the other person."

Taking Action

Communication is the real work of leadership; you simply can't become a great leader until you are a great communicator. Great communicators inspire people. They create a connection that is real, emotional, and personal. And great communicators forge this connection through an understanding of people and an ability to speak directly to their needs in a manner that they are ready to hear.

The eight strategies that follow will help you to overcome the communication bias that tends to hold us back with everyone we encounter, especially those we know well. Apply these strategies and watch your communication skills reach new heights:

- Speak to groups as individuals: As a leader, you often have to speak to groups of people. Whether a small team meeting or a company-wide gathering, you need to develop a level of intimacy in your approach that makes each individual in the room feel as if you're speaking directly to him or her. The trick is to eliminate the distraction of the crowd so that you can deliver your message just as you would if you were talking to a single person. You want to be emotionally genuine and exude the same feelings, energy, and attention you would one-on-one (as opposed to the anxiety that comes with being in front of people). The ability to pull this off is the hallmark of great leadership communication.
- Talk so people will listen: Great communicators read their audience (groups and individuals) carefully to ensure they aren't wasting their breath on a message that people aren't ready to hear. Talking so people will listen means you adjust your message on the fly to stay with your audience (what they're ready to hear and how they're ready to hear it). Droning on to ensure you've said what you wanted to say does not have the same effect on people as engaging them in a meaningful dialogue in which there is an exchange of ideas. Resist the urge to drive your point home at all costs. When you are talking leads to people asking good questions, you know you're on the right track.
- Listen so people will talk: One of the most disastrous temptations for a leader is to treat communication as a one-way street. When you communicate, you must give people ample opportunity to speak their minds. If you find that you're often having the last word in conversations, then this is likely something you need to work on.
- Listening isn't just about hearing words: It's also about listening to the tone, speed, and volume of the voice. What is being said? Anything not being said? What hidden messages below the surface exist? When someone is talking to you, stop everything else and listen fully until the other person has finished speaking. When you are on a phone call, don't type an email. When you're meeting with someone, close the door and sit near the person so you can focus and listen. Simple behaviors like these will help you stay in the present moment, pick up on the cues the other person sends, and make it clear that you will really hear what he or she is saying.
- Connect emotionally, Maya Angelou said it best: "People will forget what you said and did, but they will never forget how you made them feel." As a leader, your communication is impotent if people don't connect with it on an emotional level. This is hard for many leaders to pull off because they feel they need to project a certain persona. Let that go. To connect with your people emotionally, you need to be transparent. Be human. Show them what drives you, what you care about, what makes you get out of bed in the morning. Express these feelings openly, and you'll forge an emotional connection with your people.
- Read body language: Your authority makes it hard for people to say what's really on their minds. No matter how good a relationship you have with your subordinates, you are kidding yourself if you think they are as open with you as they are with their peers. So, you must become adept at understanding unspoken messages. The greatest wealth of information lies in people's body language. The body communicates nonstop and is an abundant source of information, so purposefully watch body language during meetings and casual

conversation. Once you tune into body language, the messages will become loud and clear. Pay as much attention to what isn't said as what is said, and you'll uncover facts and opinions that people are unwilling to express directly.

- Prepare your intent: A little preparation goes a long way toward saying what you wanted to say and having a conversation achieve its intended impact. Don't prepare a speech; develop an understanding of what the focus of a conversation needs to be (in order for people to hear the message) and how you will accomplish this. Your communication will be more persuasive and on point when you prepare your intent ahead of time.
- Skip the jargon: The business world is filled with jargon and metaphors that are harmless when people can relate to them. Problem is, most leaders overuse jargon and alienate their subordinates and customers with their "business speak." Use it sparingly if you want to connect with your people. Otherwise, you'll come across as insincere.
- Practice active listening: Active listening is a simple technique that ensures people feel heard, an essential component of good communication. To practice active listening:
    - Spend more time listening than you do talking.
    - Do not answer questions with questions.
    - Avoid finishing other people's sentences.
    - Focus more on the other person than you do on yourself.
    - Focus on what people are saying right now, not on what their interests are.
- Reframe what the other person has said to make sure you understand him or her correctly ("So you're telling me that this budget needs further consideration, right?").
- Think about what you're going to say after someone has finished speaking, not while he or she is speaking.
    - Ask plenty of questions.
    - Never interrupt.
    - Don't take notes.

Theories of Communication

Imagine a world without communication. You have a brilliant idea with you but you don't possess the power of communication. You have a strong desire for something, but cannot express your desires. Life would be dull, blank and the world would not be worth living. Such is the power of communication.

Communication is the essence of life. It is a necessity. To express themselves, human beings need to communicate. An individual has to communicate to express his feelings, pass on information to the other human beings and share his thoughts and feelings.

Do only Human Beings Communicate?

Let us go through the following examples:

1. Ted spotted a poor weak pup lying almost lifeless on the streets and crying meekly. He took no time in taking the pup to a nearby vet and giving him the basic medical treatment the poor creature required. Have you ever thought how did Ted come to know that the pup requires immediate attention? The pup couldn't speak.

The answer to the above question is through communication.

Ted came to know about the condition of the pup through communication only. The crying of pup was actually an indication that the creature needs to be immediately attended by the doctor. Through his crying the pup tried to communicate Ted about his deteriorating condition and requirement of medical aid.

2. A gardener waters the plants when the leaves start turning brown, become dry and start showing withering signs. Turning brown, drying of leaves are actually ways the tree tries to communicate to the gardener that it is dying and needs to be watered immediately.

All the above examples support the communication theory.

Communication theories come from research and thought that define how information is conveyed and received between two parties. These theories apply to verbal and written communication between people as well as mass and broadcast communications. Some researchers apply the concepts to communication between animals and across computer networks. Dozens of communication theories exist, but most fall into several broader categories:

Models of Communication

The simplest communication theories describe how information is sent and received. These model the differences, for example, between a conversation among two individuals and the exchange of ideas in a six-person staff meeting, and what affects those exchanges. Five Forms of Communication theory lists different communication models, while Relational Dialectics explores how the conflicting desire for autonomy and connection affects interpersonal communication.

Theories of Effective Communication

In efforts to improve the quality of communication, some researchers develop theories about what makes communication effective. These theories explore what goes right when ideas pass between two parties, and how to repeat that success more easily and reliably. Examples include Cutlip and Center's seven Cs of communication, which holds that attention to clarity, credibility, content, context, continuity, capability and channels improves the quality and effectiveness of communication. The Narrative Paradigm theory holds that humans pay more attention to stories than to data or logic, so communicating with a narrative structure is often more effective and convincing.

Theories of Ineffective Communication

Other researchers work to identify what goes wrong with communication in order to avoid those pitfalls when developing communication strategies. These look at situational, cultural and cognitive reasons why communication might fail, or break down, between groups. The Groupthink theory explores why cohesive groups rarely consider or communicate all options when solving problems. Cognitive Dissonance Theory states that communication breakdowns often happen because people don't like and will act to ignore or avoid information incompatible with their opinions and beliefs.

Structural Theories

Structural theories of communication investigate the components of communication, both to understand meta-communication and how to improve the effectiveness of those components. Cultural Approach to Organization explores how cultures organize communication around shared symbols, experiences and archetypes. Muted Group Theory defines how communication is different for minorities in a society than for the majority in the same culture using the same language.

Economic and Political Theories

Some communication theories focus on how to apply communication toward achieving specific economic or political goals. Rhetoric theories are the most basic of these, exploring how a speaker can persuade an audience. More advanced theories such as Uses and Gratifications investigate specific applications of communication to business and government, and many of these theories have to do with the effects and application of television and other media on our lives. Cultivation Analysis is one such theory; it explores how people gain knowledge through curated mass media rather than through direct experience or research.

Authoritarian Theory of Mass Communication

Authoritarian theory of mass communication originated from the philosophy of Plato. The English monarchs used this approach when the printing press was invented by censoring, licensing, taxation and making laws.

It is a normative theory of mass communication where mass media is influenced and overpowered by power and authority in the nations. Media must respect what authorities want and work according to the wishes of the authorities though, not under direct control of the state or ruling classes. The press and media cannot work independently and their works are suspected to censorship.

Concepts of Authoritarian Theory of Mass Communication

Authoritarian theory is taken as a theory used by the dictatorship governments, but can also be seen in democratic as well as dictatorial nations. Here, the media cannot offend or go against the majority or dominant groups. Media must remain subordinate to the authorities in authoritarian theory.

It is believed that state information, when distributed, might put security at risk and cause to be a national threat. Thus, the theory is justified by saying that state is greater than individual rights where state controls the media, especially in the time of emergencies like wars and conflicts. These situations might be internal or external.

Democratic governments also use this approach as the only option in these types of conditions. They also justify the process as to preserve social order and harmony but minority views are not censored unless the authorities do not take it as a threat to their power.

Press is taken as a weapon of the powerful. It is used to increase the power of the rulers. The authorities control media by providing rights and license to some media and not to some. Ambiguous rights are given to media and harm journalists if they do not agree to the understood censorship rules. The authorities can also cancel the license.

Sensitive issues are mostly not published or are published through press releases. There are many kinds of censorship like political censorship, military censorship, religious censorship, economic censorship, etc. Having said, the theory does not encourage homogeneous and national culture like Totalitarianism.

Major Features of Authoritarian Theory of Mass Communication

- Direct control of the media by government and authorities
- Power exercised to control media
- Control by the powerful ruling minorities or a group of ruling majorities
- Media has no power to criticize the government, its work, decisions and policies
- Media cannot offend the ruling parties in any way
- Punishment and threats are given to the people who try to offend the government and the powerful
- Licensing of media by the state and giving limited rights (registration)
- Cancelation of license if the media does anything wrong to the government
- Clear limits on what media can publish
- Ownership is mostly private
- Concept of propaganda
- Control might be on all issues or just some particular issues
- Media is used as a weapon or an instrument to strengthen the power of the government

Examples of Authoritarian Theory of Mass Communication

Engels and many other scholars have talked about authoritative theory. Kings used this approach in the past by granting royal charters and licenses. The whole part of Western Europe used this approach to control the middle class from starting a revolution after printing press was started.

Germany and Italy were also following it before the Second World War because of Hitler and Mussolini.

All propaganda should be popular and should adapt its intellectual level to the receptive ability of the least intellectual of those whom it is desired to address.

Taliban government practiced Authoritarian media approach in Afghanistan. Burmese media was also made to follow authoritarianism till 2011. Media who published against the government were punished and imprisoned. Today it is being applied in developing countries in the form of National Security Act and Official Secret Act.

Many writers have been imprisoned and published books have been banned like Salman Rushdie's Satanic Verses due to censorship, showing Authoritarianism.

There are still several countries who follow Authoritarianism in media today which are Israel, Bahrain, Qatar, Syria, Uzbekistan, Belarus, Zimbabwe, China, North Korea, Iran, etc.

Strengths of Authoritarian Theory of Mass Communication

- This approach is sometimes better for resolving social and cultural conflicts.
- It is also better sometimes because it motivates people to work for the country and its people.
- This theory can act as a gatekeeper and prevent the media that act irresponsibly.
- The theory can be used for establishing propaganda.

Weaknesses of Authoritarian Theory of Mass Communication

- Common people are taken as less intelligent and as an easy target to manipulate.
- The ruling class uses the media only for their own benefits.
- The freedom of expression and information of normal people is attacked.

Libertarianism or Free Press Theory

This theory is regarded as a western theory. The underlying principle of the libertarian theory of the press is that the press should be free to perform its functions but in the authoritarian theory, the press was under governments' licensing, and censorship. If the media is free to write, and publish. It will provide truthful, comprehensive and intelligent account of the day.

In the same line of thought, but a slightly different angle, writes that, "In this theory man is being looked upon as a rational being with inherited natural rights. One of these rights was the right to pursue truth. There is also the obligation to keep public about governmental activities and the media are seen as the fourth estate of the realm". Libertarians basically follows dictates if their conscience, seek truth, engage in public debate and create a better life for themselves strength of the free press theory lies in the following:

- Freedom of the press will give more freedom to media to reveal the real thing happening in the society without censorship or any authority blockades.
- Is reliable with U.S media traditions, as the principle is duly enshrined in the first amendment to the constitution.
- It gives more values for individuals to express their thoughts in media.
- Is too positive about individual ethics and rationality. Theory also has its weakness, these include.
- Theory is excessively positive about media's willing to meet responsibilities which may lead.
- People into negative aspects.
- Ignores need for reasonable control of media. It gives more values for individuals to express their thoughts in media.

If the media power were radically shifted to individuals, parochial local interests would predominate at the expense of the whole, and hat this would exacerbate current problems with collective action. Perhaps, this is one weakness inherent in the theory at the earliest stages. In today's world, ignoring dilemma posed by conflicting freedoms. The fundamental principles of the libertarian theory could be summarized thus: seek to maximize political freedom and autonomy, emphasizing freedom of choice, voluntary association, individual judgment and self-ownership. It gives more values for individuals to express their thoughts in media is too positive about individual ethics and rationality. Theory also has its weakness, these include; Theory is excessively positive about media's willing to meet responsibilities which may lead people into negative aspects.

Ignores need for reasonable control of media. These goals according to Nerone, (1995) argues that if the media power were radically shifted to individuals, parochial local interests would predominate at the expense of the whole, and that this would exacerbate current problems with collective action. Perhaps, this is one weakness inherent in the theory at the earliest stages.

In today's world, ignoring dilemma posed by conflicting freedoms. The fundamental principles of the libertarian theory could be summarized thus: seek to maximize political freedom and autonomy, emphasizing freedom of choice, voluntary association, individual judgment and self-ownership.

Libertarian Theory: A Theory of Media Ethics

The libertarian theory came in when democracy arrived (i.e. when people had the right to vote), this theory is adopted in England after 1688 and in U.S and it is influential elsewhere in the world. In journalistic practice there are core ethics and they as follows: Truth and Accuracy, Independence, Fairness and impartiality, Humanity and Accountability. Toeing this line, Okunna (2003) emphasizes that ethics is self-legislation as opposed to official or government legislation through outside compulsion, which is characteristic of law". In the libertarian theory, control is only exercised when the media impinge on the rights of others for example, publishing libelous reports, committing treason, endangering national security. Ownership is private with editorial self-determination (autonomy). Siebert pointed out that Libertarian theory is an idea of free expression from any authority. The media have been entrusted to discharge certain public –interest functions to a democratic society and by, conferring trust, society is entitled to judge. Borrowing a clue from Keane (1991), he explains that the right to free publication has been viewed as an essential instrument for achieving democracy and a precondition of its adequate practice, especially as means for holding those who have power accountable. Freedom of publication is necessary if critical and alternative voices are to be heard. Indeed, the libertarian theory of the press summarizes what the press should be, as the words of Jeremy Bentham and John Stuart Mill as cited in, "the realization of Bentham's principle of the 'greatest good for the greatest number' requires that government be guided by the wishes of the citizens, which have to be freely expressed. Mill (in On Liberty) argued that the progress and welfare depended on free circulation of ideas by means of which truth and utility would be maximized.

Libertarian Theory Today

The libertarian theory of media has referred to the conscience and the voice of the people which is significantly one important role of the press. Regardless of the ideological differences in the various socio-political systems of the world, the freedom of the press, a logical extension of man's inalienable freedom of expression is today a universal phenomenon. Although the modern press began in Belgium in 1605 (and Sweden is generally believed to be the first country to constitutionally ordain press freedom Moemeka the idea of press freedom evolved from libertarian social philosophy which originated in England after the Revolution of 1688. Altschull notes that in much of Africa and Asia where we have a large concentration of developing countries, an indigenous press was slow in developing and tended to follow models provided by colonial rulers. Kenyan journalist and publisher, Hilary Ng'weno puts it more graphically: The challenge to the press in young countries is the challenge of laying down the foundation upon which future freedoms will thrive. In Nigeria today, recent international press freedom index, with six percent between 2016 and 2017. According to 2017 World Press Freedom ranking compiled by Reporters Without Borders (RSF), Nigeria's record of press freedom came down 111 in 2016 to 122 in 2017, out of 180 countries graded. With new record, Nigeria continues to rank alongside other countries hostile to free press such as Afghanistan, Chad, Philippines, Zimbabwe, Colombia and others. In Nigeria, it is nearly impossible to cover stories involving politics, terrorism, or financial embezzlement.

Journalists are often threatened, subjected to physical violence, or denied access to information by government officials, police, and sometimes the public itself. Online freedom was recently curbed by a cyber-crime law that punishes bloggers in arbitrary manner; RSF said eight journalists have been killed across the world in 2017, while 193 are currently imprisoned. On Monday 24th of April2 017, President Buhari, Chief Security Officer, Bashir Abubakar, chased out the state house correspondent of PUNCH newspaper, Lekan Adetayo, from the presidential villa for reporting about President Muhammadu Buhari's ill health. libertarian theory of the press should be adopted for free market of ideas and a better society. Libertarianism can also be ethical theory or stance that holds that the best- i.e., best ethically speaking, or what "ought to" or " should" exist or be upheld –political, social, economic. It provides man with the greatest individual liberty, initiative, and entrepreneurship.

Social Responsibility Theory

This theory, regarded as a western theory incorporates part of the libertarian principle and introduces some new elements as well. The underlying principle of the social responsibility theory of the press is that the press should be free to perform the functions which the libertarian theory granted it freedom to perform, but that this freedom should be exercised with responsibility. If the media fail to meet their responsibilities to society, the social responsibility theory holds that the government should encourage the media to comply by way of controlling them. Bittner has it that the theory held that "a press has the right to criticize government and institutions but also has certain basic responsibilities to maintain the stability of society". In the same vein, but in a slightly different angle, Dominick writes that, This approach holds that the press has a right to criticize government and other institutions, but it also has a responsibility to preserve democracy by properly informing the public and by responding to society's needs and interests. The press does not have the freedom to do as it pleases; it is obligated to respond to society's requirements.

The Commission on Freedom of the Press which formulated the Social Responsibility theory while noting that the press does not fulfill her basic societal roles of providing information, enlightenment, serving as watchdog, advertising, entertainment, and self-sufficiency, called on the media to:

- Provide a truthful, comprehensive and intelligent account of the day's event in a context which gives them meaning.
- Serve as a forum for exchange of comment and criticism.
- Project a representative picture of the constituent groups in society. Be responsible for the presentation and clarification of the goals and values of the society.
- Provide full access to the day's intelligence.

These goals according to Peterson and Wilkins were troublesome to journalists who think that these goals are ambiguous and unattainable at the time. How should the forums operate? Whose values should be presented and clarified? How could they provide 'intelligent discourse about the day's events' in a nightly newscast of less than 23 minutes? And on and on the confusion went. Perhaps this is one weakness inherent in the theory at the earliest stages.

From the foregoing, it is palpable that the fundamental principles of the social responsibility theory could be summarized thus: "be self-regulated, practice responsibly, or the government will control you". In other words, freedom should be exercised with utmost responsibility to societal interest.

Social Responsibility Theory: A Theory of Media Ethics

Without question, the social responsibility theory of the press bothers on journalistic ethics. Its introduction was what gave rise to professional journalistic associations who have self-formulated codes of ethics and official journalistic standards designed to encourage responsible behavior by their members.

As Moemeka pointed out "this theory places due emphasis on the moral and social responsibilities of persons who, and institutions which, operate the mass media". Let us remember that its provision for self-regulation revolve around the concept of ethics. Ethics generally is the moral philosophy concerned with the standards of good and bad conduct, the rightness or wrongness of an action. Toeing this line, Okunna emphasizes that ethics is self-legislation as opposed to official or government legislation through outside compulsion, which is characteristic of law". McQuail cited in Okunna & Omenugha (2012) gave a list of basic tenets guiding this theory and which further drive home this ethical dimension of the social responsibility principle, to include accepting and carrying out certain societal duties; setting high professional standards of truth, accuracy, objectivity, balance and informativeness; regulating itself in accordance with the law; having media pluralism – multiplicity of voices – to represent divergent viewpoints; accountability to society, their medium and others; and that people have the right to expect them to perform creditably. The media have been entrusted to discharge certain public-interest functions essential to a democratic society and, by conferring this trust, society is entitled to judge whether it is being honoured. In Western liberal democracies, the media enter into an inherent compact with the societies they serve. Under this compact, the media promise that in return for the freedom to publish, they will meet certain core functional obligations: the terms of this compact are embodied in the Social Responsibility theory of the press as earlier argued. They may be thought of as ethical or "soft obligations", not enforceable at law, as opposed to "hard obligations". The soft obligations require attention to be paid to issues that are central to recurring controversies about media performance: bias, invasion of privacy, dishonest or careless presentation of information, violations of standards of public taste, suppression of material which it is not in the publisher's interest to publish, and incapacity to penetrate public-relations spin.

Indeed, there is no other better way to then summarize this theory in relation to media ethics, as the argument has shown, than with the words of Bittner (1989) which affirm that "within the framework of open and free press criticism, codes of ethics or government regulation, and guidelines for responsible action on the part of members of the press, lies the Social Responsibility Theory".

Difference between Social Responsibility Theory and Libertarianism

Social responsibility theory rests on a concept of positive liberty unlike the Libertarian theory that was born of a concept of negative liberty. Hocking (1947) say of positive liberty, positive freedom is a defining feature of our humanness but must constantly be etched out of our tendency to serve ourselves rather than use our liberty for the common good". The social responsibility theory differs from libertarian theory on the view it takes of the nature and functions of government: the social responsibility theory holds that the government should help society to obtain the services it requires from the mass media if self-regulated and self-righting features of community life are insufficient to provide them.

They also differ on the nature of freedom of expression as well: the libertarian theory considers this a natural right while the social responsibility theory considers it a moral right, rather than an absolute right. They also differ fundamentally in their view of the nature of man. The libertarian principle regards man as primarily a moral and rational being who will hunt for and be guided by truth; whereas the social responsibility views man as being lethargic. More alert elements of the community must goad him into the exercise of his reason.

Communist Theory of Communication

After the revolution of 1917, the Soviet Union was restructured with new political system based on the Marxist-Leninist principles. The newly formed communist party by Lenin shows much interest in the media which serves to the working class in the country and their welfares. So the Soviet originates a theory from Marxist, Leninist and Stalinist thoughts, with mixture of Georg Wilhelm Friedrich Hegel ideology is called "Soviet Media Theory" is also known as "The Communist Media Theory". The same theory was developed and followed by Adolf Hitler's Nazi in Germany and Benito Mussolini in Italy.

Soviet Media Theory

Soviet media theory is imitative of Leninist principles which based on the Carl Marx and Engel's ideology. The government undertake or controls the total media and communication to serve working classes and their interest. Theory says the state have absolute power to control any media for the benefits of people. They put end to the private ownership of the press and other media. The government media provide positive thoughts to create a strong socialized society as well as providing information, education, entertainment, motivation and mobilization. The theory describe the whole purpose of the mass media is to educate the greater masses of working class or workers. Here, the public was encouraged to give feedback which would able to create interests towards the media.

According to authoritarian theory, the media controlled and censored by the ministries in the country but libertarian is fully free without any intervention of any authority or government, Social responsibility theory – press freedom in one hand but other hand they controlled the press by raising question and Soviet media theory, the whole control of the media is under the leader of the nation.

Critics of Soviet Media Theory

1. Soviet media theory looks similar like authoritarian theory but the core part is different from each other. In authoritarian theory is a one way communication, there is no feedback allowed from the public but in Soviet media theory is a two way communication at the same time the whole media is controlled or works under the leadership.
2. Private ownership is not allowed which leads the press without any restriction and it can serve people without any authoritative blockades.
3. Soviet media theory allows some restriction based on the nation interest rather than personal.
4. Under communist theories like soviet media theory, the journalist or press should support the leadership rather than a watchdog.
5. If the leadership is wrong the whole nation will suffer a lot.

Development Communication Theory

The main idea behind development communication theory is media for development of people in a nation or to help the target population. Communication seeks to serve the people without manipulation and encourage genuine response.

There is no propaganda as ulterior motive of communication. Communication is to develop Conscientization or critical consciousness which can be about self-responsibility, social conscience and self-determination for right judgments and for social communication. The theory was used for social change.

Explanation of Development Communication Theory

Development used to be taken as bridging the disparity between the so-called 1st world and the 3rd world countries before the 20th century. Development was believed to be the process which made the third world countries follow the first world countries/ western countries, which were considered to be fully developed.

The under-developed countries had to follow their kind of political and economic systems, like heavy industries, capital intensive technology, etc. All other countries had to replicate a single form of development process which was practiced in some specific countries.

Thus, development was linked with Westernization. Development communication was at first based on the developmental theory of westernization but later had its own basis in the developmental theory of modernization.

The definition of development communication has been evolving with time from considering people as audiences who were to be influenced (one way) and the process rooted in the SMCR model. The unilateral communication flow was criticized for cultural imperialism. The socially engineered messages were disseminated for propaganda to control the culture of the poor countries by glorifying the conditions of the rich nations.

The theory focused on passive audience which was not participatory. This gave the notion that development was being, like the developed countries, one way influence. After that, the aspect of feedback was added.

Then, communication was said to be horizontal. Today, development communication is about working for local development and creating opportunities. Its objective is to uplift the quality of life of people not only economically but also socially, culturally, politically, etc. by using the tools of development communication.

The theory later became known for its use in the developing and under developed countries. The concept of participation was later added which paved the way for model to be used for social change, development communication and democratic-participant communication theory.

"Interpersonal communication as the base for participation of communities in their liberation from the unjust structures of their societies was part of this radical rethinking of communication—and eventually in how communication for social change might be defined"

– McAnany

Development communications process can be adjusted according to the needs, which improves the program as a learning process, as the concept of development communication is continuously evolving. Development of different digital technologies have made the concept broader and more participatory.

The implementation of this theory plays an important role in the overall development of a country. If done for international development projects, the communication process becomes a catalyst for the project to be successful.

Major Features of Development Communication Theory

- Development roles and objectives
- To help people
- No manipulation or propaganda
- Generates genuine response from the audience
- Used to develop critical consciousness
- Self-responsibility and self-determination

- Two way communication flow
- Uses development communication tools

Examples of Development Communication Theory

The reports and brochures of international development projects along with the Information Education Communication and Behavioral Change Communication materials can be taken as the examples of development communication tools. The posters, brochures, documentaries, etc. used for development projects like awareness in rural areas are development communication tools.

Strengths of Development Communication Theory

- Specified tools for communication makes communication effective
- Helps in international development projects
- Participation in communication media makes it inclusive

Weaknesses of Development Communication Theory

- It enforces westernization more than modernization
- Cultural hegemony is occurred through development communication implementation

Democratization/Democratic Participant Media Theory

This theory is the latest in the field of media theories, and Professor McQuail is its proponent. Its location is mainly in rich, developed countries where the citizens have the scientific, technological and financial means to put the latest innovations in inter-personal communication to practical and regular use.

It is by no means confined to the rich developed countries because science and technology is universal; all countries can make use of them provided there is a will to do so, particularly among the financially well-off sector. Cyber systems are prevalent everywhere and India is no exception. From the early 1990s, or at least from mid-1990s, Internet is part of media and communication system.

For a while advanced countries in the West witnessed citizens' apathy towards democratic politics, especially at the time of periodic elections in the 1970s and 1980s. Their voting behavior changed and this was reflected in the low percentage in voter-turnout. Political scientists found an explanation for this alteration in voter-behaviour. It was concluded that citizens' apathy was caused by their conviction that not many things could be changed by voting once in five years or so. The government establishment and the political system appeared immutable.

The democratic participant theory is, in a way, the technological version of the libertarian theory. People can and must express their views freely, exchange ideas without fear, and with absolute freedom, making use of innovations in technology. The Internet came in handy, and with it came the interpersonal device of electronic mail (e-mail), without any central authority to control it.

The theory challenges commercialization and monopolization of privately-owned media; it reacts against the centralism and bureaucratization of media institutions, as pointed out by McQuail. It emphasizes communitarianism, and encourages citizens' participation in community affairs. The dominance of mainstream mass media owned by private or public monopolies was the reason behind the emergence of "underground" publications during the 1960s and 1970s, The alternative media were technically made more efficient with the arrival of the Internet.

Underlying the theory under discussion is the assumption that mass communication need not be "uniform, centralized, high-cost, commercialized, professionalized, state controlled or privately controlled. Mass communication can take place without the mass media.

In fact, this is what happened in Egypt, Tunisia and other Arab countries where people organized protests and popular movements against authoritarian regimes. This is what can enthuse people to clamour for more freedom, and accountability from ruling governments. Properly directed, such movements are desirable in all States under repressive governments. The new media can come to the aid of citizens wanting more political and social freedom, and personal expression of freedom for desirable action for the welfare and safety of citizens.

Mass communication can be multiple, small-scale, local, non-institutional, run by small communities (or even individuals?) having similar aims and goals.

Not only newspapers, but radio, ham radio, mobile phones, smart phones and all devices that can be used conveniently by the ordinary citizens can effectively apply this theory of participation in democracy, without interference from government. Since technology is now available to all informed groups and persons even in poor countries, the New Media including wall newspapers, bro-adsheets with jumbo-size messages printed in big fonts, wall posters similarly printed, little ma-gazines, etc., can serve the pu-rpose. The neo-literate millions in China and India can benefit from this unconventional journalism.

Local issues can be more effectively handled by local media, particularly interactive media where and when available and a revolution of some sort in communication in socioeconomic, political and cultural matters can be achieved in poor countries. Panchaayats and municipal towns can benefit from such novel methods of communication for people's mobilization and active participaton.

Nonverbal Communication

The Nonverbal Communication is the process of conveying meaning without the use of words either written or spoken. In other words, any communication made between two or more persons through the use of facial expressions, hand movements, body language, postures, and gestures is called as non-verbal communication.

The Nonverbal Communication, unlike the verbal communication, helps in establishing and maintaining the interpersonal relationships while the verbals only help in communicating the external events. People use nonverbals to express emotions and interpersonal attitudes, conduct rituals such as greetings and bring forward one's personality.

The nonverbal communication in the form of signals, expressions add meaning over the verbals and help people to communicate more efficiently. It supplements whatever is said in words, such as people nod to acknowledge and move their hands to give directions.

The non-verbal communication defines the distance between the communicators and helps them to exchange their emotional state of mind. Also, it regulates the flow of communication, for example, an individual can give signals to convey that he had finished speaking or else he wants to speak.

Sometimes, the nonverbals acts as a barrier to communicating effectively as the recipient could not understand what the sender is trying to say and may interpret it wrongly.

Five Nonverbal Abilities

How is it that non-verbal communication is the element of the in-person presentation that has caused it to be the default response when responses matter most: inaugural addresses, States of the Union, getting big accounts, keeping big accounts–the list goes on and on. Perhaps because this form of communication shares so much more than dialogue. There are five main effects that nonverbal communication can have:

- Repetition: They can reinforce what is already being said
- Contradiction: They can contradict the message and make the speaker seem untruthful
- Substitution: They can take the place of words
- Complementing: They can compliment a verbal message, for instance, a pat on the back
- Accenting: They can underline a certain point in the message

First Impression

Meeting a new business contact can be nerve-wracking. Just like a first date, your first impression is of the utmost importance, as it can determine the trajectory of the arrangement. And while rehearsing what you are going to say and arguments you intend to make can be helpful, a major part of making a good first impression has to do with unspoken qualities such as body language, hygiene, and preparedness. Below you will find a few aspects that should always be at the front of your mind when you schedule a meeting.

Research before the Meeting

Find out as much as you can about the client and company involved in the meeting. Learn about their goals, values, and interests.

Keep your Nonverbals in Check

Your body language is capable of communicating almost as much as your actual words, so it's important to be intentional with it. Remember to maintain good posture—no slouching. Not only will slouching communicate a lack of confidence and composure, but also it isn't great for your back. You may have also guessed that a firm handshake is important, too. Make sure that your handshake is indeed firm, but also keep in mind that it isn't a test of strength and should not be overly firm.

Dress Appropriately

While meetings often take place outside of the office, that's no excuse to go uber casual on the clothing front. Take some time to consider the right outfit, whether it be a full suit or something business casual. Of course, this will depend on the industry. Silicon Valley is a good example of the shift in attitudes toward dress, as jeans paired with blazers or black turtleneck sweaters grow in popularity, even among people in leadership positions. But when in doubt, dress up.

Demonstrate that you're Listening

You can use both verbal and non-verbal cues to show your interlocutor that you are listening and that they have your full attention. Eye contact is one of the easiest ways to show such respect, so long as it does not cross the line into staring. You can also align your body to face the other person. Without interrupting, verbal cues are effective, too. Ask thoughtful questions and be solutions-oriented when appropriate.

Be Prepared for Impromptu Meetings

Sometimes you won't get much notice before a meeting is scheduled because circumstances aren't always in your control. For this reason, it's best to keep a 'go bag' on hand at all times. In it, be sure to include a tie and clean shirt, personal hygiene products, breath mints (not gum), and a pen and paper. If you have time, try to get some base-level research in, too.

In general, and regardless of the topic of the meeting, one of the main goals is to build trust and rapport. A positive first impression is the perfect starting point to cultivate a relationship, as your interlocutor will feel comfortable working with you from the start. It can also boost your professional reputation, as word of mouth travels far and can result in new leads and connections. So always try to put your best foot forward.

Posture

What you say is more than the words that come out of your mouth. Posture and how you move your body are important elements of nonverbal communication, which can affect how you are perceived by others. The body language may reveal even more about a person than verbal communication does. Being aware of your posture can help you make the right impression in many areas of your life.

Open Posture

Open posture portrays friendliness and positivity. In an open position, your feet are spread wide and the palms of your hands are facing outward. That people with open postures are perceived as being more persuasive than those with other postures. To achieve an open posture, sit or stand up straight with your head raised, and keep your chest and abdomen exposed, advises the "Body Language." Combine this pose with a relaxed facial expression and good eye contact to come across as approachable and composed. During conversation, keep your body facing toward the other person.

Closed Posture

Crossing your arms across your chest, crossing your legs away from someone, sitting in a hunched forward position, showing the backs of your hands and clenching your fists are all signs of closed posture. That a closed posture may give the impression of boredom, hostility or detachment.

Confident Posture

If you want to come across as confident, even if you are feeling anxious, stressed or nervous, make subtle changes to your posture. Pull yourself up to your full height, hold your head high and keep your gaze at eye level. Pull your shoulders back and keep your arms and legs relaxed by your sides.

Mirroring

Notice the way a loving couple relate to each other. You might like to observe a close relationship in person or on television. You will see that the partners' postures will match, as if one partner is a mirror reflection of the other. For example, if one partner drapes an arm over the back of a chair this might be replicated in the other person's position. If one partner frowns, it could be reflected in the other partner's facial expression. This 'mirroring' indicates interest and approval between people.

Clothing

The body as an instrument of communication does not just mean that the mouth speaks, the hands mold or the feet move. We communicate even further on a nonverbal level by what we chose to cover ourselves with. For centuries, people have used the language of dress to express personal things such as race, class, gender, ethnicity and religion but also larger social and political movements.

Every language has a vocabulary and grammar, which act as rules of communicating with others. We learn the rules of our spoken language at a very young age, not only in school but also from hearing people speak around us, and participating in conversation. The way in which we know how to speak was not entirely taught to us, as we develop a subconscious understanding of what is grammatically correct through the lived experience of speaking and listening to others.

Fashion, just as any other language, has its own grammar. There are unspoken rules about what matches, what is appropriate, what to wear in certain situations and what is unacceptable. And while every language has different accents and dialects, so does fashion. Different cultures, religions and groups of people have different ways of constructing outfits to communicate their beliefs, customs and history. Similar to spoken language, these rules are learned from our family, friends, groups to which we belong, and the media.

The "words" that make up the language of fashion include hair styles, make up, jewelry, shoes, clothing, and accessories. Just as words are put together to create sentences, the building blocks of the speech of fashion are put together to create outfits or certain looks. Some people have a very large vocabulary of clothing and can create a plethora of outfits to communicate different things at different times. Others have a limited vocabulary, whether because of economic restrictions or by choice, and have limited options for conveying messages using clothing

Choosing the right words to express your thoughts is critical in making sure you get your message across the way you want it to be understood. Saying the wrong thing can cause a lot of damage to yourself and the person who hears you. While you may use a more formal way of speaking with teachers and employers, you may use a more casual form of speech with family and friends.

Fashion plays the same role. Certain outfits, hair styles or make up may be appropriate at specific times and places, and offensive at others. You may wear one thing in front of your parents, and another thing out with your friends. For example, a mini skirt, high heals and heavy eye shadow are perfect for going to a bar, but may be detrimental to a job interview at a law firm. Choosing the right attire to give off the impression you desire is just as important as finding the right words to deliver a message.

The rules of grammar can be, and very often are, broken. They way we speak English today would be appalling to our great, great grandparents. Different dialects come about by people breaking the rules of the language and creating a new way of speaking. The rules of "dress grammar" are often broken as well.

Some rules, however, are taken very seriously. Women are not allowed to go topless in most parts of the United States, and men are not allowed to walk around without pants on. Some cultures, such as the Amish and religious Jews, have very strict dress rules that cannot be broken. These rules stem from deeply rooted religious beliefs, and serve as a form of identification for individuals who are members of that community.

On a less serious level, every subculture has unspoken rules about what to wear. Just as a group of preppy students from Vaderbilt University, a black gang from Compton, New York and a sorority from University of Hartford would all have different ways of communicating within their groups and with other groups, those same subcultures have implicit rules for what to wear and how to wear it. There are also rules about what not to wear.

Often times people use slang or curse words to emphasize a feeling, get attention or signify emotions. While this type of speech has become increasingly accepted in our culture, it is still disapproved of in many situations. Slang is a more casual form of speech while curse words give emphasis and demand attention. Jeans, t-shirts and sweatpants are the slang of dress, and give a relaxed, loose feel to your appearance.

There are also ways of dressing that can be compared to curse words. The attire of the punk movement, which consists of bold hair, ripped clothing and dark colors, can be seen as the curse words of dress. In verbal speech, slang and curse words often become accepted parts of the language, and the same occurs for clothing. While jeans were once worn as work clothes, they are now a staple item in most people's wardrobes, and can be dressed up or dressed down for almost any occasion. Similarly, the mohawk, which used to be associated with punk culture, has meshed into the "faux-hawk" and is a popular hairstyle for teens and young men today.

"In dress as in language, there is a possible range of expression from the most eccentric statement to the most conventional." A woman who cannot properly form sentences and strings together words incongruently may be recognized as deranged and her outfits will probably look the way her speech sounds. Mismatched, random articles of clothing and wild, messy hair gives the mark of insanity. On the other hand, a polished, matching, expensive suit identifies the person as wealthy, professional and together.

Our culture believes strongly in first impressions. Whether a blind date, meeting your boss, or being introduced to your significant other's parents, there is a great emphasis on coming off the right way to people. Long before you are close enough to someone to speak to them, you are aware of what they look like. What someone wears can be an instant marker of age, gender and class. It can also give information as to profession, ethnicity, mood and background.

We all consciously and subconsciously absorb the information others give us via their clothing, and create opinions based on attire. We also carefully choose our outfits depending on how we want to appear to others. If fashion is a language, and therefore a way of communicating, then clothing is the medium through which we send messages to other people. Whether the message others receive was what we intended or not, we dress with intention. While a designer may have created an article of clothing for one intention, someone may buy it with another intention. The meaning that is put into clothing during production changes drastically by the time it is perceived by someone passing by on the street.

The act of deciding what to wear on any given day has repercussions that go far beyond simply reaching into the closet and putting together an outfit. Whether your selections are made out of impulse or calculation, your choices are always profoundly revealing- whether you know it or not.

All clothing sends a message, whether we intend it to or not. It expresses every aspect of an individual. In order for people to respond to us the way we want, we must understand how our clothing is a representation of who we are and what we communicate through what we wear.

Fashion is often used to create a sense of community amongst a group of people, and to separate between those in the group and those outside the group. This is true for cultural clothing, such as Sari's worn by traditional Indian women, but also for smaller subcultures such as sports teams. Wearing a Yankee's hat is a way of telling others something about you, and identifying with people who are also fans. The traditional white robe with a pointed hood acts as a way for Ku Klux Klan members to differentiate themselves from the rest of the culture and recognize other group members. Wearing a t-shirt stamped with a brand name lets others know that you identify with that brand and whatever reputation comes along with it.

In the well loved 2004 movie Mean Girls, the popular girls of North Shore High School have very strict rules about what they could wear. "On Wednesdays we wear pink. You can't wear a tank top two days in a row and you can only wear your hair in a ponytail once a week. We only wear jeans or track pants on Fridays." Breaking these rules meant that you could not sit at their table that day. While this seems like a fabrication to enhance a move plot, it reflects real life attitudes and thoughts about how clothing is a form of group identification that is taken very seriously.

Clothing serves multiple functions. It is worn for modesty, to protect the body against the elements and to provide comfort. Perhaps the most intriguing purpose clothing serves is to communicate with others. It allows us to express parts of ourselves that we want people to see, and we can reveal different aspects of our character every day. Just as verbal language, fashion has the power to evoke emotion, tell a story, convey a message, reveal an identity and form a community. "Fashion is free speech, and one of the privileges, of not always one of the pleasures, of a free world."

Gestures

A gesture is a specific bodily movement that reinforces a verbal message or conveys a particular thought or emotion. Although gestures may be made with the head, shoulders, or even the legs and feet, most are made with the hands and arms.

Your hands can be marvelous tools of communication when you speak. But many inexperienced speakers are unsure what to do with their hands. Some try to get them out of the way by putting them in their pockets or behind their backs. Others unconsciously relieve nervous tension by performing awkward, distracting movements. A few speakers over-gesture out of nervousness, waving their arms and hands wildly.

A speaker's gestures can suggest very precise meaning to an audience. The Indians of North America devised a sign language that enabled people with entirely different spoken languages to converse. Sign language has also made it possible for deaf people to communicate without speaking.

The use of gestures in communication varies from one culture to the next. In some cultures, such as those of Southern Europe and the Middle East, people use their hands freely and expressively when they speak. In other cultures, people use gestures less frequently and in a more subdued way.

The specific gesture we make and the meanings we attach to them are products of our cultural training. Just as cultures differ, so do the perceived meanings of gestures. For example, nodding one's head up and down signifies agreement or assent in Western cultures – but in some parts of India this gesture means the exact opposite. A common gesture used in the United States – that of making a circle with the thumb and forefinger to indicate approval – is considered an insult and an obscenity in many areas of the world.

To be effective, a speaker's gestures must be purposeful – even if they're performed unconsciously. They must be visible to the audience. They must mean the same thing to the audience that they mean to the speaker. And they must reflect what's being said, as well as the total personality behind the message.

Importance of Gestures

All good speakers use gestures. Why? Gestures are probably the most evocative form of nonverbal communication a speaker can employ. No other kind of physical action can enhance your speeches in as many ways as gestures. They:

- Clarify and support your words. Gestures strengthen the audience's understanding of your verbal message.
- Dramatize your ideas. Together with what you say, gestures help paint vivid pictures in your listeners' minds.
- Lend emphasis and vitality to the spoken word. Gestures convey your feelings and attitudes more clearly than what you say.
- Help dissipate nervous tension. Purposeful gestures are a good outlet for the nervous energy inherent in a speaking situation.
- Function as visual aids. Gestures enhance audience attentiveness and retention.
- Stimulate audience participation. Gestures help you indicate the response you seek from your listeners.
- Are highly visible. Gestures provide visual support when you address a large number of people and the entire audience may not see your eyes.

Types of Gestures

Despite the vast number of movements that qualify as gestures, all gestures can be grouped into one of the following major categories:

1. Descriptive gestures clarify or enhance a verbal message. They help the audience understand comparisons and contrasts, and visualize the size, shape, movement, location, function, and number of objects.

2. Emphatic gestures underscore what's being said. They indicate earnestness and conviction. For example, a clenched fist suggests strong feeling, such as anger or determination.

3. Suggestive gestures are symbols of ideas and emotions. They help a speaker create a desired mood or express a particular thought. An open palm suggests giving or receiving, usually of an idea, while a shrug of the shoulders indicates ignorance, perplexity, or irony.

4. Prompting gestures are used to help evoke a desired response from the audience. If you want listeners to raise their hands, applaud, or perform some specific action, you'll have to enhance the response by doing it yourself as an example.

Gestures made above the shoulder level suggest physical height, inspiration, or emotional exultation. Gestures made below shoulder level indicate rejection, apathy, or condemnation. Those made at or near shoulder level suggest calmness or serenity.

The most frequently used gestures involve an open palm held outward toward the audience. The meaning of this type of gesture depends on the position of the palm. Holding the palm upward implies giving or receiving, although this gesture is sometimes used as an unconscious movement, with no specific intended meaning. A palm held downward can express uppression, secrecy, completion, or stability. A palm held outward toward the audience suggests halting, repulsion, negation, or abhorrence. If the palm is held perpendicular to the speaker's body, it tends to imply measurement, limits in space or time, comparisons, or contrasts.

Proper use of Gestures

Gestures reflect each speaker's individual personality. What's right for one speaker probably won't work for you. However, the following six rules apply to almost everyone who seeks to become a dynamic, effective speaker.

1. Respond naturally to what you think, feel and say

When you present a speech, you naturally express yourself though gestures. No matter what our personality or cultural background may be, every one of us has a natural impulse to punctuate and strengthen our words with gestures.

The trick is not to suppress that impulse by retreating behind a mask of impassiveness; this can only create a buildup of tension. At the same time, don't get gestures out of a book or from another speaker. Be genuinely and spontaneously yourself. If you impose artificial gestures onto your natural style, your audience will sense it and label you a phony.

Some people are naturally animated, while others are naturally reserved. If you naturally use your hands freely when you converse informally, use them freely when you give a speech. If you're by nature a reserved, low-key person, don't change your personality just to suit public speaking situations.

2. Create the conditions for gesturing – not the gesture

Your gestures should be a natural outgrowth of your own unique thoughts and feelings. They should arise naturally and habitually from your attitude toward the message you present.

When you speak, you should be totally involved in communicating – not in thinking about your hands. Your gestures need to be motivated by the content of your presentation. By immersing yourself in your subject matter, you will create the conditions that will enable you to respond naturally with appropriate gestures.

3. Suit the action to the word and the occasion

Your visual and verbal messages must act as partners in communicating the same thought or feeling. When a speaker fails to match gestures with words, the outcome can be wooden, artificial, and sometimes comical. Every gesture you make should be purposeful and reflective of your words. In this way your listeners will note the effect rather than the gesture.

Make sure the vigor and frequency of your gestures are appropriate for your words. Use strong, emphatic gestures only when your feeling for the message calls for them. On occasion, you may need to adapt your gestures to fit the size and nature of your audience. Generally speaking, the larger the audience, the broader and slower your gestures should be. Also keep in mind that young audiences are usually attracted to a speaker who uses vigorous gestures, but older, more conservative groups may feel irritated or threatened by a speaker whose physical actions are too powerful.

Your gestures during a speech are also affected by the logistics of the speaking situation. When you speak from a physically confining position, you may be restricted from using broad, sweeping gestures. A common example of a confining speaking position is a head table, where people are seated close to the speaker.

4. Make your gestures convincing

Your gestures should be lively and distinct if they're to convey the intended impression. A gesture performed in a half-hearted manner suggests that the speaker lacks conviction and earnestness. Every hand gesture should be a total body movement that starts from the shoulder – never from the elbow. Move your entire arm outward from your body freely and easily. Keep your wrists and fingers supple, rather than stiff or tense. Effective gestures are vigorous enough to be convincing, yet slow enough and broad enough to be clearly visible. Your gestures should be distinct but not jerky, and they should never follow a set pattern.

5. Make your gestures smooth and well-timed

Any single gesture has three parts: the approach, the stroke, and the return. During the approach, your body begins to move in anticipation of the gesture. The stroke is the gesture itself, and the return brings your body back to a balanced speaking posture. The flow of a gesture – balance, approach, stroke, return, balance – must be smoothly executed in such a way that only the stroke is evident to the audience. Just as timing is an essential ingredient of comedy, a gesture's timing is just as important as its quality. The stroke must come on the correct word – neither before nor after it. However, the approach can be initiated well before the stroke; in fact, you can obtain an especially powerful effect by approaching a gesture several seconds in advance, then holding the approach until the exact instant of the stroke. The return simply involves dropping your hands smoothly to your sides – it doesn't have to be rushed. Don't try to memorize gestures and incorporate them into a speech. Memorized gestures usually fail, because the speaker cues himself or her-self by the word the gesture is designed to punctuate. This results in the gesture following the word, which looks artificial and foolish.

6. Make natural, spontaneous gesturing a habit

To improve your gestures, practice – but don't wait until the day of your speech. Work on enhancing your gesturing abilities in front of friends, family members, and co-workers. Relax your inhibitions, gesture when you feel like it, and let yourself respond naturally to what you think, feel, and say. Through awareness and practice, you can make appropriate gesturing a part of your habitual behavior.

Eye Contact

The old saying that "eyes are a reflection of your inner self" holds true in most cases. There are a lot of meanings to eye contact. It can be a glaring look when a person is defiant or angry. A stare when we see something unusual about the person. A glazed over look when we are hopelessly in love with the person. It can also be a direct look when we are talking and trying to make a point.

Importance of Eyes in Communication

In all instances we use our eyes as a level of communication with the other person. We also avoid a direct look from another person if we have something to hide. The police use it as a means to detect if the person is telling the truth or not. So unless you are a very accomplished liar in most cases you will feel uneasy when you lie. Also sometimes a person feels uncomfortable looking another person in the eye due to shyness. This trait is also present with other signs of shyness such as a slight stammer and sometimes blushing. Otherwise it could just be that the person has a short attention span for anything you have to say.

Eye Contact in Events

Our eyes also reflect our sincerity, integrity and comfort when communicating with another person. Which is why having good eye contact while conversing is the indication that the communication has gone on well. How is eye contact related to events? Well, events are a form and means of communication, be it to send out a message, to educate or even to introduce. A good event management company will realize that eye contact during communication and speech is important.

Take for instance a presentation event where you have a speaker and an audience. One of the main items of importance during event planning will be the camera and projection screen. Another item of importance is the cameraman. One point to note is that you can obtain a good event management app to manage your checklist for all these items. Notice how during the presentation the cameraman will focus on the face of the speaker. On cue when the speaker makes a point, the cameraman will focus on the speaker's eyes. This is to establish a contact between speaker and audience through the big screen so that the audience can feel a connection between the speaker and his or her audience. When you notice this in any presentation that you go to, make sure to take note of the event solution company and the cameraman. They have their act well-rehearsed.

Eyes and the Body Language

Eye contact is a form of body language which is important during communication. How we present ourselves and communicate with others aside from talking is by our body language. Our body language speaks more than words which then logically accounts for a bigger percentage of our communication skills. Therefore our eyes speaks volumes about us and how we communicate.

Some points to remember while communicating and why eye contact is important are:

- Surprise, eye contact is a sign that you happen to be a good listener. Now what has the eye got to do with listening? When you keep eye contact with the person you are talking to it indicates that you are focused and paying attention. It means that you are actually listening to what the person has to say. That is where the saying "Don't just listen with your ears" comes from. So "listen" more than talk, everyone loves a good listener especially the opposite gender.
- Your eyes are a way of building a connection with the other person. This could mean you like that person. You feel comfortable talking and communicating with the person or you just are plain falling in love with the person. Either way, the eyes say it all.
- Avoiding eye contact could also mean that you do not want the person you are speaking with to know too much. It could be that you may not like the person. You do not want the person to know you like them or you do not feel comfortable with that person. These are the negative impacts of avoiding eye contact. Sometimes the other person might read it wrongly and therefore produce a negative feeling towards you as well.
- A big part of eye contact is building trust. A person with whom you are talking to will be more likely to trust and respect you as eye contact indicates an openness in communication. It also tells the other person "Hey, I am confident and self-assured, you can trust me". So if you hope to land that big contract or project, be trust-worthy.

Practising good eye contact is a skill for effective and vital communication and is mostly under-rated and under-utilized. Keeping eye contact with the person you are talking to indicates interest and saying to the person "You are important and I am listening". It is one of the "unseen" tools used in any event communication.

Reasons to Practice Strong Eye Contact

- Respect: In Western countries like the United States, eye contact in order to show and earn respect. From talking to your boss at work to thanking your grandmother for a birthday gift, eye contact shows that you see the person as equal or someone you view as important. Of course there are other ways to show respect, such as staying eye-level with the person and positioning yourself as leaning into them when you're talking, but eye contact shows that you're on the same page in the most straight-forward way. As they say, "eyes are the window to the soul." Sincerity can be felt through eye contact, therefore, genuine respect will be received if you pay strong attention through your eyes.
- Interest: If you like someone in any way, shape, or form, why not look them in the eye when you're talking to them? Looking down or away from them can come off as aloof, especially if the person is telling you about something important or trying to get your attention. In order to put the most effort into showing interest, look the person in the eye and smile. This can be taken different ways depending on what you and the other person are intending – interest could mean familial, friendship, a respectful authoritarian interest, love interest, or even just a strong bond that you and the other person have. Eye contact can say so much, yet leave so much to assumptions and analyzing body language.
- Appreciation: You can convey appreciation quite easily with the eyes – just give a meaningful look into their eyes while you're thanking them and the other person is able to recognize how you feel. Showing emotions like appreciation is quite important in terms of friends and family members if they do something nice or helpful for you, so eye contact is vital in these situations. It's a socially constructed way to keep up a positive image with people in your life, yet also an extremely good way to show your thanks with sincerity.
- Understanding: A locking of eyes can be all you need to have some understand something you mean. If you're trying to get a point across or just want some reassurance, eye contact can be an important asset in communicating your thoughts.
- Eye contact can be the difference between seeming aloof and a new friendship: If you're giving someone eye contact, this could be the start of friendly, warm communication with a new person. By keeping yourself open to locking eyes with a stranger, you're inviting them to look at you and perhaps start a conversation. You're leaving yourself open to people if you're willing to make eye contact and keep up a friendly face. While there's a clear difference between good eye contact and glaring, it's important that you know when it's appropriate to use either. Warm, friendly eyes could be the deciding factor in whether you make a possible friend or scare someone away. While there are exceptions to leaving yourself open with your eyes (when you're somewhere new and you feel rather sketched out), it's important to not let opportunities where eye contact could help you to pass you by. Surprising things could happen if you just open your eyes.

In general, eye contact is something people don't think enough about. It's important to teach children from a young age to look people in the eye when they're talking to them or they could develop a habit of seeming aloof or disinterested in communicating with other people. Locking eyes and knowing when to look away is a good people skill to possess. Use your eyes to project a positive image and one look could be the catalyst for change in your life.

Movement and Body Position

Body language is nonverbal communication that involves body movement. "Gesturing" can also be termed as body language which is absolutely non-verbal means of communication. People in the workplace can convey a great deal of information without even speaking; through nonverbal communication.

Not all of our values, beliefs, thoughts and intentions are communicated verbally. In an ongoing communication, most of those are communicated non-verbally. In Nonverbal communication, our human body expresses our feelings and intentions through conscious and unconscious movements and postures, accompanied by gestures, facial expressions, eye contacts and touch. This collectively forms a separate language of the body within the ongoing communication. This is called Body Language.

Communication of The Body

Our human body speaks through the conscious and unconscious movements and postures, hand gestures, facial expressions, eye movements and touch. Each of these physical movements of the body parts could be seen as separate words and can be interpreted differently by other human beings within a given context of communication.

Importance of Body Language

Since interpretations of body language differ from people to people and cultures to countries it is important to learn about them. Body language alone comprises of 55% of total communication whereas spoken words comprise of 7% and tone of voice comprise 38%.

Types of Body Language

Body language is usually grouped along two lines:

1. Parts of the body.

2. Intent.

Parts of the Body

From head to toe, here are the groups when grouped for body parts:

- The Head: Movement and placement of the head, back to front, left to right, side to side, including the shaking of hair.
- Facial Expressions: The face has many muscles (anywhere between 54 and 98, depending on who you ask) that move several areas of the face. Each combination of movements of the following face elements communicates a state of mind:
  - Eyebrows - Up, down, frowning.
  - Eyes - Left, right, up, down, blinking, eye dialiation.
  - Nose - Wrinkle (at the top), flaring of the nostrills.
  - Lips - Smiling, snarling, puckered, kissing, opened, closed, tight.
  - Tongue - In, out, rolled, tip up or down, licking of lips.
  - Jaw - Open, closed, clinched, lower jaw left or right.
- Body Posture: The way you place your body and arms and legs, in relation to each other, and in relation to other people:
  - Body proximity: How far or close to other people.
  - Shoulder movements: Up, down, hanging, hunched.
  - Arm placement: Up, down, crossed, straight.
- Leg and feet placement: Straight, crossed, weight placement, feet towards speaking partner or pointing elsewhere, dangling of shoes.
- Hand and finger gestures: How you hold and move your hands and fingures are particularly insightful in reading people.
- Handling and placement of objects (eg. pens, papers, etc.): The odd one out...technically not a body part, but objects do play a big role in reading body language.

Intent

Another way to group types of body language is along Intent:

- Voluntary/Intentional movements usually called "Gestures". These are movements you intended to make, like shaking a hand, giving the finger, blinking with one eye.
- Involuntary movements usually called "tells", but "ticks" also fall into this category. Any body movement you have no cotrol over falls in this category. While technically not a body movement, sweating also applies.

So where is Tone of Voice

While usually seen as body language, tone of voice and intonation are a separate group from body language.

These are the groups that are found in tone of voice:

- Pitch of voice, high voice, low voice, intonation.
  - Loudness, everything from shouting to whispering.
  - Breathing slow, fast breathing, shaky voice.

Body Language of Movement

Facial Expression

- All facial organs on human face indicates facially expressive message.
  - These are hair, forehead, eyebrows, eyes, mouth, chin, nose, lips, ears, teethe, tongue etc.
  - Facial expressions comes naturally hence it is beyond the control of speaker.

Examples of Facial Expression

A Smile expresses friendliness and Affection,

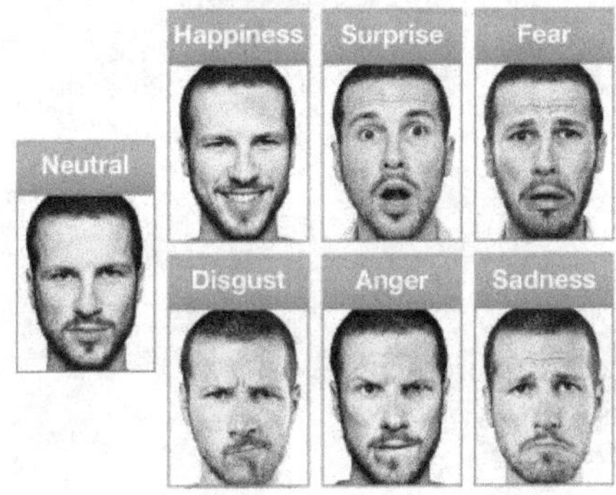

Examples of Facial Expression: Raised eyebrows convey surprise,

Examples of Facial Expression: Furrowed forehead expresses worries & Anxiety,

Examples of Facial Expression: Frown shows dislike or suspicion,

Silence

- "speech is silver but silence is golden".
- It establishes the relationship between the communicators.
- Moments of silence – do not know how to continue.

Voice Modulation

- The speaker must use his voice effectively.

- Someone wants to become a effective speaker, a good is must.
- A good voice is natural gift.
- One can take the training of phonetics to improve his own voice.

More Body Language Examples and Their Meaning

Arms Crossed in Front of The Chest

This is one of the body language examples that indicate that one is being defensive. The body language meaning of crossed arms may also show disagreement with opinions and actions of other people with whom you are communicating.

Biting of Nails

Nail biting demonstrates nervousness, stress, or insecurity. Many people bite nails without realizing they have the habit.

Hand on Cheek

This body language example indicates that one is lost in thought, maybe considering something. When your hand is on your cheek and your brows are furrowed you may be in deep concentration.

Finger Tapping or Drumming

This action demonstrates that one is growing tried or impatient while waiting.

Touching the Nose

Touching or rubbing the nose signifies disbelief, rejection, or lying about something.

Prisk Rubbing of the Hands

This may show that the hands are cold, which may mean that one is excited about something, or waiting eagerly.

Placing Finger Tips Together

This is called "steepling" or placing fingertips together to demonstrate control or authority.

Open Palms, Facing Upward

This gesture is a sign of honesty, submission, and innocence. This is how some people show submission and respect.

Head in Hands

The body language meaning of this gesture may be that of boredom, being upset, or being ashamed, so one does not want to show their face.

Locking of Ankles

Whether you are sitting or standing, when your ankles are locked, you are communicating apprehension or nervousness.

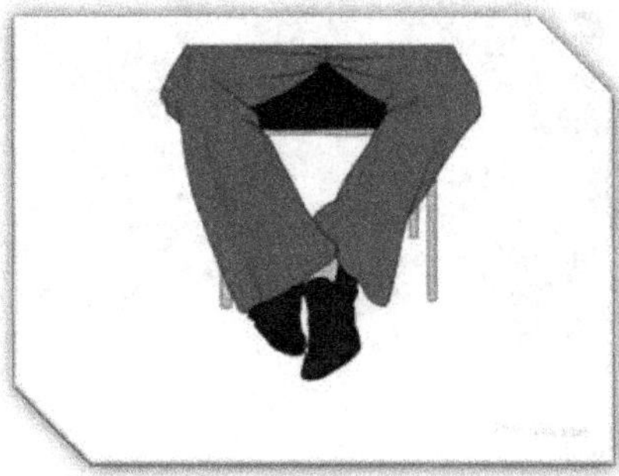

Stroking the Chin or Beard

This communicates that one is in deep thought. This action is often done unintentionally when one is trying to come up with some decision.

Ear Pulling

Pulling an ear lobe can mean one is trying to make a decision, but remains indecisive about something.

Head Nodding

This gesture usually signifies agreement or bowing, s submissive gesture that shows one is going along with another person's opinions.

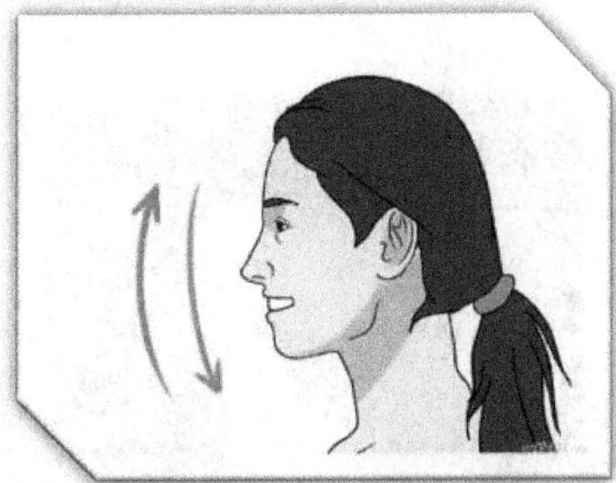

Lint Picking

Picking of imaginary lint is another one of the body language examples of displacement gestures, which one uses to show disapproval of the attitudes or opinions of other. This action makes one look away from the other person while doing some irrelevant action.

Catapult Posture

This seated version of the "Hand-on-Hip" male poster with the hands behind the head and elbows pointed out is used to intimidate or show a relaxed attitude. Thus giving a false sense of security before an ambush is made

Lowered Head

This indicates one is hiding something. When you lower your head while you are being complimented, you may be showing shyness, shame, or timidity. It may also convey that you are keeping distance from another person, showing disbelief, or thinking to yourself.

Proxemics

Proxemics is a theory of non-verbal communication that explains how people perceive and use space to achieve communication goals. Introduced by anthropologist Edward T. Hall in the 1960s, the theory emerged from studies of animal behavior conducted in the 19th and early 20th centuries. Just as animals use urine and physical posturing to define their territory, Hall posited, so do humans use personal space and concrete objects to establish theirs.

Core Concepts and Assumptions

Following are the ideas behind proxemic theory:

1. There are four types of distances people keep: Intimate (0 to 18 inches), personal (18 inches to 4 feet), social (4 to 10 feet), and public (over 10 feet).

2. The distances outlined are those deliberately chosen by individuals: Forced closeness doesn't factor in proxemics.

3. Proxemic behavior is learned mostly from observing others rather than from explicit instruction, which is why personal distance and physical contact varies by culture.

4. The physical distance between communicators indicates the type of relationship they have. Body angles, touch and eye contact further reveal the familiarity between people.

5. Americans generally prefer 18 inches of personal space.

Proxemics could not only help illuminate relationships and communication goals, but also explain other cultural and anthropological phenomena, such as the organization of towns and living spaces. Furniture, walls, streets, buildings and fences are arranged in ways that delineate one's territory, whether for living, working or meeting others. Territories are designed to provide comfort for their owners and produce anxiety within intruders.

Even color is used to identify certain kinds of territories and the behavior expected from those who enter them. For instance, a bright purple sofa in a small apartment would encourage a fun, carefree attitude, while a pristine white sofa in the same apartment would indicate an owner who prefers formality and restraint. Restaurants painted in soothing pastels invite diners to linger over their meals; those decorated with loud, obnoxious tones say, "Eat quickly and leave."

Types of Territories

There are four main kinds of territories in proxemics:

1. Body Territory: It refers to the personal space, or "bubble," that one maintains around their person.

2. Primary Territory: One's home, vehicle or other living space.

3. Secondary Territory: A structured place where entry is reserved for particular individuals and certain norms are expected, such as a school, office or church.

4. Public Territory: An open space where anyone can come and go, such as a park or shopping mall.

Territories can overlap. For example, a book club might meet in a person's home. For the homeowner, the home is a primary territory. For the book club members, it's a secondary territory. Territories function as a way to protect their owners' comfort, interests and possessions from unwelcome invaders.

Proxemics and Anxiety

Encountering proxemic behavior different from one's own has been known to trigger anxiety, or a fight-or-flight response. Researchers have conducted experiments that prove whenever an animal experiences a violation of its personal territory, it reacts by either running away or attacking the intruder. The same holds true for humans in most cases.

The exception comes in instances where people voluntarily give up their personal space to, for example, ride a crowded train or elevator. Research has shown that humans can put aside their personal discomfort to achieve certain goals day after day (i.e., getting to the office on time) without becoming overtly anxious, hostile or violent in the process. The key, researchers found, is withholding eye contact from others. Those who averted their eyes while in close physical contact with strangers exhibited markedly less anxiety. Thus, eye contact plays a significant role in proxemics research.

Culture Types

For the purposes of understanding how different people communicate non-verbally, Edward Hall separated cultures into two basic categories: contact and non-contact. In contact cultures, physical touching between acquaintances is permitted and even necessary for establishing interpersonal relationships. Such cultures include Arab, Italian, French, Latin America, and Turkish. For non-contact cultures, touching is reserved for only the most intimate acquaintances. Examples include the U.S., Norway, Japan, and most Southeast Asian cultures.

British linguist and businessman Richard D. Lewis later expanded upon this idea by outlining three specific types of cultures based upon communication styles:

1. Linear-active: Cool, logical and decisive (non-contact). Speakers tend to be direct and occasionally impatient, but otherwise remain reserved and deal mostly in facts. Examples include the U.S. and most Northern European cultures.

2. Multi-active: Warm and impulsive (contact). Speakers communicate enthusiastically, readily express emotion and prefer personal stories to facts. They tend to interrupt during conversation and display impatience more openly. Examples include Brazil, Mexico and Greece.

3. Reactive: Accommodating and non-confrontational (non-contact). Speakers value decorum and diplomacy over facts or emotions. They're usually very patient listeners who remain reserved in their body language and expressions. Examples include Vietnam, China and Japan.

Lewis' cultural classification is known as The Lewis Model. It even includes a test individuals can take to identify their cultural communication style.

Measuring Proxemics

Researchers must consider many factors when studying proxemics. Edward Hall, for instance, measured posture, body angle, physical distance, touch, eye contact, thermal heat, smell and vocal volume when defining the different types of distances people create between themselves and others. Though some of Hall's successors discounted heat, smell and volume as somewhat extraneous, they discovered several additional variables that often affect conversational distance: age, gender, social status, conversation topic, available space and environmental noise.

Such a reality begs many questions. For instance, were two women whispering in the corner because they're close friends or because they're coworkers planning a surprise party for their boss? Would those strangers on the corner still be talking loudly if there weren't a siren going off one block away? As a result of so many variables, researchers now treat distance as part of an integrated system of communication rather than a stand-alone phenomenon. They also select which measures to include and isolate the variables for individual analysis.

Most proxemics research is conducted through observation, either in a laboratory or a natural setting. During observation, the actual distance subjects maintain between each other is measured, along with duration of eye contact and instances of touching. However, some researchers use a method called projection, in which subjects must simulate proxemic behavior by arranging dolls or similar objects on a flat surface. Researchers then measure the distance between the objects according to scale.

Approaches to Proxemic Theory

Research into proxemics has yielded two divergent theories about why people use space in communication:

1. Equilibrium Theory: Proxemics aids humans in maintaining a status quo. People will adjust proxemic factors during conversation to keep their relationships at a consistent level of intimacy.
2. Expectancy Violation Model: Proxemics helps people to obtain what they want. Those who violate the spatial expectations of others can often achieve specific, desirable communication goals. Violation has a better outcome than equilibrium.

Applications

Proxemics research has proved useful in several different fields. Film analysts have discovered that by decreasing the distance between the camera and the actor, audiences become more emotionally attached to the actor's character. People in business have found that increasing face-to-face interactions between employees strengthens corporate culture.

Perhaps its most important application, though, is in the field of communication technology. Studies have shown that people naturally gravitate toward media in which proximity can be accurately simulated in the virtual world. The greater the perceived proximity, the more successful and effective the technology becomes.

Verbal Communication

The Verbal Communication is a type of oral communication wherein the message is transmitted through the spoken words. Here the sender gives words to his feelings, thoughts, ideas and opinions and expresses them in the form of speeches, discussions, presentations, and conversations.

The effectiveness of the verbal communication depends on the tone of the speaker, clarity of speech, volume, speed, body language and the quality of words used in the conversation. In the case of the verbal communication, the feedback is immediate since there are a simultaneous transmission and receipt of the message by the sender and receiver respectively.

The sender must keep his speech tone high and clearly audible to all and must design the subject matter keeping the target audience in mind. The sender should always cross check with the receiver to ensure that the message is understood in absolutely the same way as it was intended. Such communication is more prone to errors as sometimes the words are not sufficient to express the feelings and emotions of a person.

The success of the verbal communication depends not only on the speaking ability of an individual but also on the listening skills. How effectively an individual listens to the subject matter decides the effectiveness of the communication. The verbal communication is applicable in both the formal and informal kind of situations.

Verbal Communication Skills

Almost every job requires workers to use verbal communication skills. That's why verbal skills are highly ranked on the candidate evaluation checklists used by many job interviewers.

The stronger your communication skills, the better your chances of getting hired regardless of the job for which you're applying. You'll do better during the interview, as well as on the job.

Effective verbal communication skills include more than just talking. Verbal communication encompasses both how you deliver messages and how you receive them. Communication is a soft skill, and it's one that is important to every employer.

Workers who can convey information clearly and effectively are highly valued by employers. Employees who can interpret messages and act appropriately on the information that they receive have a better chance of excelling on the job.

Verbal Communication Skills in the Workplace

What constitutes effective verbal communication on the job depends on the relationships between communication partners and the work context. Verbal communication in a work setting takes place between many different individuals and groups such as co-workers, bosses and subordinates, employees, customers, clients, teachers and students, and speakers and their audiences.

Verbal communication occurs in many different contexts including training sessions, presentations, group meetings, performance appraisals, one-on-one discussions, interviews, disciplinary sessions, sales pitches and consulting engagements.

Examples of Verbal Communication Skills

Review examples of effective workplace verbal communication skills:

- Advising others regarding an appropriate course of action
- Annunciating clearly
- Anticipating the concerns of others
- Asking for clarification
- Asking open-ended questions to stimulate dialogue
- Assertiveness

- Calming an agitated customer by recognizing and responding to their complaints
- Conveying feedback in a constructive manner emphasizing specific, changeable behaviors
- Conveying messages concisely
- Disciplining employees in a direct and respectful manner
- Emphasizing benefits of a product, service or proposal to persuade an individual or group
- Encouraging reluctant group members to share input
- Enunciating each word you speak
- Explaining a difficult situation without getting angry
- Explaining that you need assistance
- Giving credit to others
- Introducing the focus of a topic at the beginning of a presentation or interaction
- Noticing non-verbal cues and responding verbally to verify confusion, defuse anger, etc.
- Paraphrasing to show understanding
- Planning communications prior to delivery
- Posing probing questions to elicit more detail about specific issues
- Projecting your voice to fill the room
- Providing concrete examples to illustrate points
- Receiving criticism without defensiveness
- Recognizing and countering objections
- Refraining from speaking too often or interrupting others
- Requesting feedback
- Restating important points towards the end of a talk
- Selecting language appropriate to the audience
- Showing an interest in others, asking about and recognizing their feelings
- Speaking calmly even when you're stressed
- Speaking at a moderate pace, not too fast or too slowly
- Speaking confidently but with modesty
- Stating your needs, wants or feelings without criticizing or blaming
- Summarizing key points made by other speakers
- Supporting statements with facts and evidence

- Tailoring messages to different audiences
- Telling stories to capture an audience
- Terminating staff
- Training others to carry out a task or role
- Using affirmative sounds and words like uh-huh, got you, I understand, for sure, I see, and yes to demonstrate understanding
- Using humor to engage an audience
- Utilizing self-disclosure to encourage sharing

Clarification

In communication, clarification involves offering back to the speaker the essential meaning, as understood by the listener, of what they have just said. Thereby checking that the listener's understanding is correct and resolving any areas of confusion or misunderstanding.

Clarification is important in many situations especially when what is being communicated is difficult in some way. Communication can be 'difficult' for many reasons, perhaps sensitive emotions are being discussed - or you are listening to some complex information or following instructions.

Clarifying reassures the speaker that the listener is attempting to understand the messages they are expressing. Clarifying can involve asking questions or occasionally summarising what the speaker has said.

A listener can ask for clarification when they cannot make sense of the speaker's responses. Sometimes, the messages that a speaker is attempting to send can be highly complex, involving many different people, issues, places and/or times. Clarifying helps you to sort these out and also to check the speaker's priorities.

Through clarification it is possible for the speaker and the listener to make sense of these often confused and complex issues. Clarifying involves genuineness on the listener's part and it shows speakers that the listener is interested in them and in what they have to say.

Some Examples of Non-directive Clarification-seeking Questions

- "I'm not quite sure I understand what you are saying."
- "I don't feel clear about the main issue here."
- "When you said what did you mean?"
- "Could you repeat?"

Clarifying Involves

- Non-judgemental questioning.
- Summarising and seeking feedback as to its accuracy.

Clarification Questions

When you are the listener in a sensitive environment, the right sort of non-directive questioning can enable the speaker to describe their viewpoint more fully.

Asking the right question at the right time can be crucial and comes with practice. The best questions are open-ended as they give the speaker choice in how to respond, whereas closed questions allow only very limited responses.

Open Questions

If your role is to assist a speaker to talk about an issue, often the most effective questioning starts with 'when', 'where', 'how' or 'why'. These questions encourage speakers to be open and expand on their thoughts. For example:

1. "When did you first start feeling like this?"
2. "Why do you feel this way?"

Closed Questions

Closed questions usually elicit a 'yes' or 'no' response and do not encourage speakers to be open and expand on their thoughts. Such questions often begin with 'did you?' or 'were you?' For example:

1. "Did you always feel like this?"
2. "Were you aware of feeling this way?"

Guidelines for Clarifying

Clarification is the skill we use to ensure that we have understood the message of the speaker in an interpersonal exchange. When using clarification follow these guidelines to help aid communication and understanding:

- Admit if you are unsure about what the speaker means.
- Ask for repetition.
- State what the speaker has said as you understand it, and check whether this is what they really said.
- Ask for specific examples.
- Use open, non-directive questions - if appropriate.
- Ask if you have got it right and be prepared to be corrected.

Questioning Skills

Unless the speaker provides you with the facts and details, you will never find out about the many other things you want to discover if you do not ask questions. Questioning is but a part of an exchange in communication between and among individuals. It is a key tool to learning new knowledge, clearing out confusions and misunderstanding, and in resolving issues.

Asking questions is a skill that needs to be honed. By mastering the art of asking the right and effective questions, other communication skills are also improved such as the ability to gather more information and acquire new knowledge, the skill in building better relationships, and people management.

Develop your question skills by understanding the various types of questioning techniques and finding out the most appropriate instances to use these techniques. Moreover, you must learn the principles governing good questioning skills and how it is characterized by the person asking the question. This makes it easier for you to throw intelligent and effective questions in an exchange of communication.

Characteristics of a Good Questioner

- A questioner has to demonstrate the need to gather information. The need for information itself fuels a person to ask questions.
- A questioner must particularly know the kind of information needed. It allows for a formulation of relevant, direct-to-the-point questions.
- A questioner must have good knowledge of terminologies and must possess wide vocabulary in relation to the context or subject matter in order to construct relevant questions. Without sufficient knowledge, a person can hardly relate to the issue and can barely ask questions pertaining to the issue.
- A questioner must have the ability to ask an array of significant questions using the various questioning techniques. Based on the information needed, that is how the questions will be created.
- A questioner must have a good list of proper and credible resources for making effective and relevant questions.
- A questioner must be able to modify, rephrase, or edit their questions as needed or when the construction does not seem clear enough to the other person.

Various Questioning Techniques

Open-Ended Questions

Asking open-ended questions simply requires further explanation or elaboration in order to gather more information from the speaker. It gets the conversation going and allows for more details of the subject matter. Open-ended questions start with Who, What, Where, When, Why, and How. Other starters also include “Can you tell me more”, “Please explain more about” and phrases that elicit more answers.

Closed-Ended Questions

In contrast to the former, closed-ended questions limit a person’s answers. These questions are asked to lead a conversation. Information needed is specific and limited, sometimes answerable by yes or no. It is also used to confirm facts. Closed-ended questions usually start with the linking verbs is, are, and am.

Funnel Questions

This questioning technique involves asking questions from a general to a deductive manner. Investigators and detectives commonly use this technique in order to dig deeper and get to the most specific answers needed. One tip to ask funnel questions is to start with closed-ended questions and then progressing using open-ended questions.

Probing Questions

In order to understand an issue better, the use of probing questions helps. These are intelligent, relevant open or closed questions based from the subject matter or issue at hand. Use probing questions to be sure you were able to capture everything and comprehend it thoroughly. These questions are also effective in gaining information from people who are hesitant to share details.

Leading Questions

Sales people are fond of using leading questions for the purpose of generating sales. It is best to use leading questions to people who cannot seem to decide over choices. Leading questions are normally closed-ended type of questions.

Rhetorical Questions

These questions are not really questions in construction because they do not require answers at all. Rhetorical questions are statements modified in the form of a question. It is intended to engage a listener into the conversation.

Advantages of Having Good Questioning Skills

You cannot be a good communicator if you do not know how to ask questions. There are so many benefits of being an effective questioner. Demonstrating effective questioning skills is useful in the following instances:

Learning new knowledge

- Information gathering
- Managing and coaching
- Conflict resolution
- Persuading people
- Winning negotiations
- Enhancing people skill

Making A Speech

To deliver an effective presentation or speech, an individual has to take care of his communication and it has to be really impressive and effective. No one will really take the pains to listen to your ideas unless and until your communication is effective and impressive. Only speaking is not the solution, how you deliver your presentation or speech is more important and thus should be taken good care of.

Before delivering any presentation, make it a habit to read your presentation aloud once or twice as it will definitely give you the needed confidence. You must be clear with each and every slide.

Never deliver your presentation in a noisy area as it would distract the audience and they would never be able to concentrate on your presentation and thus nullifying its effect. Prefer a conference room or the board room with pin drop silence for the same. It is the prime responsibility of every member in the audience as well as the speaker to keep their mobiles in the silent mode. The speaker must also be very careful about his dressing. Your dress code must be formal with light colours. Wear a formal tie, shoes must be polished and avoid wearing bracelets or any other jewellery as the clattering sound can act as a disturbing element. Never be shabby or adopt a casual approach. Look your best on the day of the presentation.

Speak clearly and convincingly and do take care of your accent. Communicate in the most convincing and impressive way. Carefully convert your thoughts into content. The content has to be very sensible, related to the topic and above all convey your information in the best possible way. Your words have to instantly hit the audience and have a long and a lasting impression on them. Take care how you speak. Don't keep half of your words in your mouth or stammer. Don't forget to take pauses in between slides. You can also include some light jokes in between to break the monotony.

The best possible way to keep the last bench audience awake is to reach out to them also. Don't just speak for the person sitting under your nose. The tone has to be loud enough so that everyone is able to hear you properly and above all understand you well. Speak slowly with the desired expressions. Don't rush. Keep your presentation interactive and ask lots of questions from the audience - a very simple way to find out whether they are attentive or not. The pie charts, graphs, tables might be very simple for you, but can be complicated for the others. Make it a point to explain the pictorial representations properly preferably with the aid of a scale or a pointer.

It is not only the verbal communication which is important but also the nonverbal communication which should never be ignored.

Your facial expressions must be in tune with the content. If your slides indicate that you have overachieved your target a particular month, smile. Never smile if there is a dip in your performance in the next slide. Look positive and promising. Learn how to keep a check on your emotions.

Take care of your postures, hand movements as well. Stand straight and never fiddle with a pen or play with your tie. It reflects your nervousness and works against you. Don't chew nails in between or yawn. It is a strict no-no in presentations or any formal meetings. Maintain an eye contact with your audience for that bangon Effect.

Always keep some time for the question answer round in the end. The listeners must also not jump in between with their questions as it can spoil the momentum of the presentation. Wait for the right moment. You must appreciate the hard work the speaker has put in preparing the presentation. Jot down your questions and always ask them once the presentation is over. The speaker must not ignore the smallest detail before the presentation, but if he is unable to answer any question he should handle the situation very smartly. Don't start sweating, be confident and answer them later. The listeners should also never criticize or make fun of the speaker. He is also a human being and can make mistakes. Give the speaker a proper feedback and do applaud him once he is through with his presentation. He will feel elated.

The content and your communication skills go hand in hand to create an effective presentation. Don't be too conscious, just be yourself, practice well and give your best and you will never fail to create wonders.

Preparation and Effective Delivery of Speech

Focus on the Main Message

If you've been asked to give a speech, the first step is to choose a focused message. Even if you've been given a theme for your speech such as "inspiration" or "strength," this is more a general umbrella under which your specific points (and point of view) will fall. Make a short list of five ideas for your speech. It can be helpful to write them in command form. "Strength" a brainstorm of five speech messages could include: "don't ever give up, "overcome failure," "build physical strength" and "know your strengths." If you feel stuck for ideas, a reference to your current political or social context can bring new insight to your theme.

Build Three Supporting Points

By focusing on your central message with supporting evidence, you strengthen it. A stronger message will resonate more with your listeners. To come up with supporting points, ask yourself "why" about the speech message you've selected. For example, for "don't ever give up," you'd ask, "Why should you never give up?" Make a list of several possible supporting ideas. Read through your finished list, and at the end, cross off the weaker ones that don't support your main point.

Keep your Audience in Mind

After looking into the central message and supporting points for your speech, you can flesh out the rest by considering your audience. Knowing who your audience are and what they are expecting from this encounter can help you pick the right tone to optimal effect.

Be a Tactful Speaker

Some speakers choose to generalize complex topics in a speech because they think it's easier for the audience to understand. It's actually better to do the opposite. Listeners tend to connect better with concrete examples and personal stories, so embrace detail in your speech. A personal anecdote about why one shouldn't give up is more effective than just saying not to. Areas where your passion and knowledge overlap are generally the richest. If appropriate to the context, don't be afraid to tell a joke about the topic. A little self-deprecating humor goes down well with the crowd, one can always give it a shot.

Brevity is The Soul of The Wit

Some of the most effective speeches of all times have been brief. "The Gettysburg Address" was only 15 minutes, while "I Have a Dream" was for 17 minutes. Aim for brevity. A good formula is to speak for less time than you've been asked to, as people tend to overestimate the attention span of their audience.

Feedback is Important

As the speech has to be delivered to an audience, it is important to get feedback from theoretical listeners. Read your speech to someone you trust and ask for some honest feedback. In particular, it can be helpful to ask if anything is confusing or unclear. Your speech will have more impact if the message is engaging.

Eye Contact is Important

During your speech, look at your audience while you are speaking. Put the content of your speech, either fully written out or in bullet points, so you are not staring straight down at a piece of paper while you speak. Engaging your audience visually makes you appear secure and confident.

Use Appropriate Gestures

A well-placed gesture can add humor or aid greater understanding of your speech. For optimal effectiveness, punctuate your speech with gestures when appropriate. If you're a very nervous public speaker, try just resting your hands against the podium. It will make you feel steadier.

Walk when Required

If your speech is informal, walking from one side of the stage to the other can help engage people sitting in different parts. It will draw your audience in and enhance your confidence.

Use Props

If appropriate, bring props to punctuate your speech for your audience. This can be anything useful such as a graph to handout to all attendees or even a personal item to drive home your speech's content. Props can personalize your speech and add interest or humor. Limit yourself to one or two props maximum per speech.

Conversation

Conversations are supposed to be fun. They involve personal interactions between two or more people about something of interest. But many people worry about having conversations. They are concerned that they won't be able to keep the conversation going, or about what they will say.

Conversation is simply talking to someone else, usually informally. So why is it considered difficult? It certainly wasn't for our grandparents' generation. Some commentators have put the problem down to the growth of social media, with its emphasis on 'broadcasting' and its 'me' focus, and this certainly doesn't make it any easier.

But all is not lost. Not only can conversational skills be learned and developed, but it is surprisingly easy to do so, especially if you follow some simple rules.

Rules of Conversation

Conversation is a Two-way Street

The first and most important rule of conversation is that it is not all about you, but it's not all about the other person either.

A monologue, in either direction, is not conversation. Try to achieve a balance between talking and listening in any conversation.

This is where social media makes life difficult. We're used to broadcasting our views, and then responding if others comment. That can feel like the start of a conversation but, when you're face to face, it's not polite to start by broadcasting your views.

Instead, try asking a question to establish common ground. For example: "What do you do?", or even "Isn't the weather beautiful?"

Be Friendly and Polite

Smiling, and being nice, will take you a long way in conversational terms. Everyone would rather chat to someone friendly and pleasant. But what are the practical elements of this?

Build Rapport

You can build rapport by establishing some common ground and by simply smiling and using positive and reinforcing body language.

Be nice

Don't say unpleasant things about anyone. After all, the person you're talking about could be your new acquaintance's best friend. And even if they're not, your new acquaintance may not relish discussion about someone behind their back (and neither should you).

Try to avoid Contentious Topics on First Acquaintance

It's fine to talk politics once you know someone a bit better. When you first meet someone, though, it's better to stick to neutral ground, which is why so many people talk about the weather. This is where 'small talk' comes in.

However dull you find someone, it is best not to say so.

Just bring the conversation to a polite close, perhaps by saying something like "I must just go and catch so-and-so before they go. It's been really nice to chat to you", or "Please excuse me, I promised to help with x and I see they need me now".

Respond to what they are Saying

To respond genuinely to what someone has just said means that you have to listen. You can't just switch off, and think about what you're going to say next. However, if we're honest, most of us would admit that we often do just that.

It's important to focus on the other person, and what they're saying. You also need to take into account their body language.

Use Signalling to Help the other Person

When a conversation is flowing well, it moves naturally from one person to the other. However, if one or both are finding it more of a struggle to 'chat', you may find it helpful to use 'signals' to show the other person that it is their turn to talk.

The most common type of signal is questions. These may be either open or closed:

1. Closed questions invite a yes/no answer.

In conversation, they might include "Don't you agree?", and "Are you enjoying the party?" They are not really inviting the other person to do more than nod and agree, rather than to share the conversation.

2. Open questions invite more information.

They open up the conversation to the other person, and invite them to participate. For this reason, in conversation, they are often called 'invitations'. Open questions often start 'How?' or 'Why?'

Create Emotional Connections

Of course it is perfectly possible to conduct a conversation entirely at the level of small talk, with nothing important being said.

But conversation is also a way to explore whether you wish to know someone better and build a relationship with them. It can therefore be useful to understand how to use conversation to create and build emotional connections.

The key is sharing appropriate information: That means being prepared to be open about what interests you, what makes you into you as a person, and inspiring the other person to share too.

Be Interested and you will be Interesting

All these ideas can perhaps be boiled down into one idea: That, in turn, will make conversations flow, because you will genuinely want to know about the other person and be able to contribute to the conversation from your own interest in the world.

On the other hand, if you take no interest in anything except yourself, you will be quite dull and people will not be keen to have any conversations with you.

References

- What-is-communication-1689877: thoughtco.com, Retrieved 12 March 2018
- What-is-communication: entrepreneurhandbook.co.uk, Retrieved 16 June 2018
- Communication-theory: managementstudyguide.com, Retrieved 15 July 2018
- Types-communication-theories-8117675: classroom.synonym.com, Retrieved 14 April 2018
- Development-communication-theory, mass-communication: businesstopia.net, Retrieved 14 May 2018
- Democratic-participant-media-theory: mediamagazine.in, Retrieved 20 March 2018
- 5-important-aspects-of-making-a-positive-first-impression: skipprichard.com, Retrieved 09 June 2018

Permissions

All chapters in this book are published with permission under the Creative Commons Attribution Share Alike License or equivalent. Every chapter published in this book has been scrutinized by our experts. Their significance has been extensively debated. The topics covered herein carry significant information for a comprehensive understanding. They may even be implemented as practical applications or may be referred to as a beginning point for further studies.

We would like to thank the editorial team for lending their expertise to make the book truly unique. They have played a crucial role in the development of this book. Without their invaluable contributions this book wouldn't have been possible. They have made vital efforts to compile up to date information on the varied aspects of this subject to make this book a valuable addition to the collection of many professionals and students.

This book was conceptualized with the vision of imparting up-to-date and integrated information in this field. To ensure the same, a matchless editorial board was set up. Every individual on the board went through rigorous rounds of assessment to prove their worth. After which they invested a large part of their time researching and compiling the most relevant data for our readers.

The editorial board has been involved in producing this book since its inception. They have spent rigorous hours researching and exploring the diverse topics which have resulted in the successful publishing of this book. They have passed on their knowledge of decades through this book. To expedite this challenging task, the publisher supported the team at every step. A small team of assistant editors was also appointed to further simplify the editing procedure and attain best results for the readers.

Apart from the editorial board, the designing team has also invested a significant amount of their time in understanding the subject and creating the most relevant covers. They scrutinized every image to scout for the most suitable representation of the subject and create an appropriate cover for the book.

The publishing team has been an ardent support to the editorial, designing and production team. Their endless efforts to recruit the best for this project, has resulted in the accomplishment of this book. They are a veteran in the field of academics and their pool of knowledge is as vast as their experience in printing. Their expertise and guidance has proved useful at every step. Their uncompromising quality standards have made this book an exceptional effort. Their encouragement from time to time has been an inspiration for everyone.

The publisher and the editorial board hope that this book will prove to be a valuable piece of knowledge for students, practitioners and scholars across the globe.

Index

CPSIA information can be obtained
at www.ICGtesting.com
Printed in the USA
BVHW011741010719
552297BV00014B/5/P

9 781641 721073